WHA ?!
KRIKK
KRIK
ペタ
SPTT
シュルル
SHWIP
NO...
KRIK
へ!!
!
KOOM
HWMM
NNIIIH
AIEEEEEEEEE
VWOOSH
SHO !!
REN— NO!
GET AWAY FROM IT!!
HHZZ
SIST ...
ZZZ

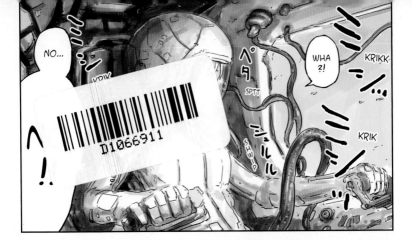

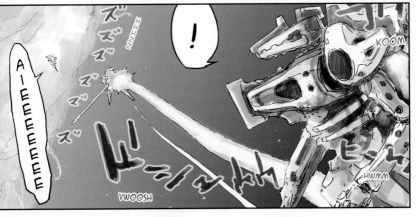

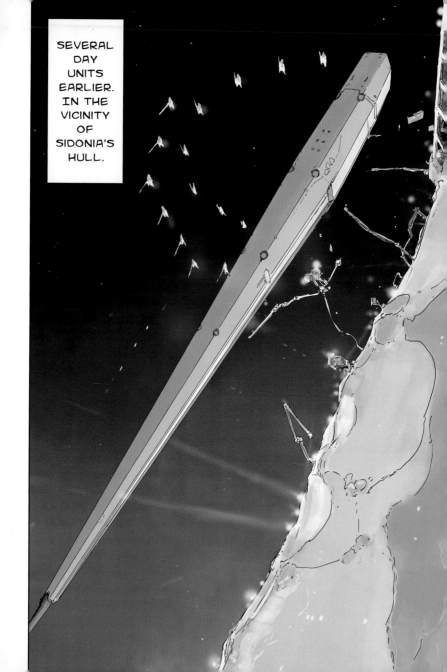

SEVERAL
DAY
UNITS
EARLIER.
IN THE
VICINITY
OF
SIDONIA'S
HULL.

#55 The Mizuki's Launch

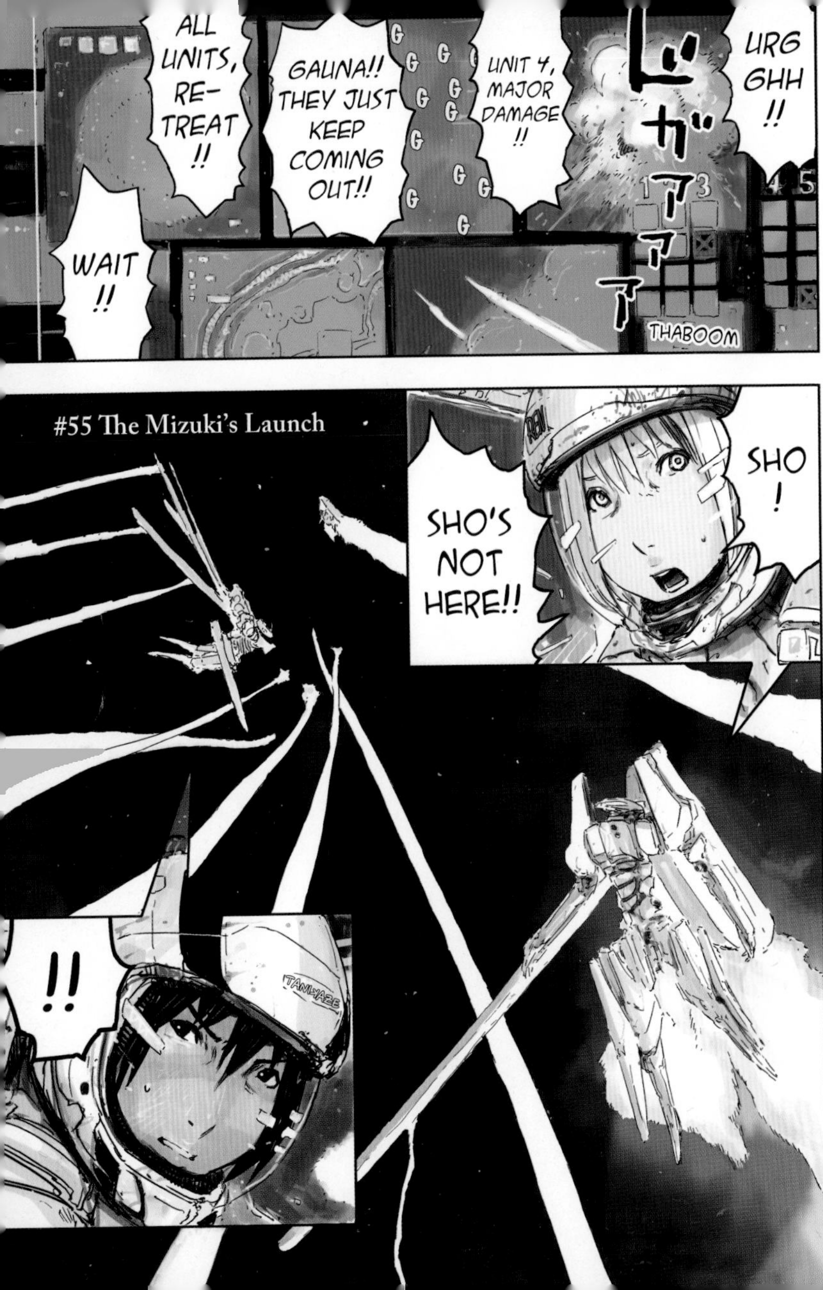

URG GHH !!
ジガアアア
THABOOM
UNIT 4, MAJOR DAMAGE !!
GAUNA!! THEY JUST KEEP COMING OUT!!
G G G G G G G G G G G G
ALL UNITS, RE-TREAT !!
WAIT !!
SHO !
SHO'S NOT HERE!!
!!

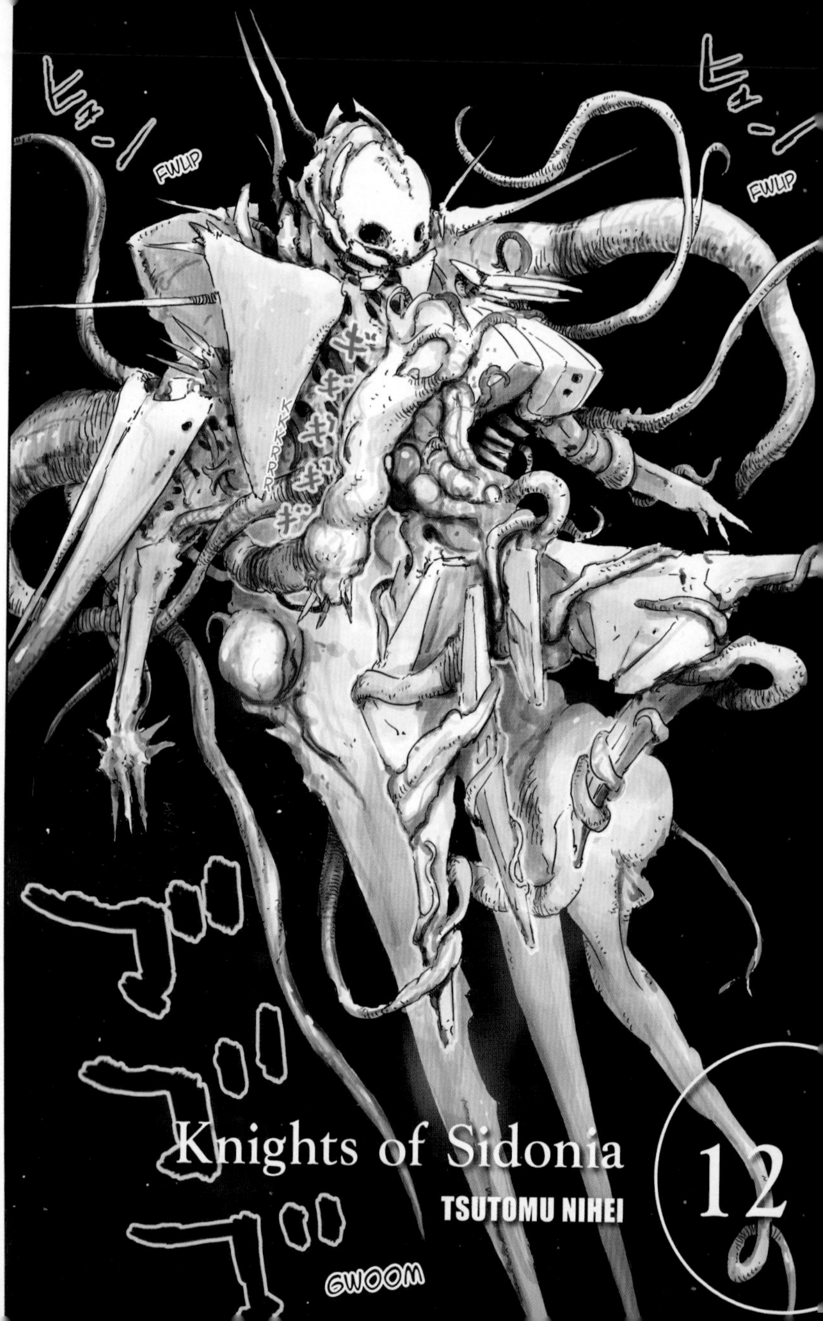
FWLIP
FWLIP
KKKRRR
Knights of Sidonia
12
TSUTOMU NIHEI
GWOOM

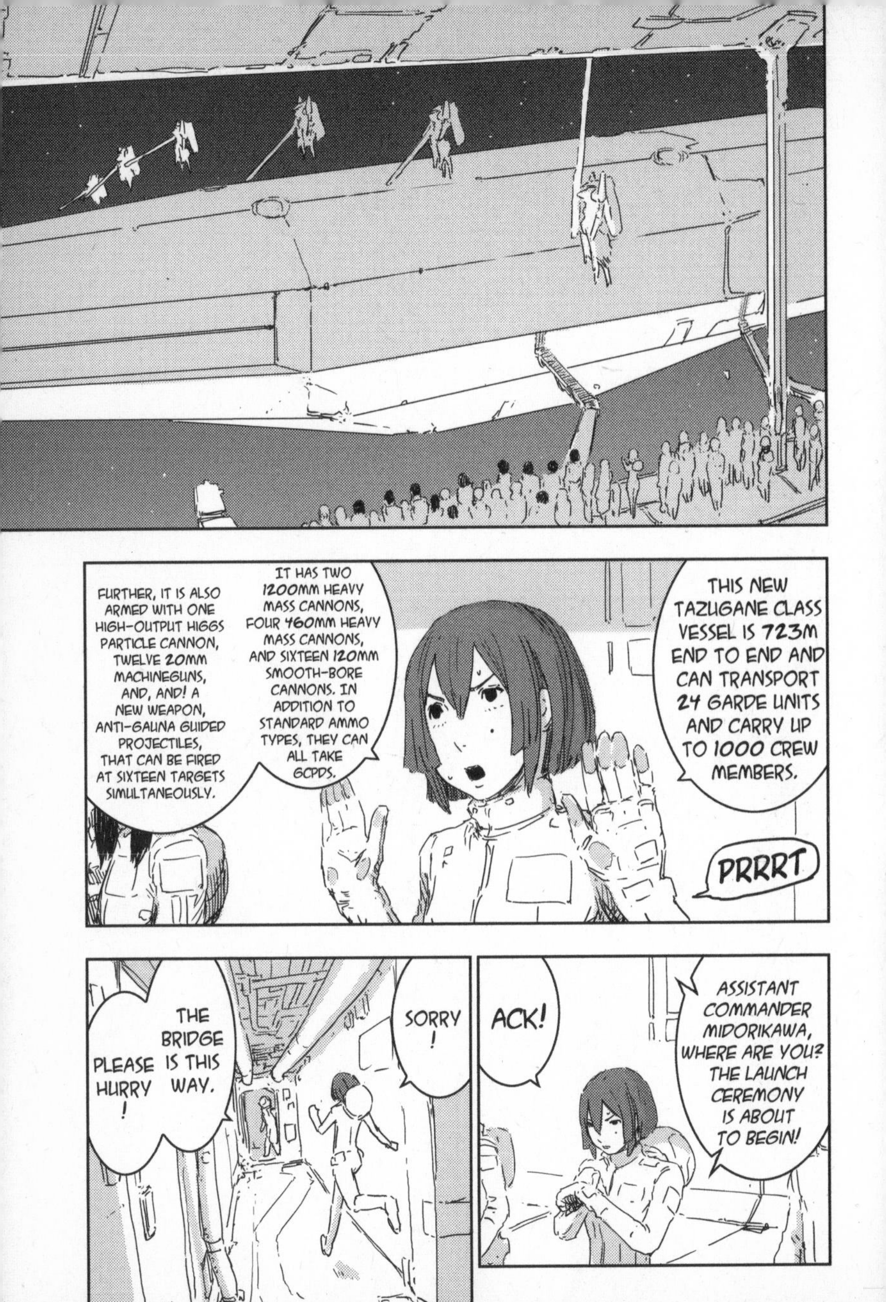

THIS NEW TAZUGANE CLASS VESSEL IS 723M END TO END AND CAN TRANSPORT 24 GARDE UNITS AND CARRY UP TO 1000 CREW MEMBERS.
IT HAS TWO 1200MM HEAVY MASS CANNONS, FOUR 460MM HEAVY MASS CANNONS, AND SIXTEEN 120MM SMOOTH-BORE CANNONS. IN ADDITION TO STANDARD AMMO TYPES, THEY CAN ALL TAKE GCPDS.
FURTHER, IT IS ALSO ARMED WITH ONE HIGH-OUTPUT HIGGS PARTICLE CANNON, TWELVE 20MM MACHINEGUNS, AND, AND! A NEW WEAPON, ANTI-GAUNA GUIDED PROJECTILES, THAT CAN BE FIRED AT SIXTEEN TARGETS SIMULTANEOUSLY.
PRRRT
ASSISTANT COMMANDER MIDORIKAWA, WHERE ARE YOU? THE LAUNCH CEREMONY IS ABOUT TO BEGIN!
ACK!
SORRY!
THE BRIDGE IS THIS WAY.
PLEASE HURRY!

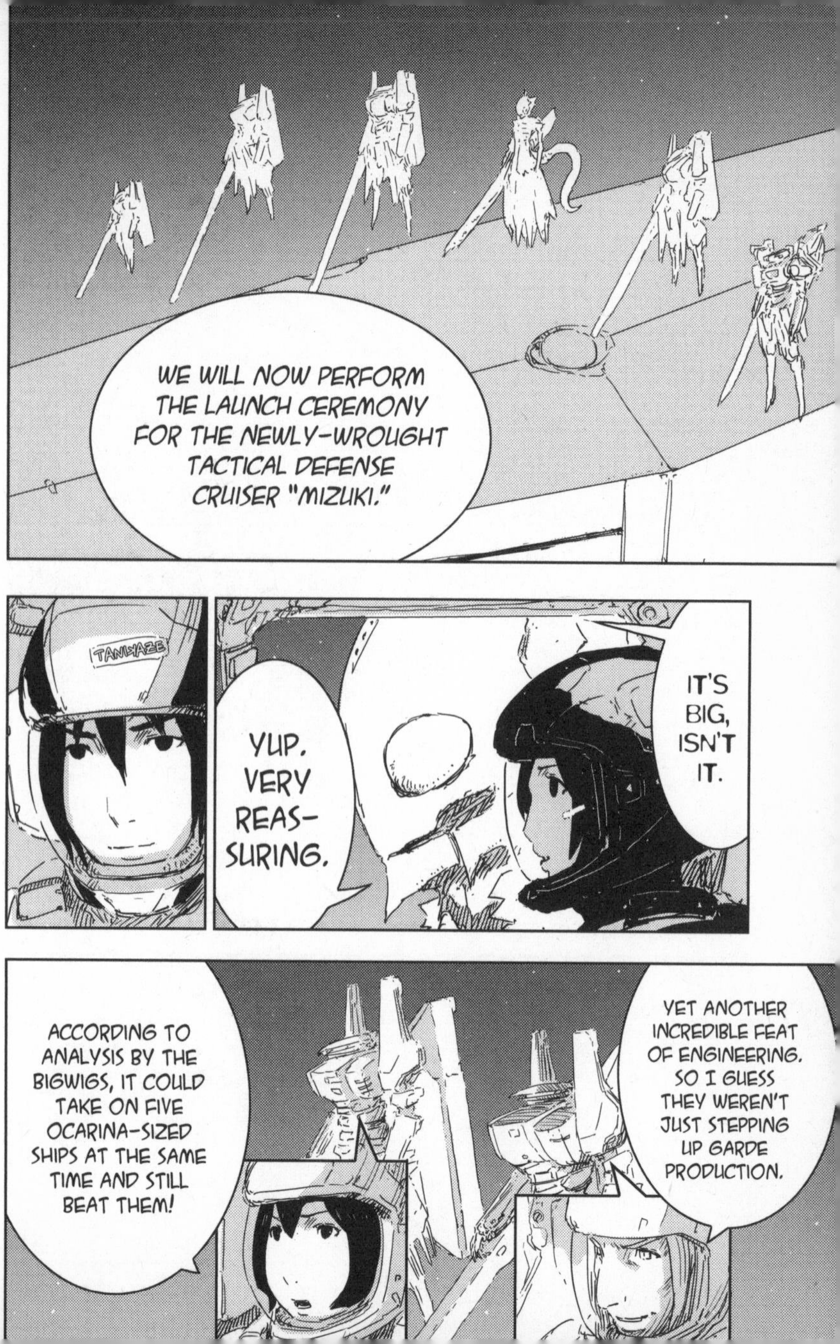
WE WILL NOW PERFORM THE LAUNCH CEREMONY FOR THE NEWLY-WROUGHT TACTICAL DEFENSE CRUISER "MIZUKI."
IT'S BIG, ISN'T IT.
YUP. VERY REAS-SURING.
YET ANOTHER INCREDIBLE FEAT OF ENGINEERING. SO I GUESS THEY WEREN'T JUST STEPPING UP GARDE PRODUCTION.
ACCORDING TO ANALYSIS BY THE BIGWIGS, IT COULD TAKE ON FIVE OCARINA-SIZED SHIPS AT THE SAME TIME AND STILL BEAT THEM!

IN OTHER WORDS, TO DEFEAT THE GREATER CLUSTER SHIP, WE'D NEED A THOUSAND OF THESE.
GGNNNN
IT'S IN YOUR HANDS, SASAKI.
AND YOU SEE THAT CAPTAIN KOBAYASHI GETS THE SUPPORT SHE NEEDS, SHINATOSE.
YES ...

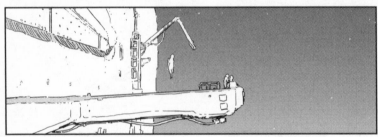

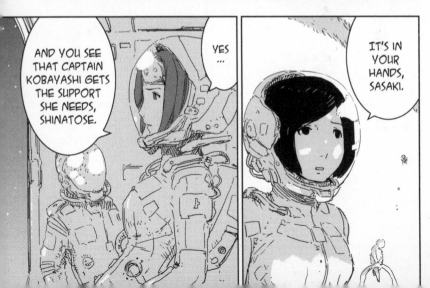

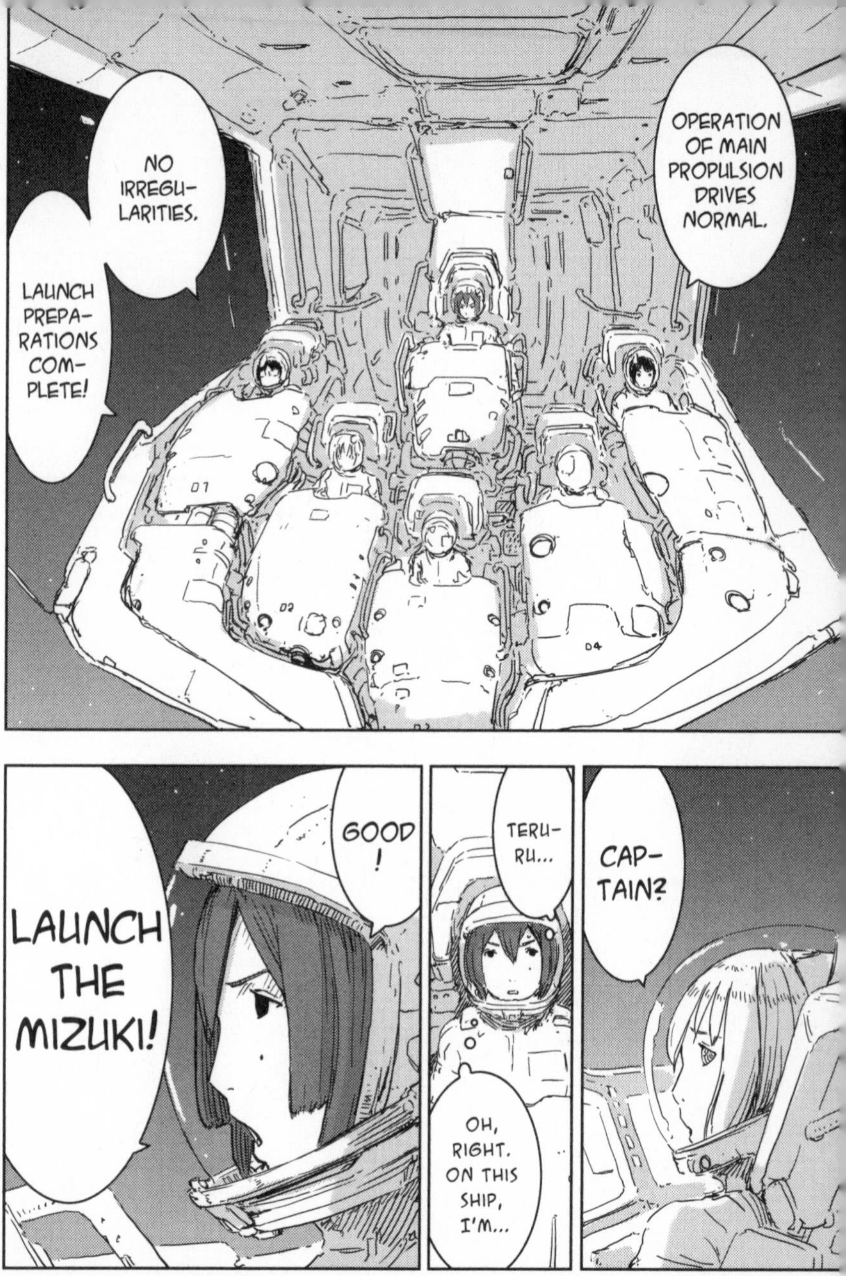
OPERATION OF MAIN PROPULSION DRIVES NORMAL.
NO IRREGULARITIES.
LAUNCH PREPARATIONS COMPLETE!
CAPTAIN?
TERU-RU...
OH, RIGHT. ON THIS SHIP, I'M...
GOOD!
LAUNCH THE MIZUKI!

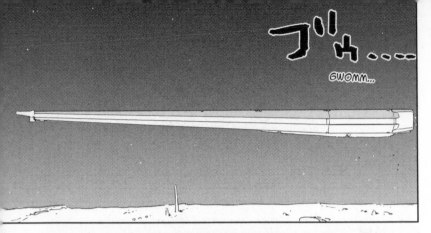

GWOMM...
STANDARD ACCELER-ATION!
ALL GARDE UNITS ACCOMPANY CRUISER!
VWOOMFF

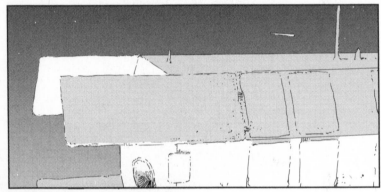

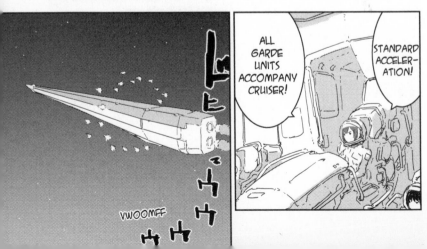

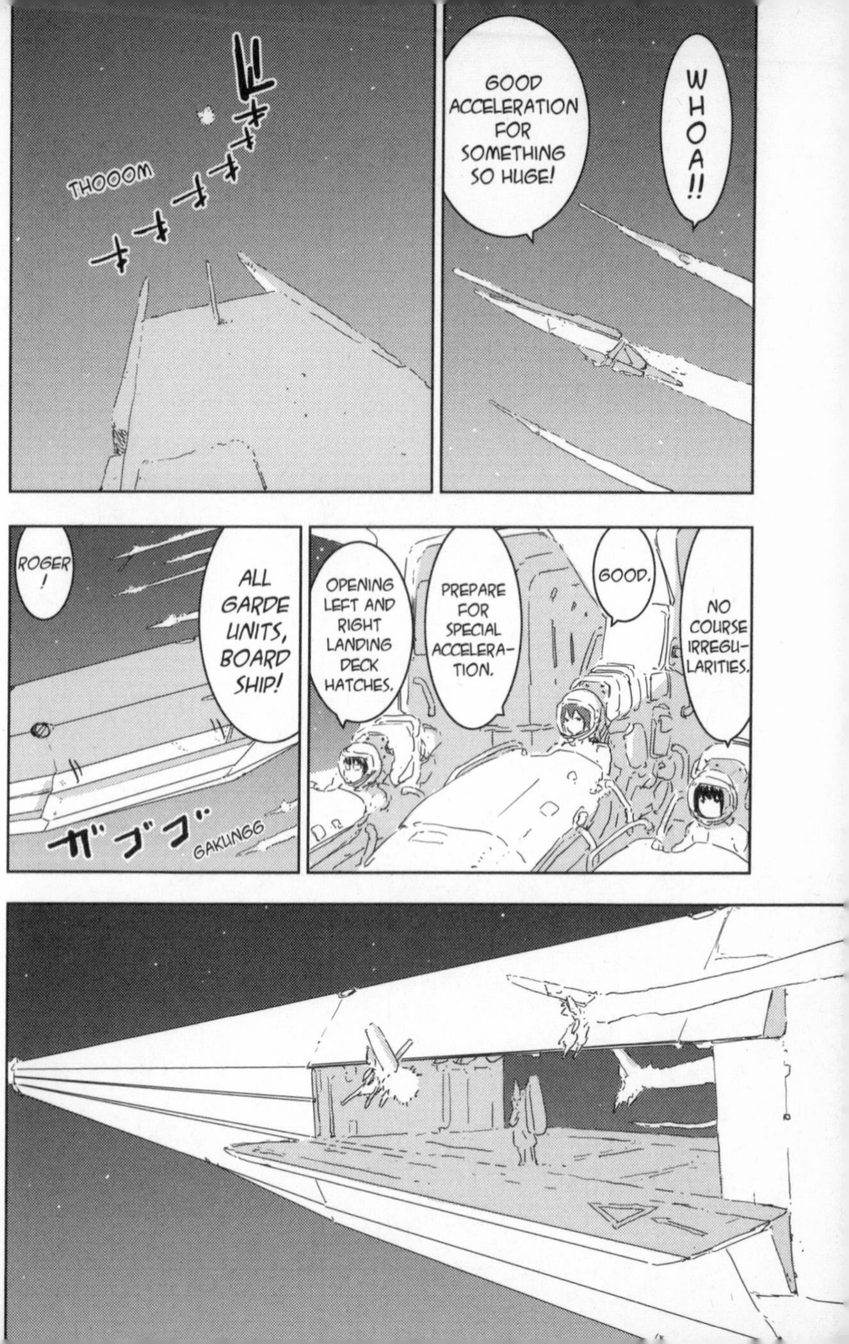
WHOA!!
GOOD ACCELERATION FOR SOMETHING SO HUGE!
THOOOM
NO COURSE IRREGULARITIES.
GOOD.
PREPARE FOR SPECIAL ACCELERATION.
OPENING LEFT AND RIGHT LANDING DECK HATCHES.
ALL GARDE UNITS, BOARD SHIP!
ROGER!
GAKUNGG

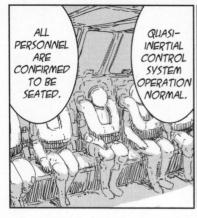

ALL GARDES ARE NOW ON BOARD!
GKUNG
QUASI-INERTIAL CONTROL SYSTEM OPERATION NORMAL.
ALL PERSONNEL ARE CONFIRMED TO BE SEATED.
COMMENCE SPECIAL ACCELERATION!!
FWOOOM
WT
KWEEEEEE

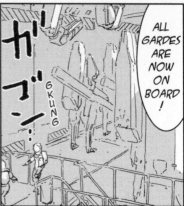

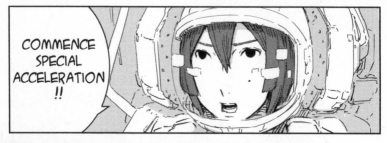

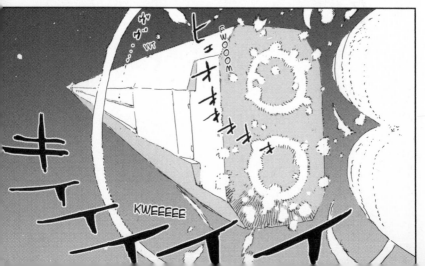

TING!!

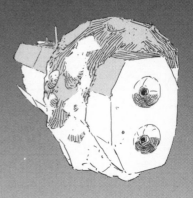

DID IT JUST VANISH ?!

WHOA!

S-SO FAST !!

GWHOOM

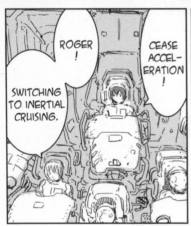

ROGER!

CEASE ACCEL- ERATION!

SWITCHING TO INERTIAL CRUISING.

GTKGTK

...

U- UNREAL ...

HHHSSSSSS

CHKNNG

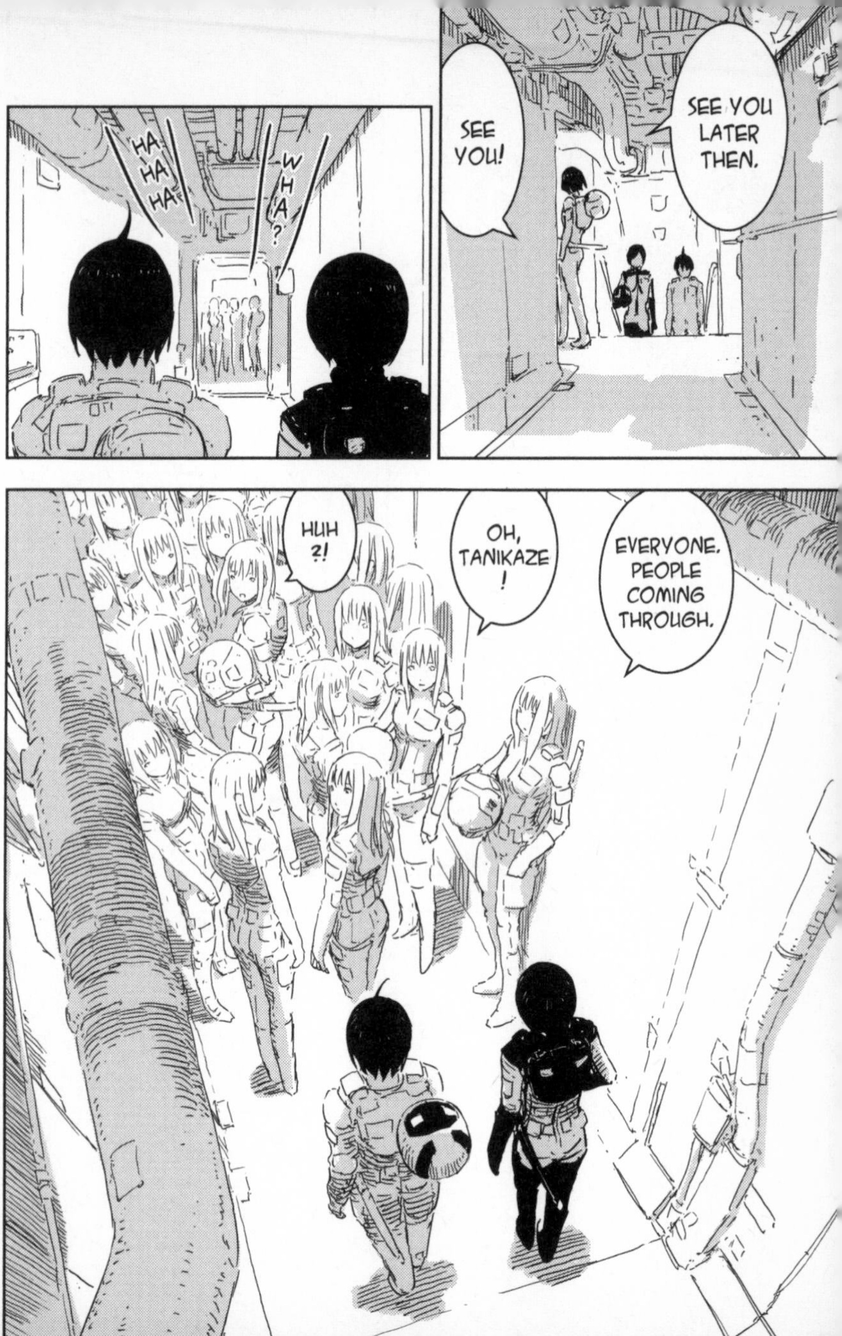
SEE YOU LATER THEN.
SEE YOU!
WHA?
HA HA HA
EVERYONE. PEOPLE COMING THROUGH.
OH, TANIKAZE!
HUH?!

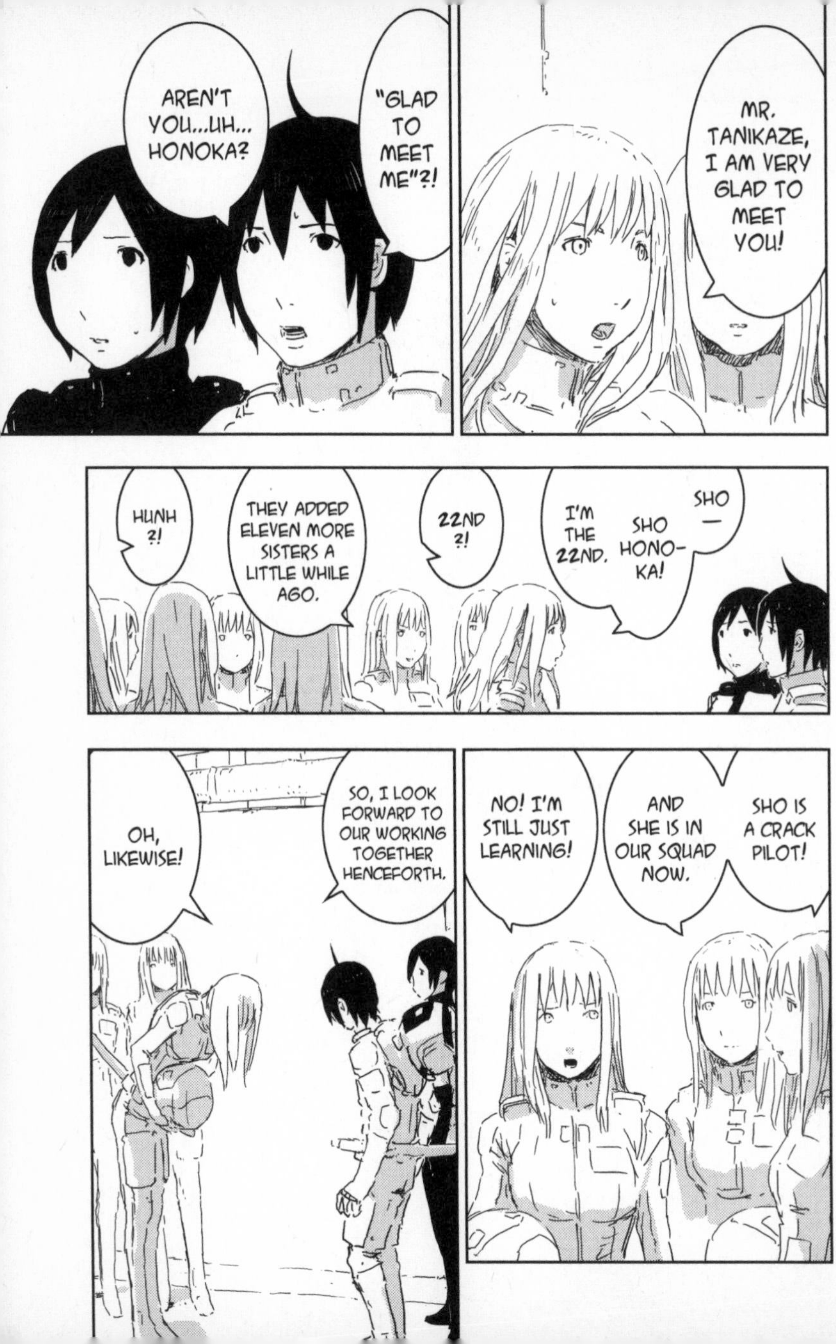
MR. TANIKAZE, I AM VERY GLAD TO MEET YOU!
"GLAD TO MEET ME"?!
AREN'T YOU...UH... HONOKA?
SHO—
SHO HONO-KA!
I'M THE 22ND.
22ND?!
THEY ADDED ELEVEN MORE SISTERS A LITTLE WHILE AGO.
HUNH?!
SHO IS A CRACK PILOT!
AND SHE IS IN OUR SQUAD NOW.
NO! I'M STILL JUST LEARNING!
SO, I LOOK FORWARD TO OUR WORKING TOGETHER HENCEFORTH.
OH, LIKEWISE!

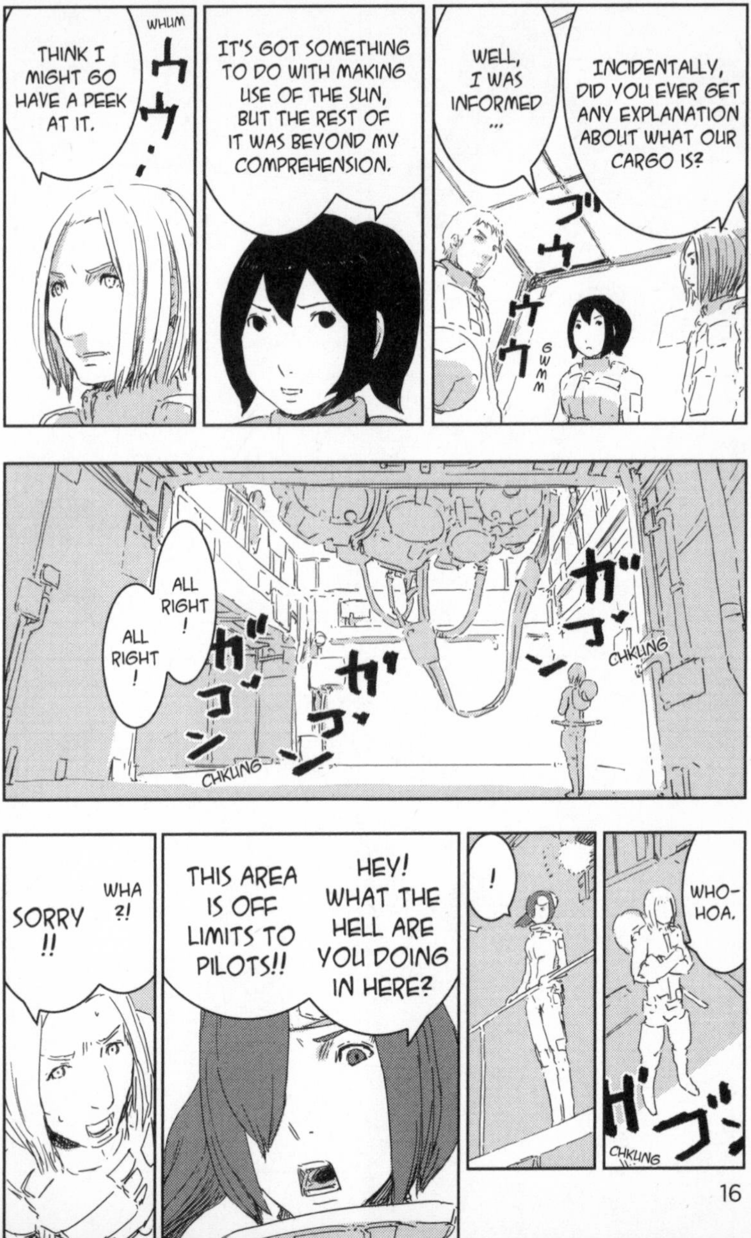
INCIDENTALLY, DID YOU EVER GET ANY EXPLANATION ABOUT WHAT OUR CARGO IS?
WELL, I WAS INFORMED ...
GWMM
IT'S GOT SOMETHING TO DO WITH MAKING USE OF THE SUN, BUT THE REST OF IT WAS BEYOND MY COMPREHENSION.
WHUM
THINK I MIGHT GO HAVE A PEEK AT IT.
ガゴン
CHKUNG
ALL RIGHT!
ALL RIGHT!
ガゴン
ガゴン
CHKUNG
WHO-HOA.
ガゴン
CHKUNG
!
HEY! WHAT THE HELL ARE YOU DOING IN HERE?
THIS AREA IS OFF LIMITS TO PILOTS!!
WHA?!
SORRY!!

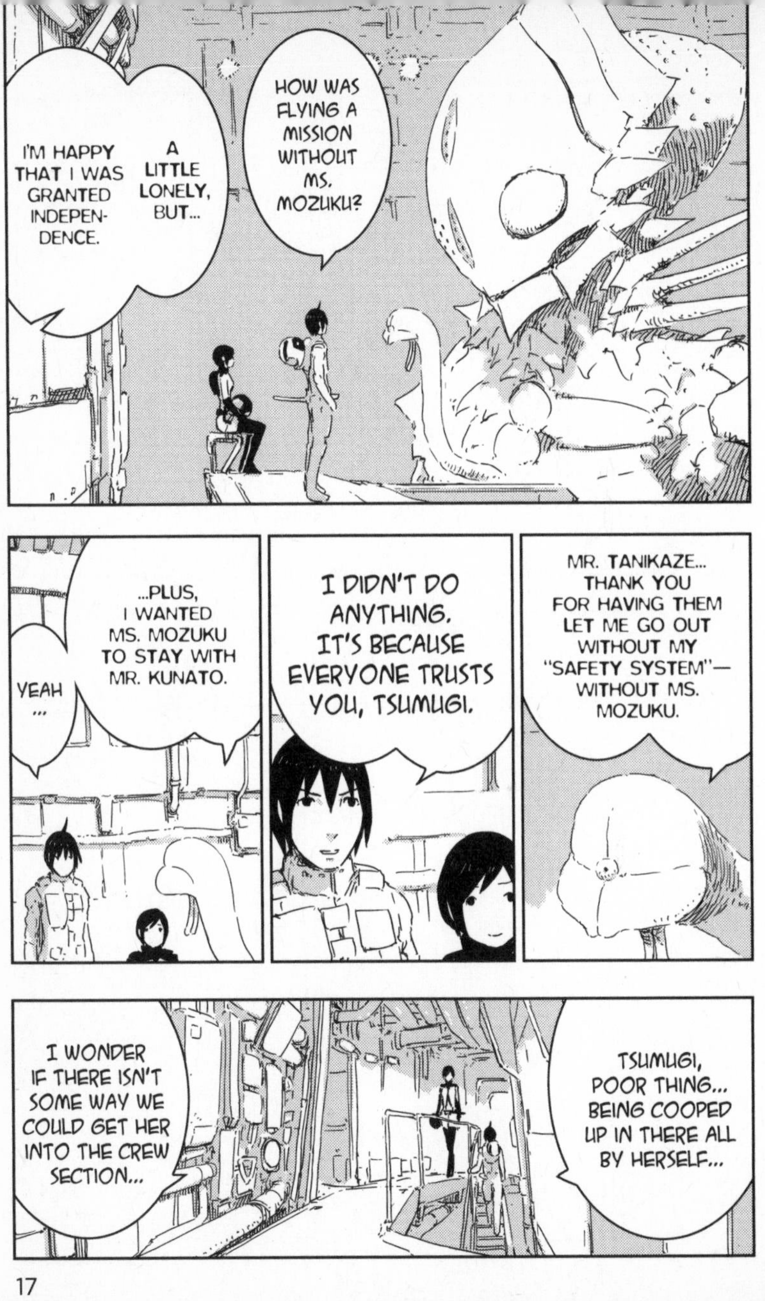

HOW WAS FLYING A MISSION WITHOUT MS. MOZUKU?
A LITTLE LONELY, BUT...
I'M HAPPY THAT I WAS GRANTED INDEPEN-DENCE.
MR. TANIKAZE... THANK YOU FOR HAVING THEM LET ME GO OUT WITHOUT MY "SAFETY SYSTEM"—WITHOUT MS. MOZUKU.
I DIDN'T DO ANYTHING. IT'S BECAUSE EVERYONE TRUSTS YOU, TSUMUGI.
...PLUS, I WANTED MS. MOZUKU TO STAY WITH MR. KUNATO.
YEAH ...
TSUMUGI, POOR THING... BEING COOPED UP IN THERE ALL BY HERSELF...
I WONDER IF THERE ISN'T SOME WAY WE COULD GET HER INTO THE CREW SECTION...

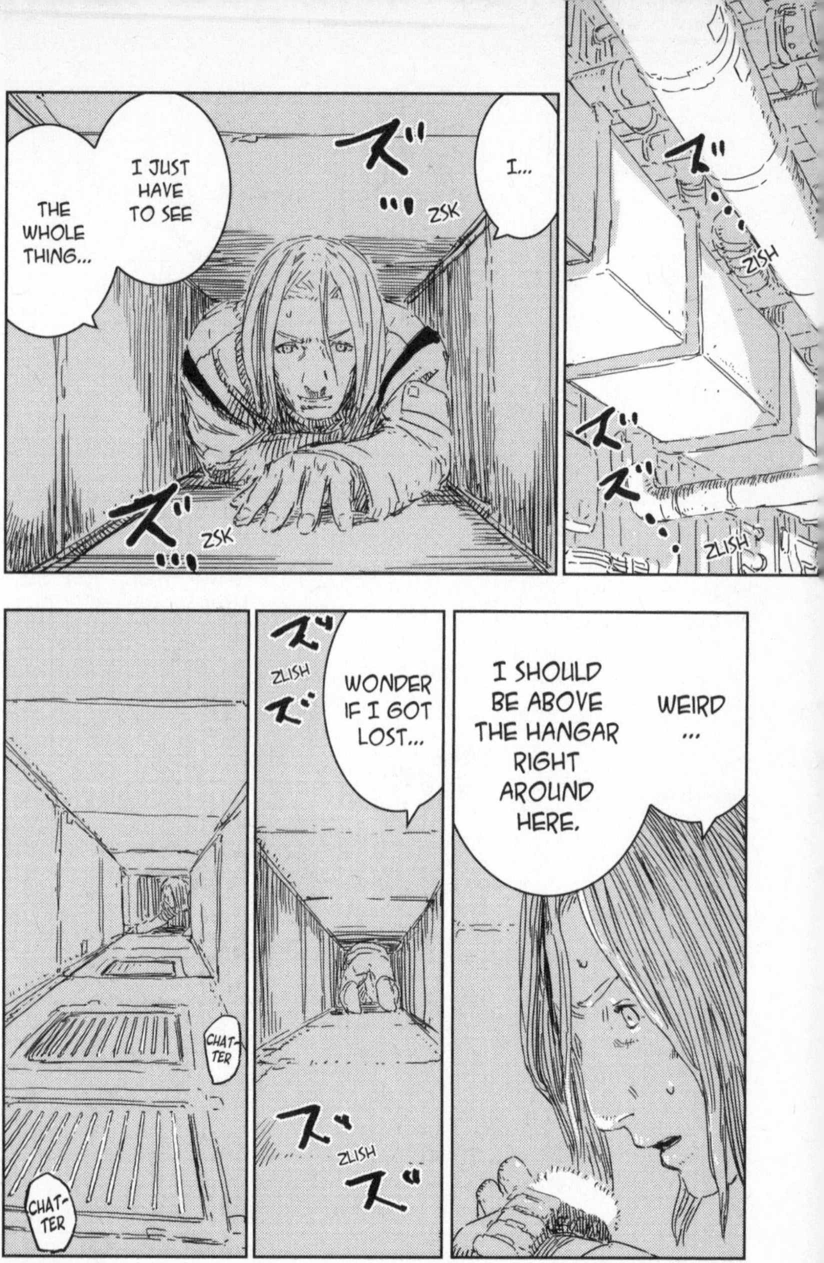
ZISH
ZLISH
I...
ZSK
THE WHOLE THING... I JUST HAVE TO SEE
ZSK
WEIRD...
I SHOULD BE ABOVE THE HANGAR RIGHT AROUND HERE.
WONDER IF I GOT LOST...
ZLISH
ZLISH
CHATTER
CHATTER

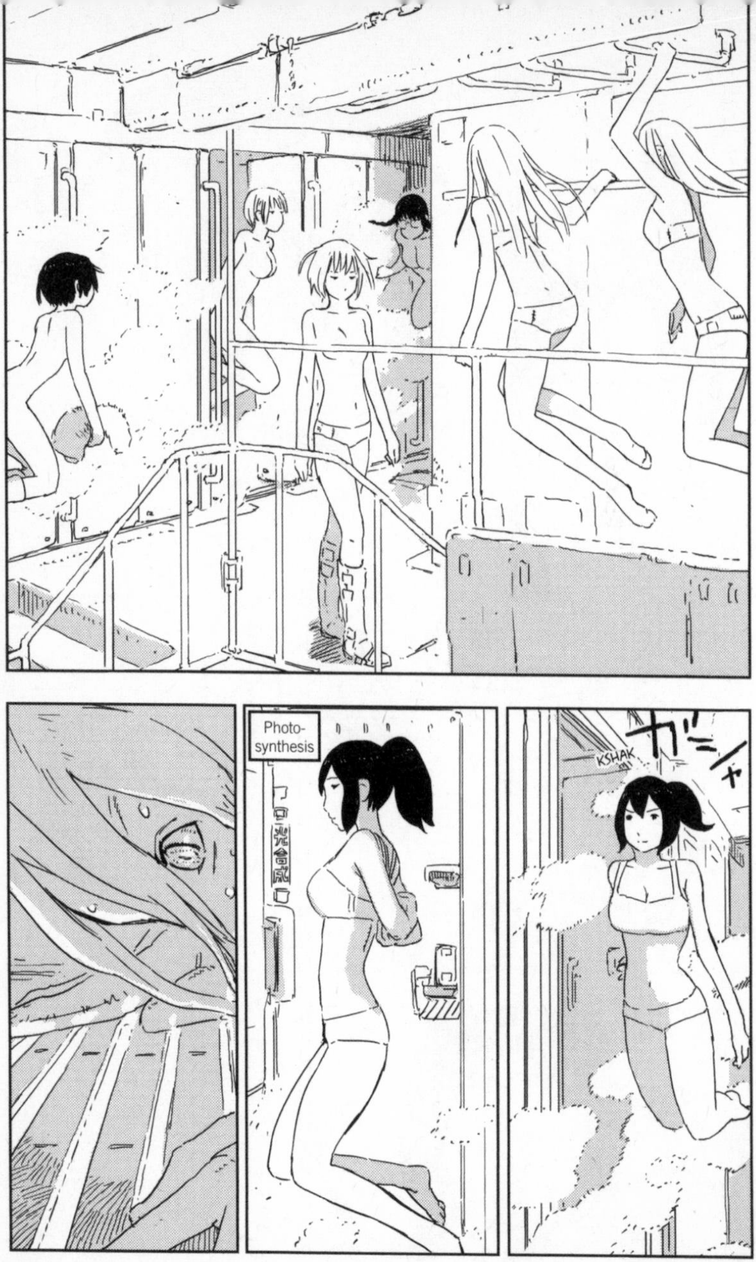
KSHAK
ガシャ
Photo-
synthesis
光合成

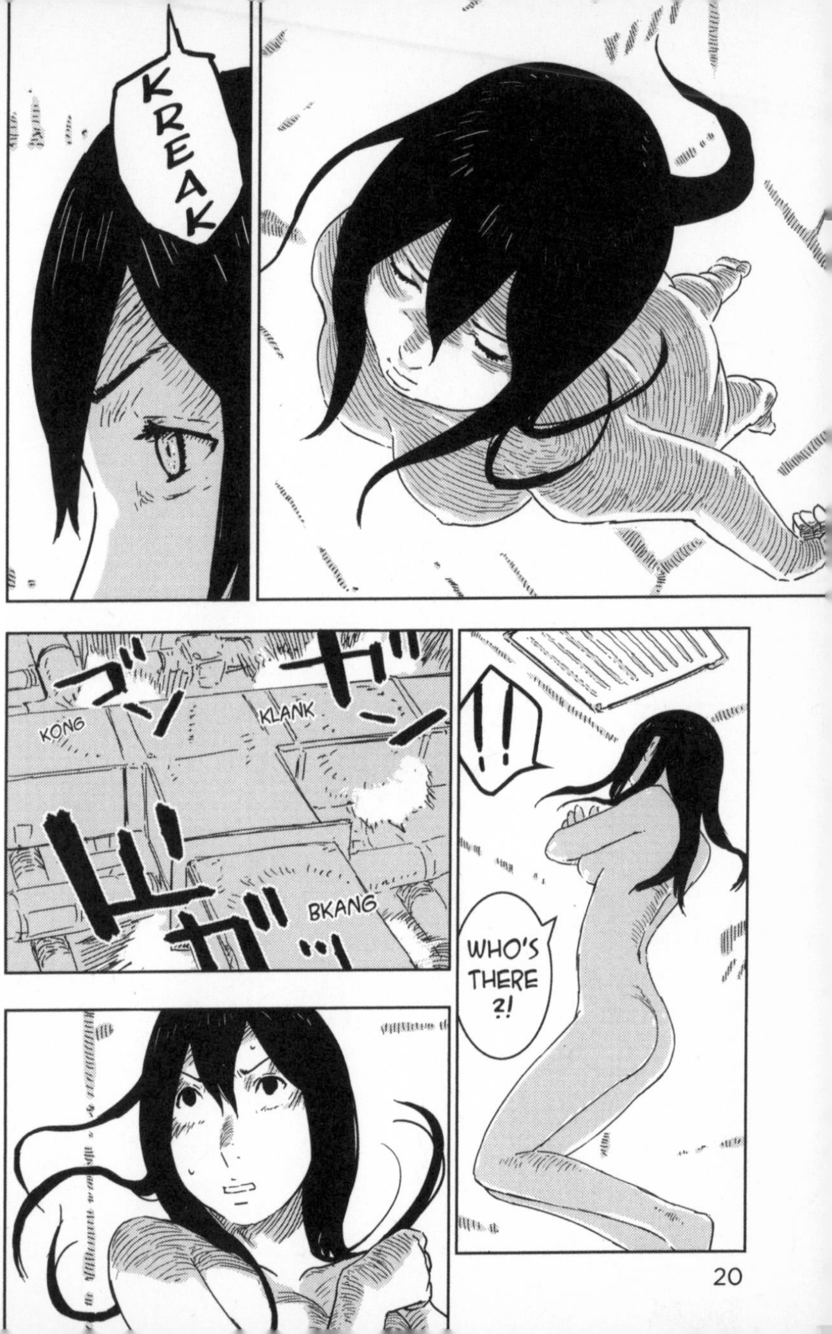
KREAK
!!
WHO'S THERE ?!
KLANK
KONG
BKANG

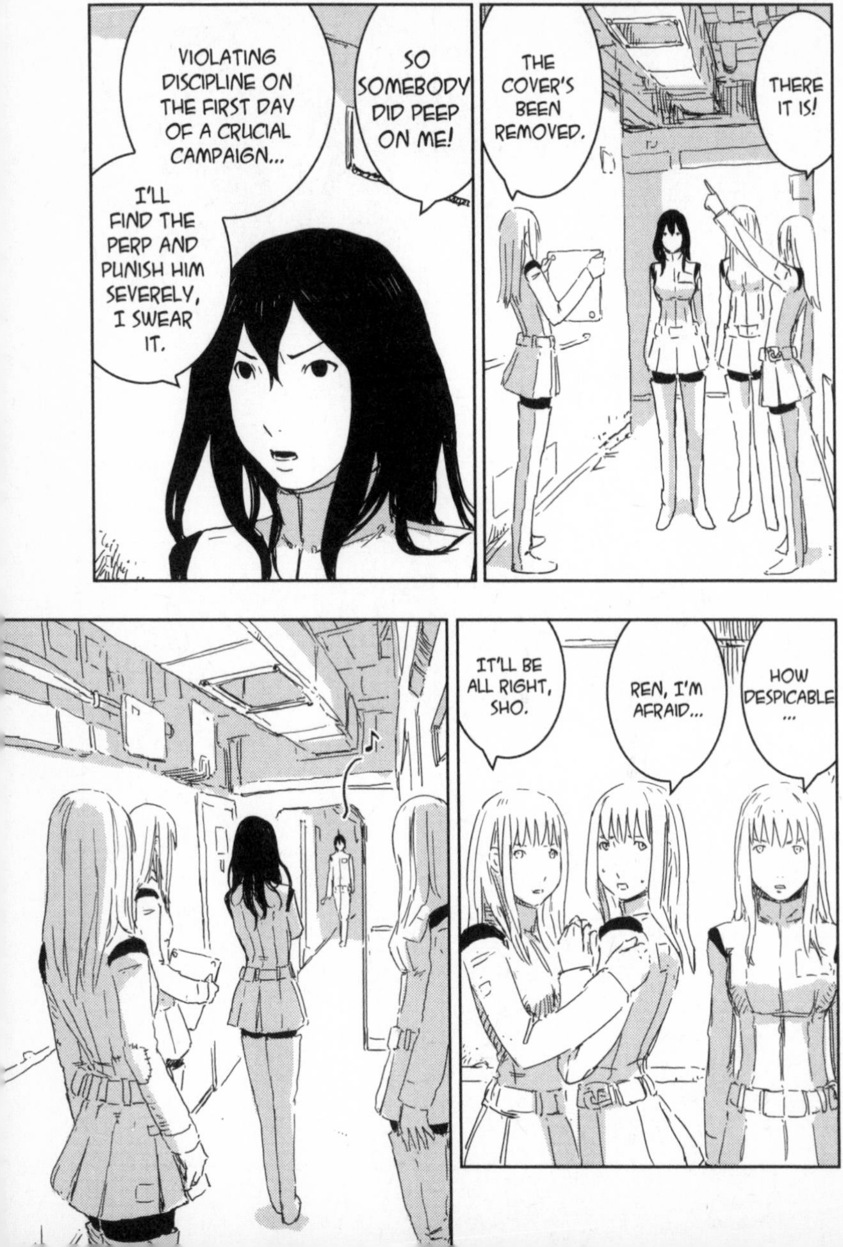
THERE IT IS!
THE COVER'S BEEN REMOVED.
SO SOMEBODY DID PEEP ON ME!
VIOLATING DISCIPLINE ON THE FIRST DAY OF A CRUCIAL CAMPAIGN...
I'LL FIND THE PERP AND PUNISH HIM SEVERELY, I SWEAR IT.
HOW DESPICABLE ...
REN, I'M AFRAID...
IT'LL BE ALL RIGHT, SHO.
♪
...

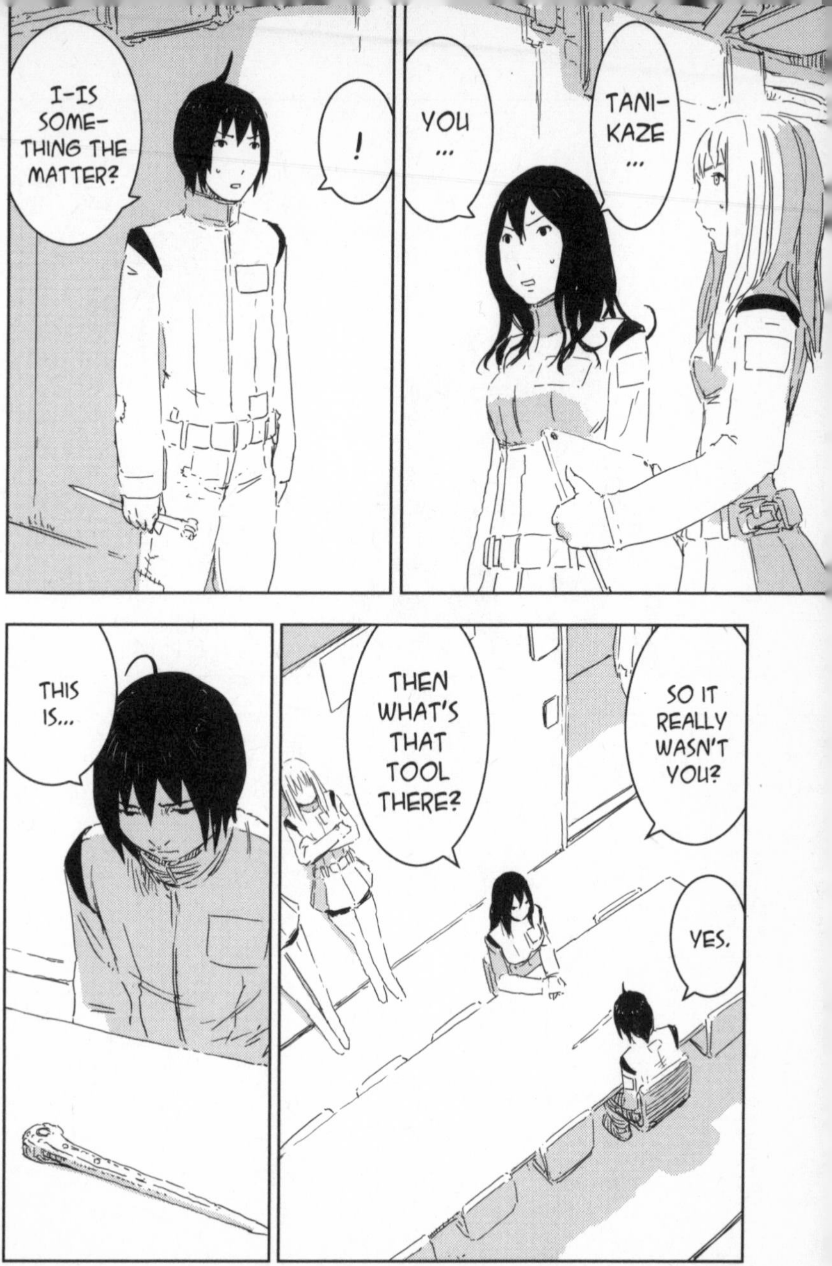
TANI-KAZE ...
YOU ...
!
I-IS SOME-THING THE MATTER?
SO IT REALLY WASN'T YOU?
YES.
THEN WHAT'S THAT TOOL THERE?
THIS IS...

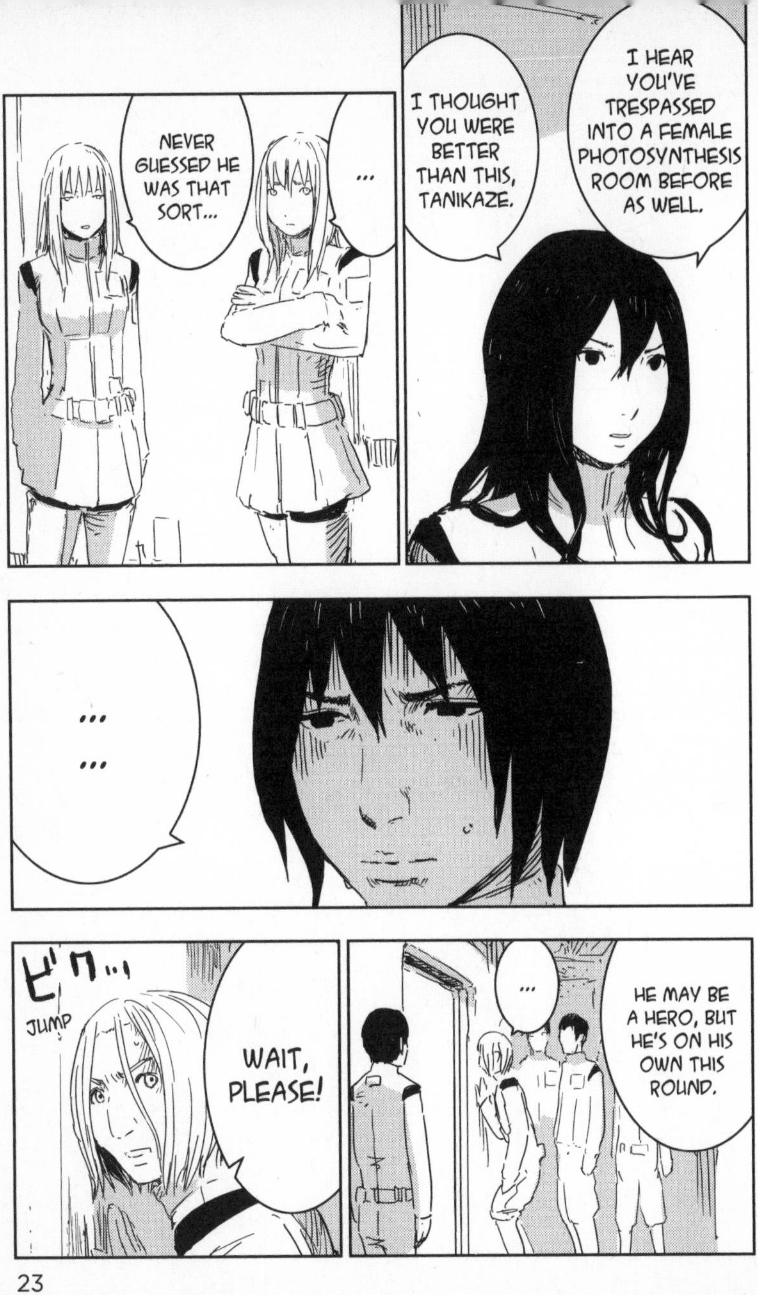

I HEAR YOU'VE TRESPASSED INTO A FEMALE PHOTOSYNTHESIS ROOM BEFORE AS WELL.
I THOUGHT YOU WERE BETTER THAN THIS, TANIKAZE.
...
NEVER GUESSED HE WAS THAT SORT...
...
...
HE MAY BE A HERO, BUT HE'S ON HIS OWN THIS ROUND.
...
WAIT, PLEASE!
ビクッ
JUMP

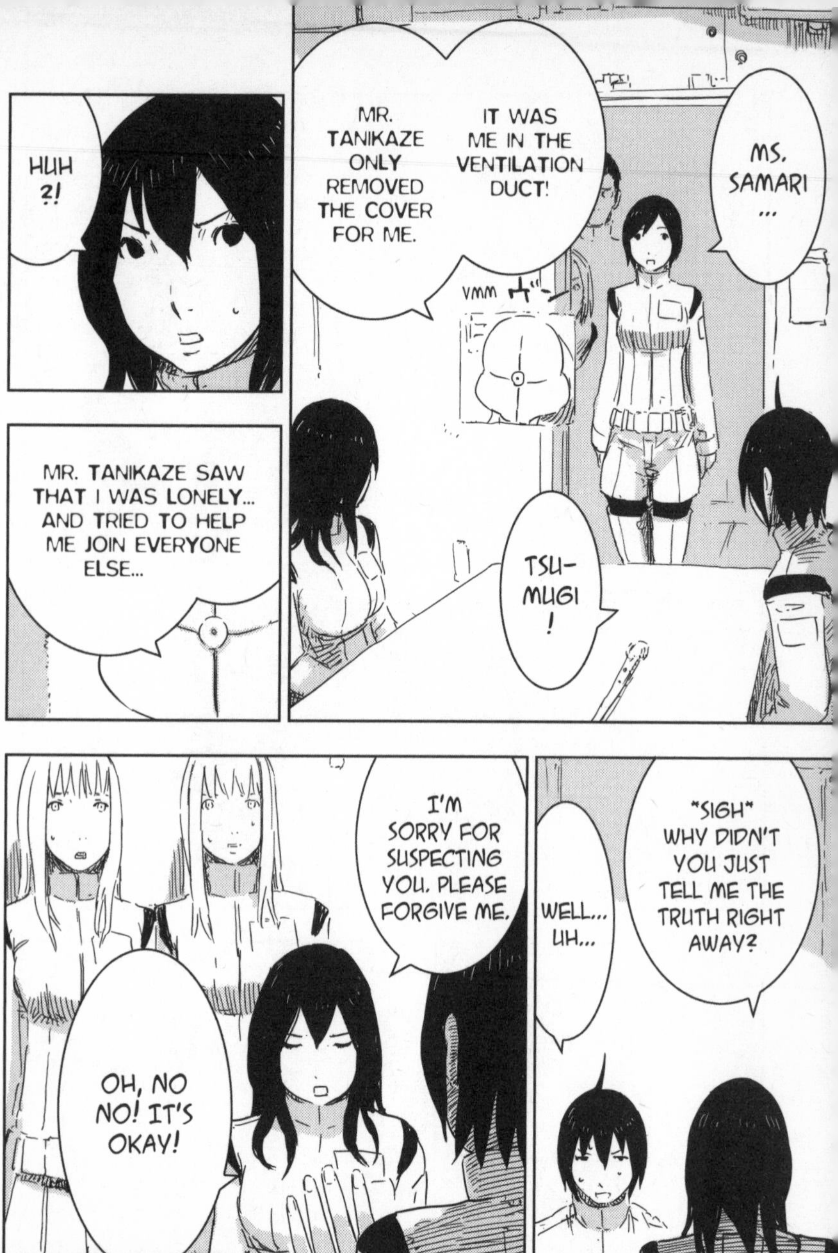
MS. SAMARI ...
IT WAS ME IN THE VENTILATION DUCT!
MR. TANIKAZE ONLY REMOVED THE COVER FOR ME.
vmm
TSU-MUGI!
HUH?!
MR. TANIKAZE SAW THAT I WAS LONELY... AND TRIED TO HELP ME JOIN EVERYONE ELSE...
SIGH WHY DIDN'T YOU JUST TELL ME THE TRUTH RIGHT AWAY?
WELL... UH...
I'M SORRY FOR SUSPECTING YOU. PLEASE FORGIVE ME.
OH, NO NO! IT'S OKAY!

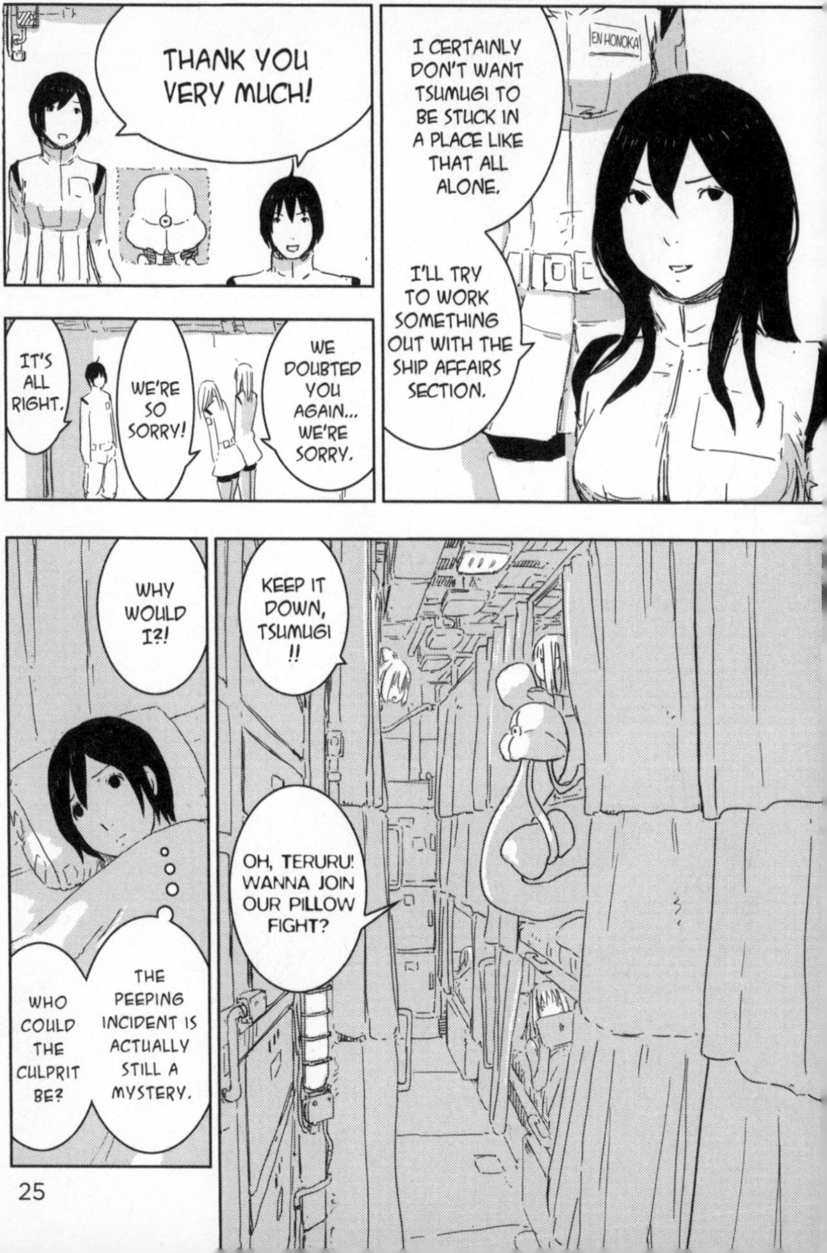
EN HONOKA
I CERTAINLY DON'T WANT TSUMUGI TO BE STUCK IN A PLACE LIKE THAT ALL ALONE.
I'LL TRY TO WORK SOMETHING OUT WITH THE SHIP AFFAIRS SECTION.
THANK YOU VERY MUCH!
WE DOUBTED YOU AGAIN... WE'RE SORRY.
WE'RE SO SORRY!
IT'S ALL RIGHT.
KEEP IT DOWN, TSUMUGI!!
OH, TERURU! WANNA JOIN OUR PILLOW FIGHT?
WHY WOULD I?!
THE PEEPING INCIDENT IS ACTUALLY STILL A MYSTERY.
WHO COULD THE CULPRIT BE?

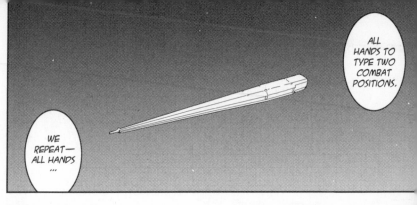

ALL HANDS TO TYPE TWO COMBAT POSITIONS.
WE REPEAT—ALL HANDS ...
I'VE COMPLETED PROCESSING THE DATA FROM THE PATROL UNIT GROUP.
SURVEYING COMPLETE HERE TOO.
DISPLAYING THE SECTOR WHERE THE DISTORTION WAS DETECTED.
LARGEST MEASURED DIAMETER APPROXI-MATELY 5 KM.
... ...
FIRE THE HIGGS PARTICLE CANNON INTO THE DISTORTED AREA—A WIDE-ANGLE BLAST!
ROGER!
KZNG

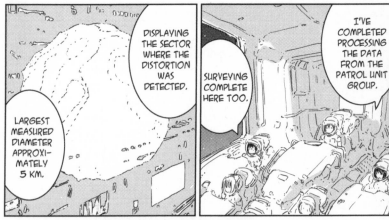

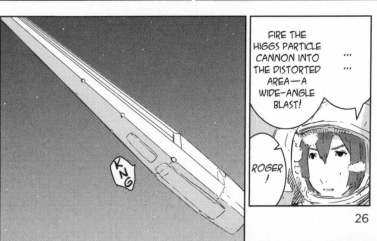

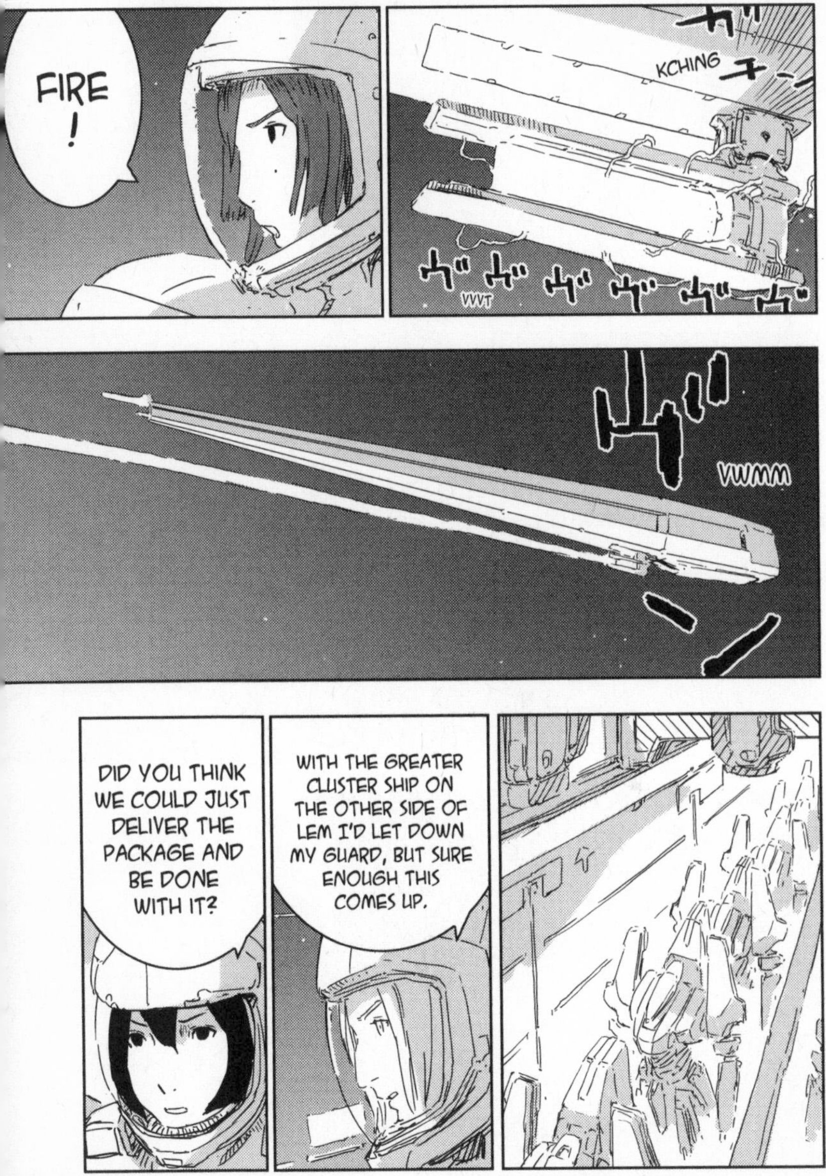
KCHING
VVVT
FIRE!
VWMM
WITH THE GREATER CLUSTER SHIP ON THE OTHER SIDE OF LEM I'D LET DOWN MY GUARD, BUT SURE ENOUGH THIS COMES UP.
DID YOU THINK WE COULD JUST DELIVER THE PACKAGE AND BE DONE WITH IT?

GKUNNG

ブゴーー

KNNG

ゴっー

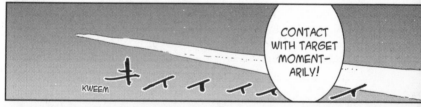

CONTACT WITH TARGET MOMENT- ARILY!

KWEEM

BWAMF

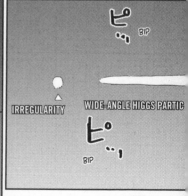

ピ BIP

IRREGULARITY

WIDE-ANGLE HIGGS PARTIC

ピ BIP

GAUNA MATERIALIZING!!

IT'S REACT-ING!!

Y-YES...

SHO, ARE YOU ALL RIGHT?

HUFF

GAUNA...

HUFF

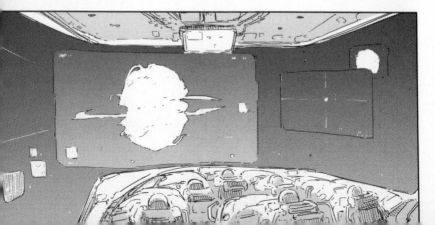

Chapter 55: END

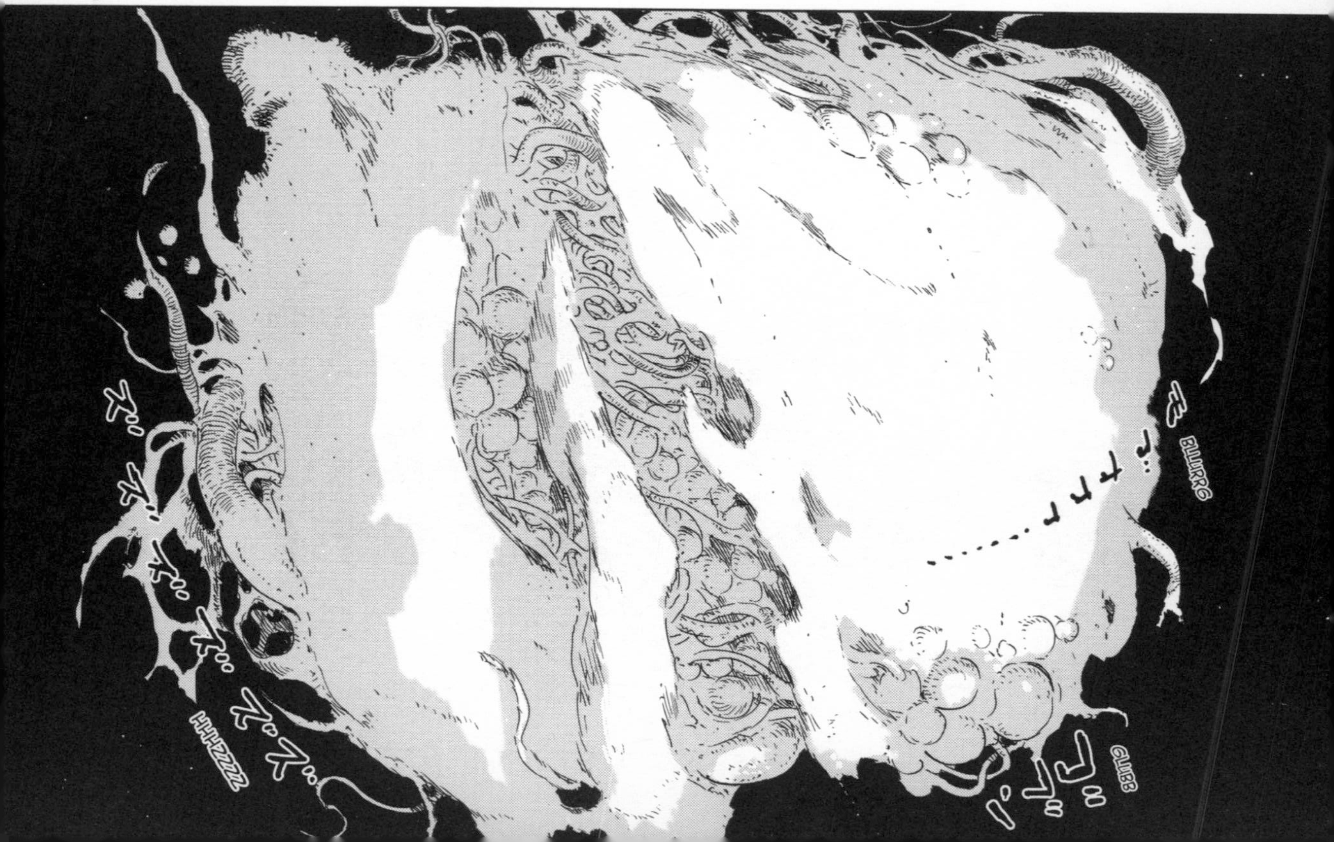

Chapter 56: The Gauna's Shapelessness

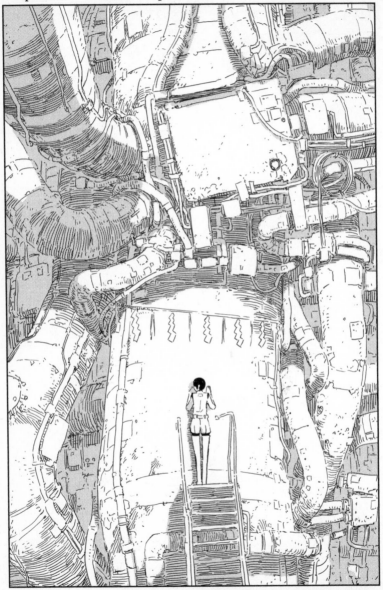

One Hundred Sights of Sidonia Part Forty-Two:
Tube of Sidonia's Oldest Conversion Reactor

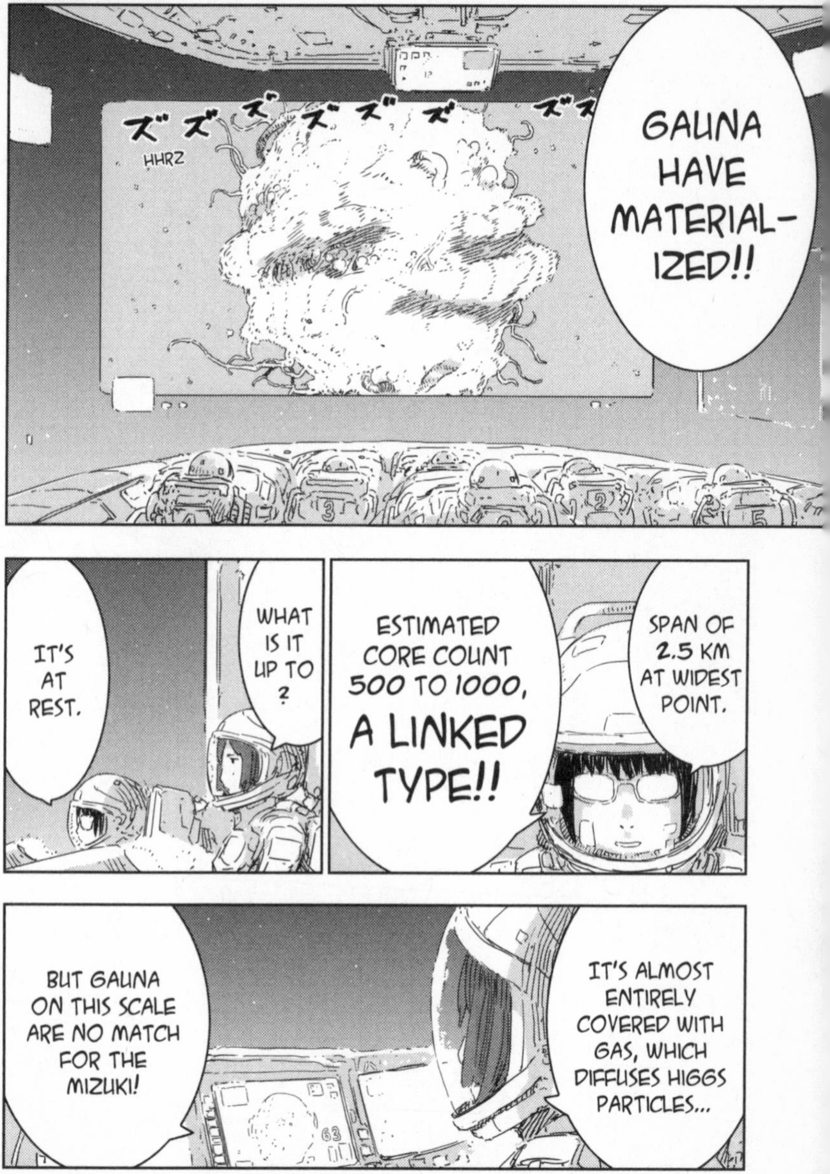
GAUNA HAVE MATERIAL-IZED!!
ズズズズズズズズ
HHRZ
SPAN OF 2.5 KM AT WIDEST POINT.
ESTIMATED CORE COUNT 500 TO 1000, A LINKED TYPE!!
WHAT IS IT UP TO?
IT'S AT REST.
IT'S ALMOST ENTIRELY COVERED WITH GAS, WHICH DIFFUSES HIGGS PARTICLES...
BUT GAUNA ON THIS SCALE ARE NO MATCH FOR THE MIZUKI!

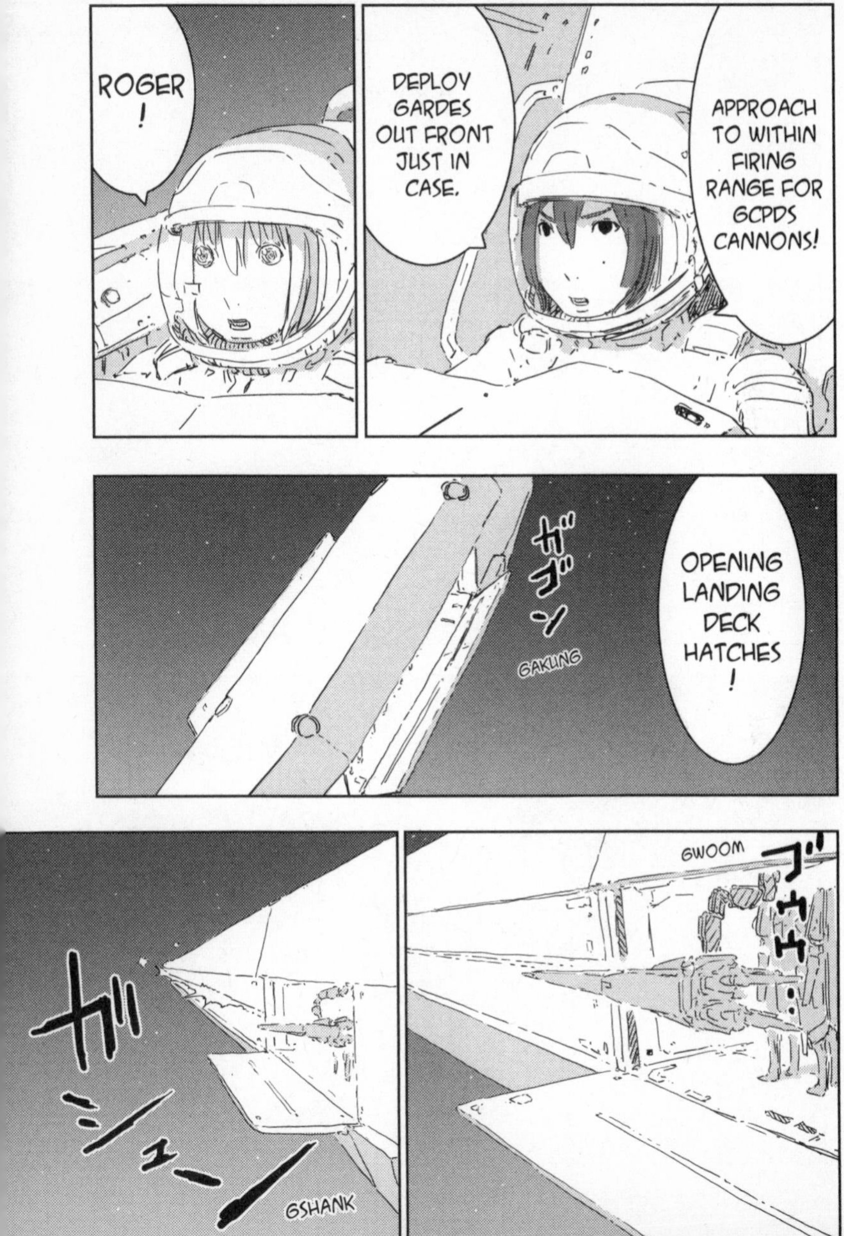
APPROACH TO WITHIN FIRING RANGE FOR GCPDS CANNONS!
DEPLOY GARDES OUT FRONT JUST IN CASE.
ROGER!
OPENING LANDING DECK HATCHES!
ガゴン
GAKUNG
GWOOM
ガシュー
GSHANK

SHUNGK
SHUNGK
VWOOOO
24-UNIT CLASP ARRAY!
ROGER!

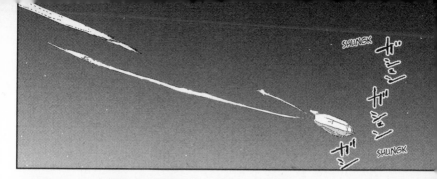

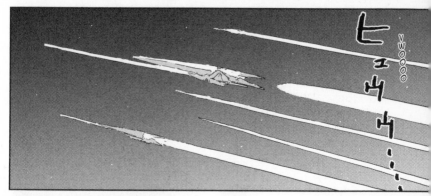

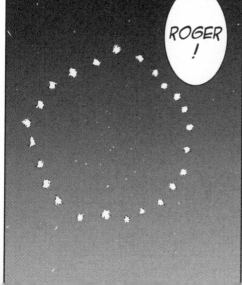

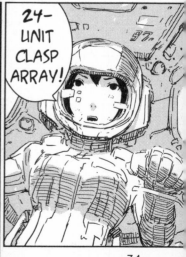

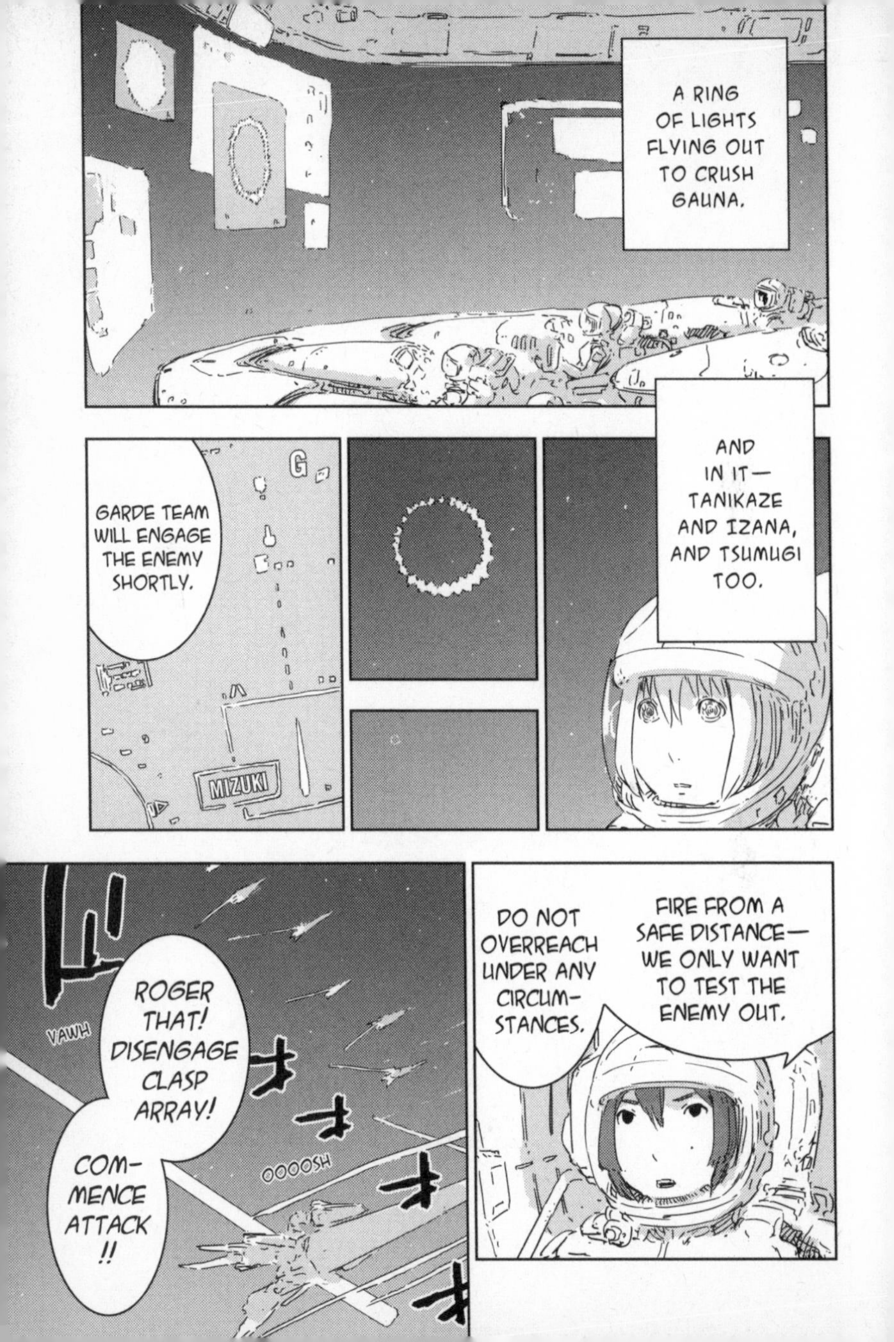
A RING OF LIGHTS FLYING OUT TO CRUSH GAUNA.
AND IN IT— TANIKAZE AND IZANA, AND TSUMUGI TOO.
G
GARDE TEAM WILL ENGAGE THE ENEMY SHORTLY.
MIZUKI
FIRE FROM A SAFE DISTANCE— WE ONLY WANT TO TEST THE ENEMY OUT.
DO NOT OVERREACH UNDER ANY CIRCUM-STANCES.
ROGER THAT! DISENGAGE CLASP ARRAY!
VAWH
COM-MENCE ATTACK!!
OOOOSH

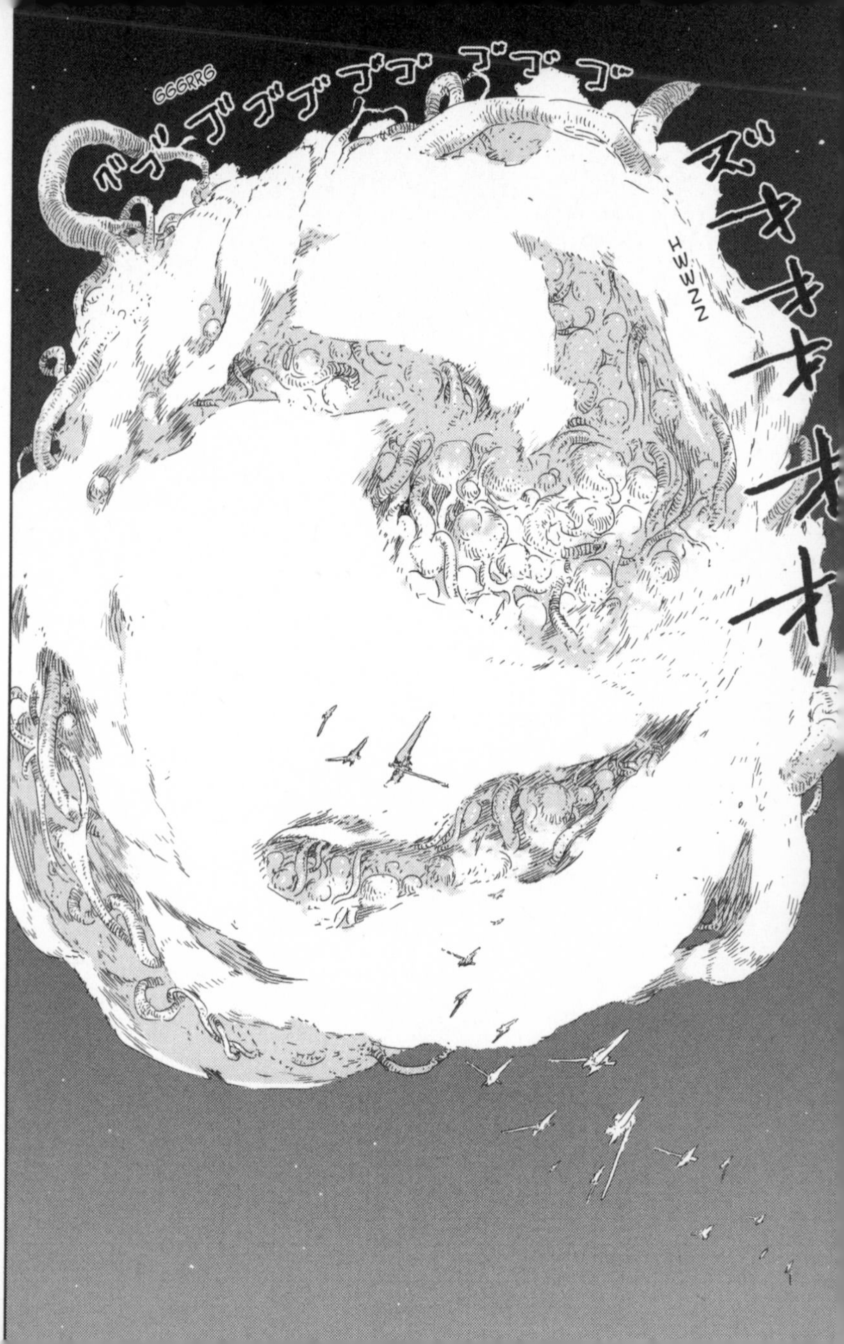
ズオオオオオ
HWWNN
グゴブブブゴゴゴゴ
GGGRRG

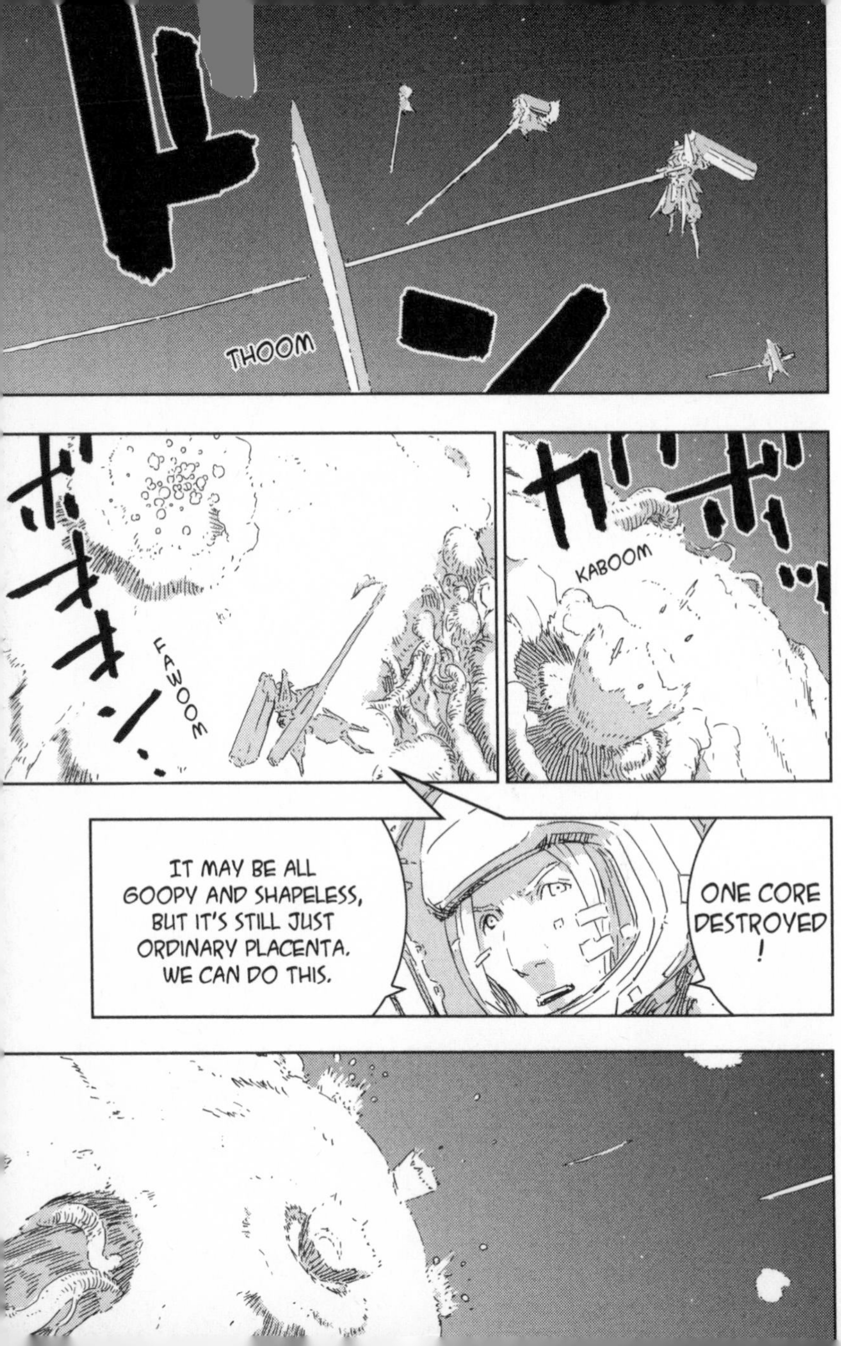
THOOM
KABOOM
FAWOOM
ONE CORE DESTROYED!
IT MAY BE ALL GOOPY AND SHAPELESS, BUT IT'S STILL JUST ORDINARY PLACENTA. WE CAN DO THIS.

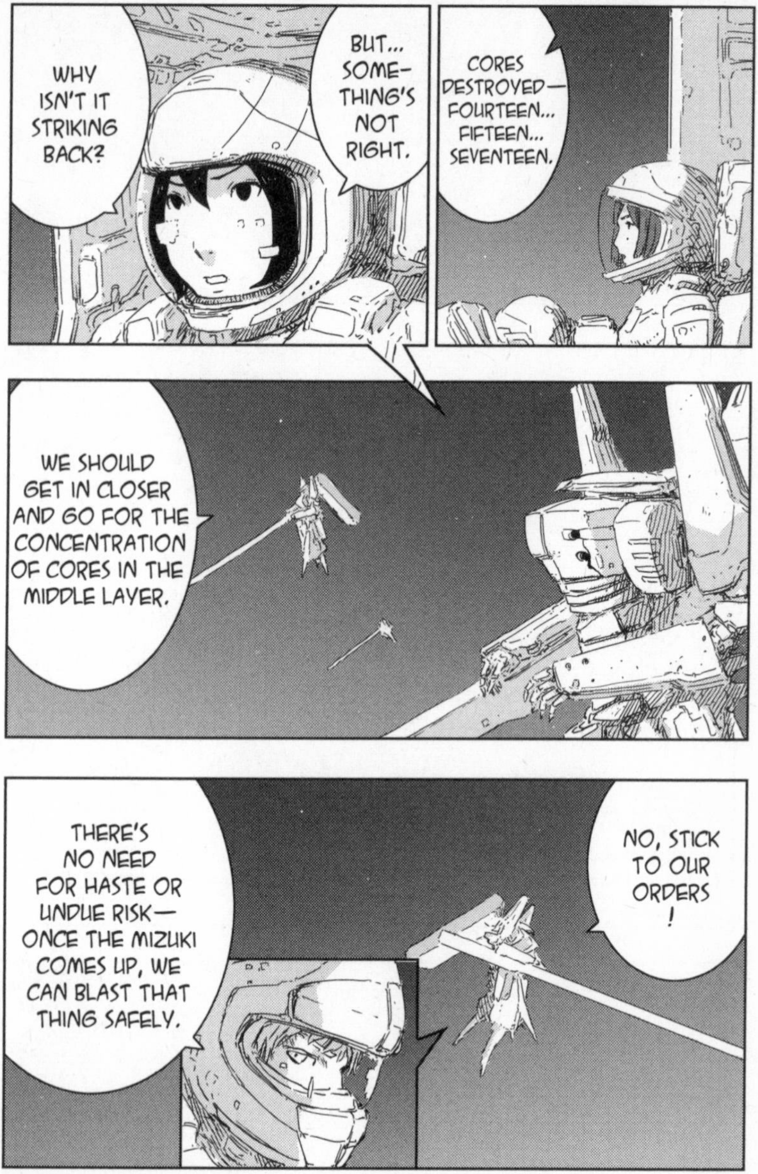
CORES DESTROYED—FOURTEEN... FIFTEEN... SEVENTEEN.
BUT... SOME-THING'S NOT RIGHT.
WHY ISN'T IT STRIKING BACK?
WE SHOULD GET IN CLOSER AND GO FOR THE CONCENTRATION OF CORES IN THE MIDDLE LAYER.
NO, STICK TO OUR ORDERS!
THERE'S NO NEED FOR HASTE OR UNDUE RISK—ONCE THE MIZUKI COMES UP, WE CAN BLAST THAT THING SAFELY.

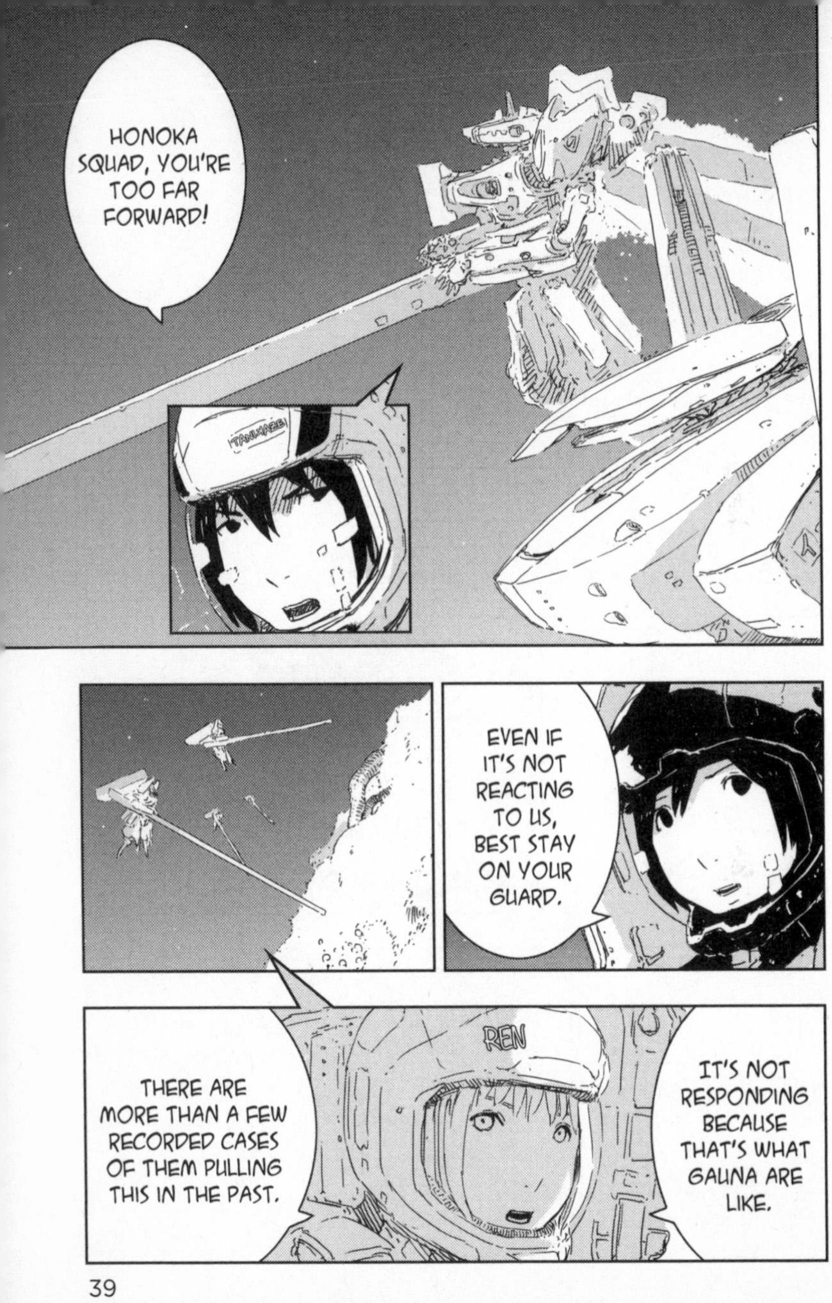
HONOKA SQUAD, YOU'RE TOO FAR FORWARD!
EVEN IF IT'S NOT REACTING TO US, BEST STAY ON YOUR GUARD.
REN
IT'S NOT RESPONDING BECAUSE THAT'S WHAT GAUNA ARE LIKE.
THERE ARE MORE THAN A FEW RECORDED CASES OF THEM PULLING THIS IN THE PAST.

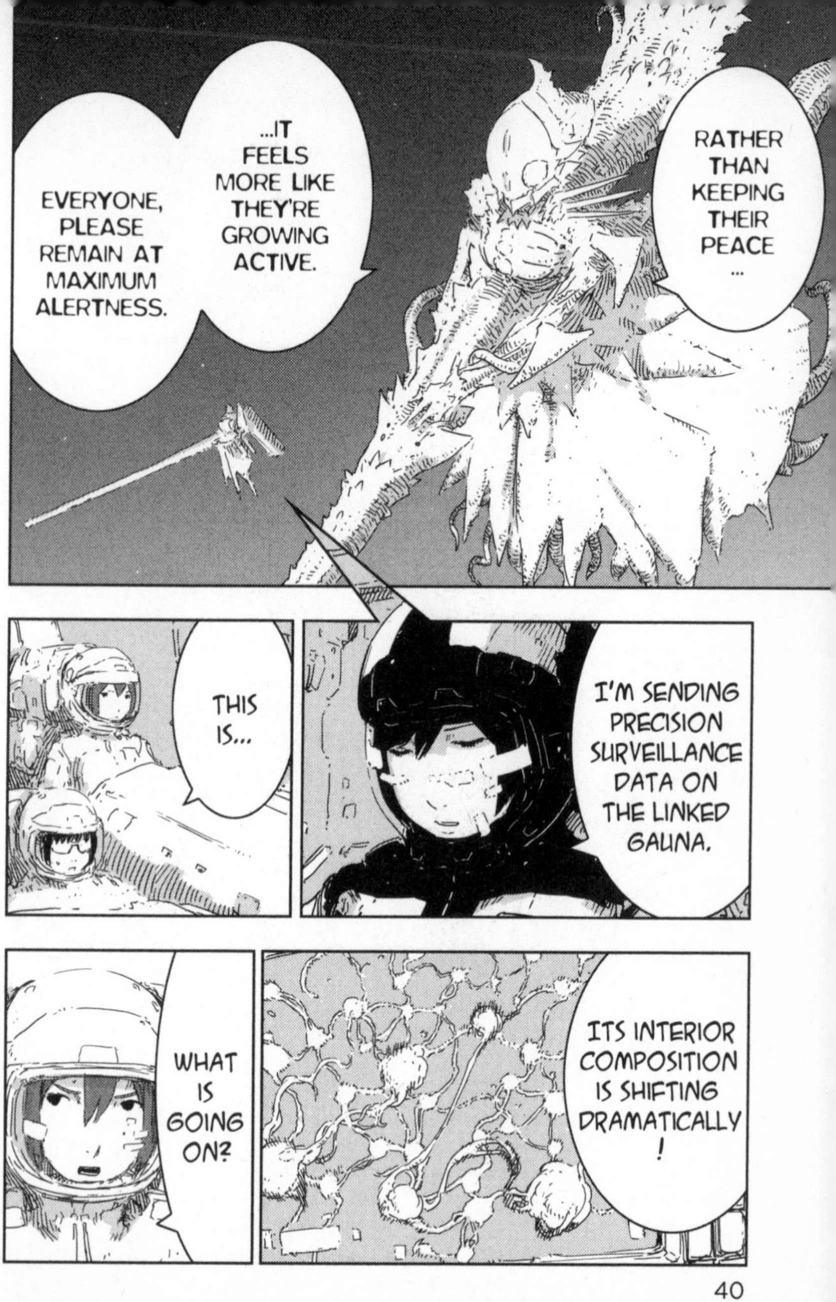
RATHER THAN KEEPING THEIR PEACE ...
...IT FEELS MORE LIKE THEY'RE GROWING ACTIVE.
EVERYONE, PLEASE REMAIN AT MAXIMUM ALERTNESS.
I'M SENDING PRECISION SURVEILLANCE DATA ON THE LINKED GAUNA.
THIS IS...
ITS INTERIOR COMPOSITION IS SHIFTING DRAMATICALLY!
WHAT IS GOING ON?

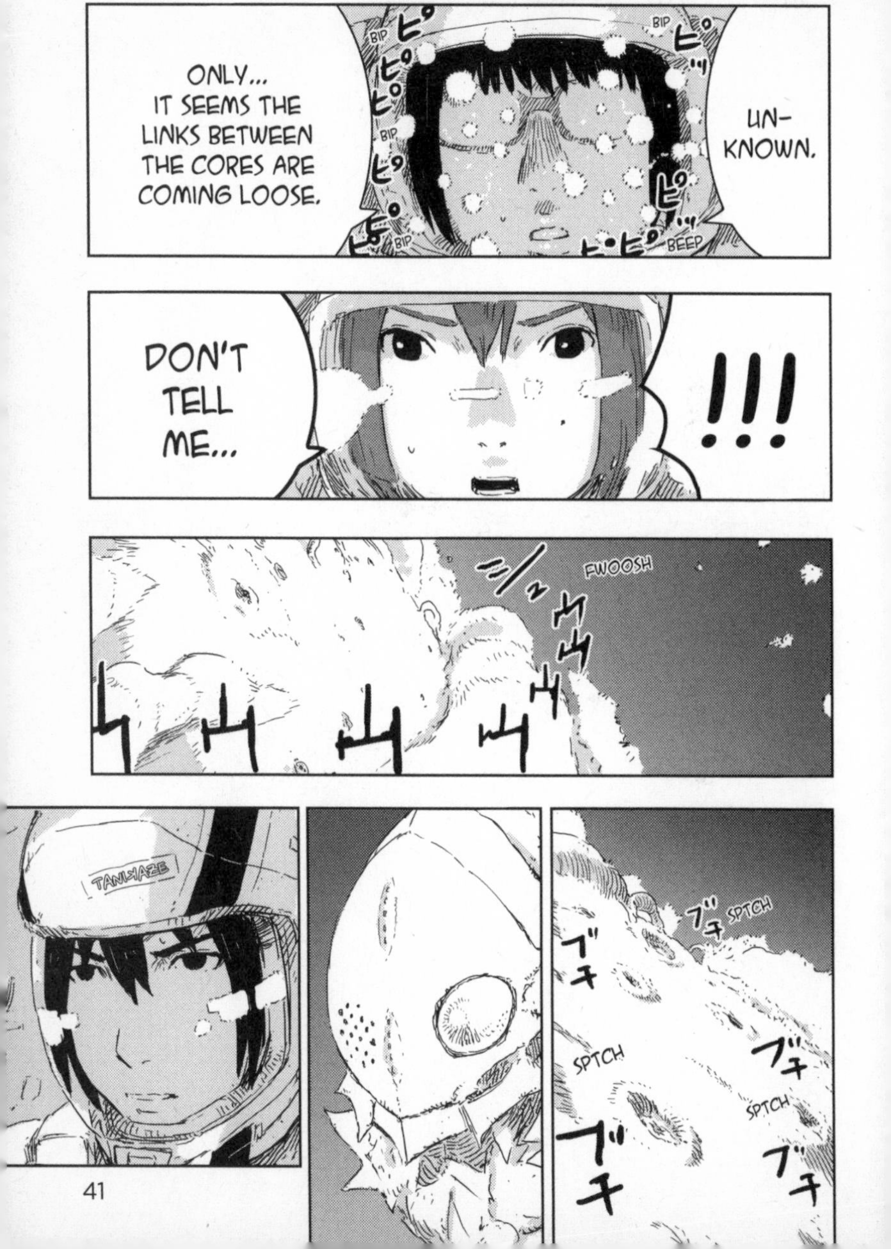
UN-KNOWN.
BIP
BIP
BIP
BIP
BEEP
ONLY... IT SEEMS THE LINKS BETWEEN THE CORES ARE COMING LOOSE.
!!!
DON'T TELL ME...
FWOOSH
SPTCH
SPTCH
SPTCH
TANIKAZE

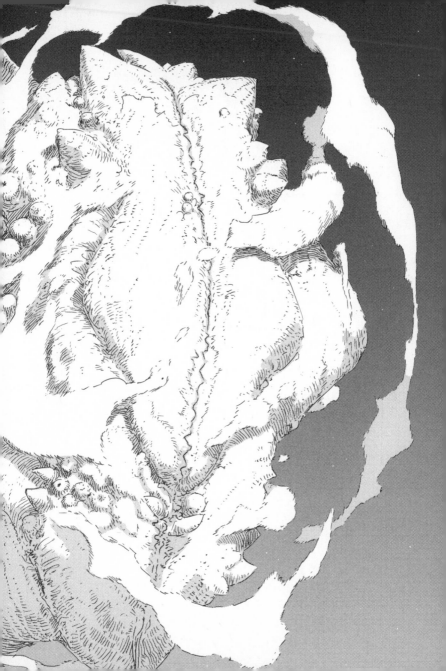

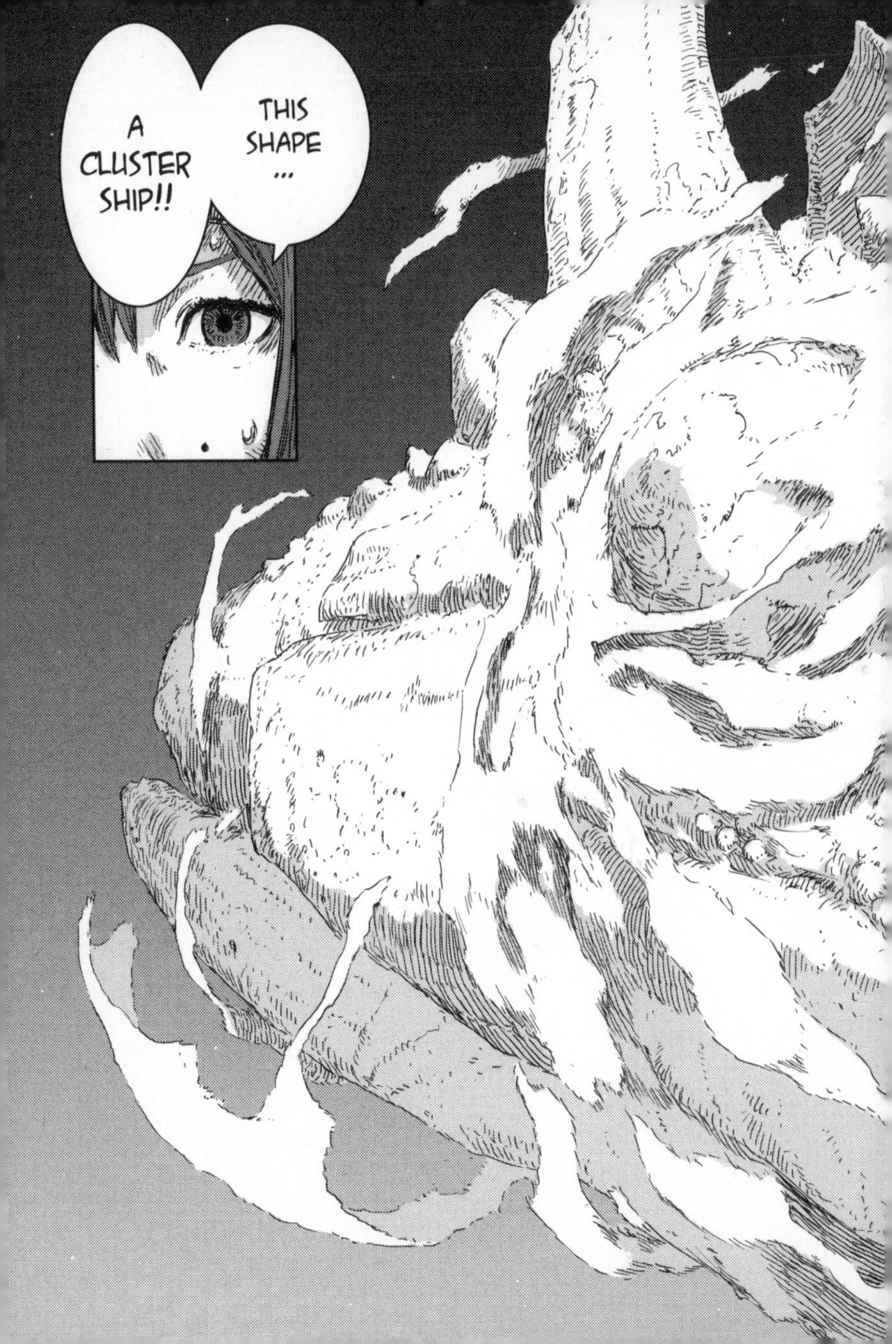
THIS SHAPE ...
A CLUSTER SHIP!!

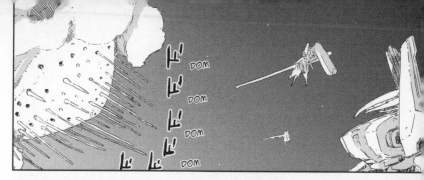

DOM
DOM
DOM
DOM
THE CLUSTER SHIP HAS LAUNCHED GAUNA!!
A HUGE NUMBER OF THEM!
RAISE MIZUKI'S SPEED!

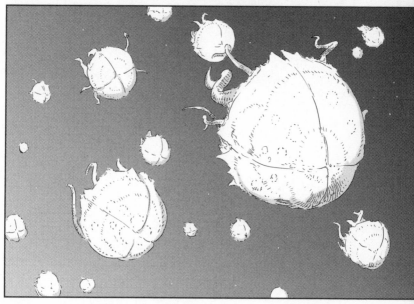

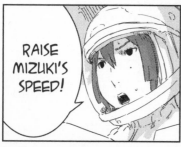

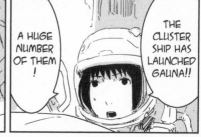

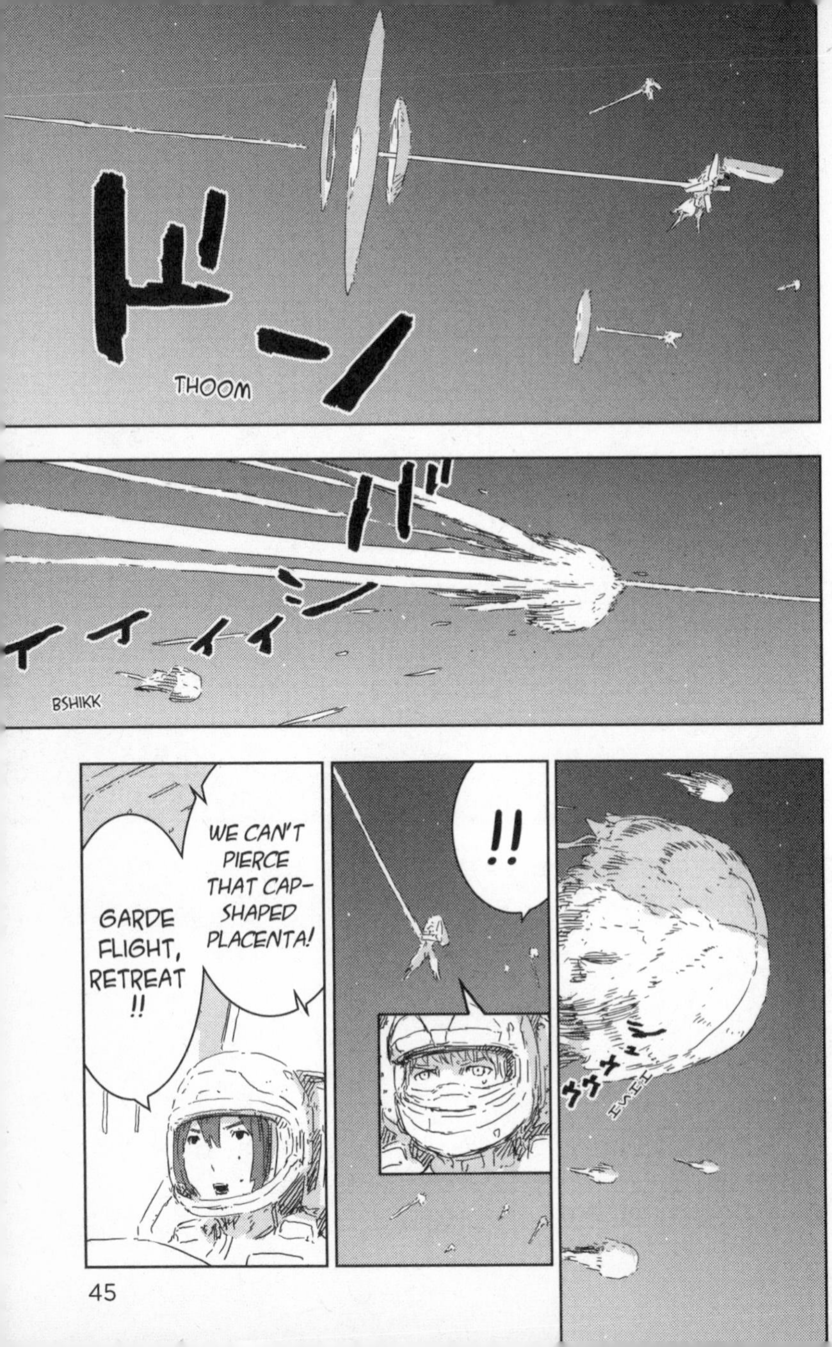
ドーン
THOOM
BSHIKK
!!
WE CAN'T PIERCE THAT CAP-SHAPED PLACENTA!
GARDE FLIGHT, RETREAT !!

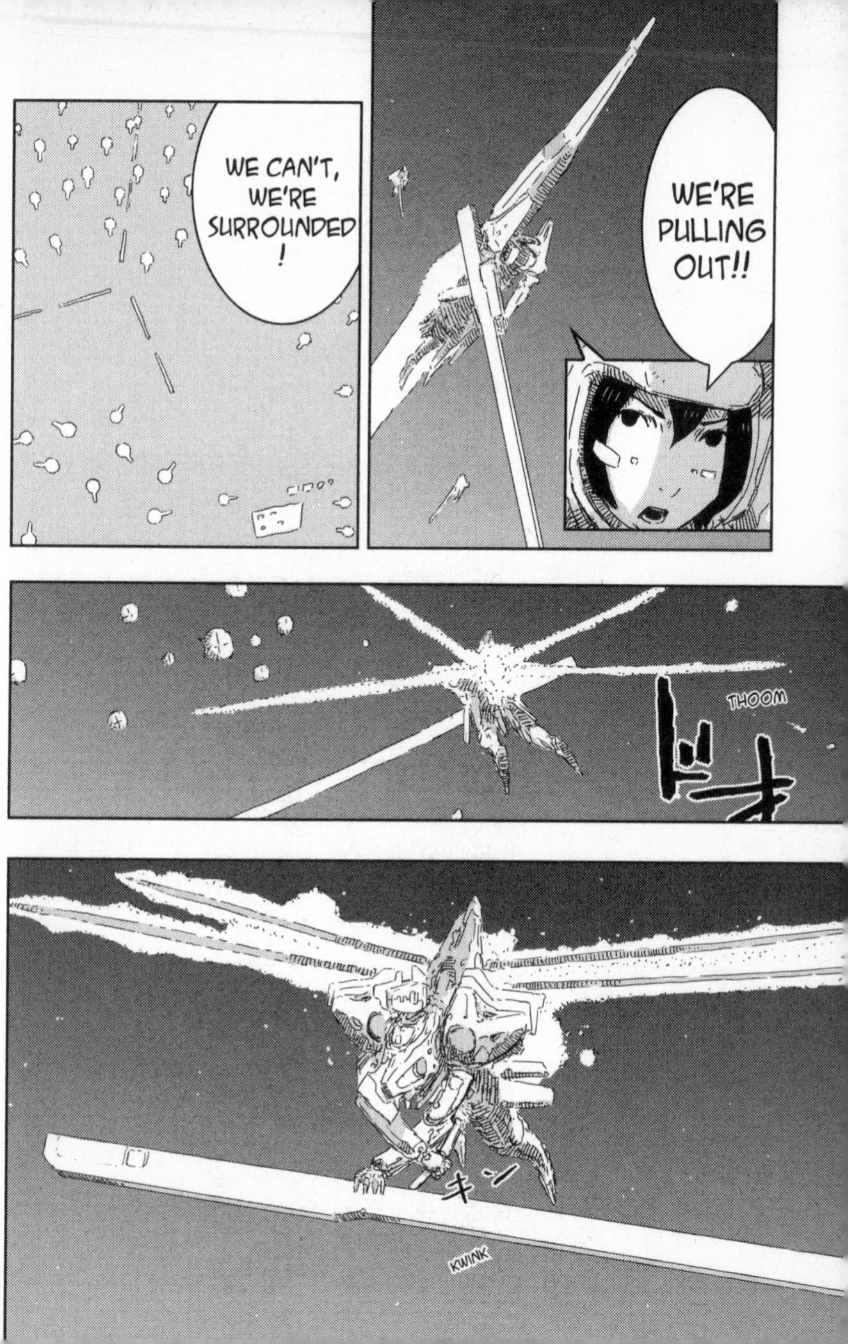

WE'RE PULLING OUT!!
WE CAN'T, WE'RE SURROUNDED!
THOOM
KWINK

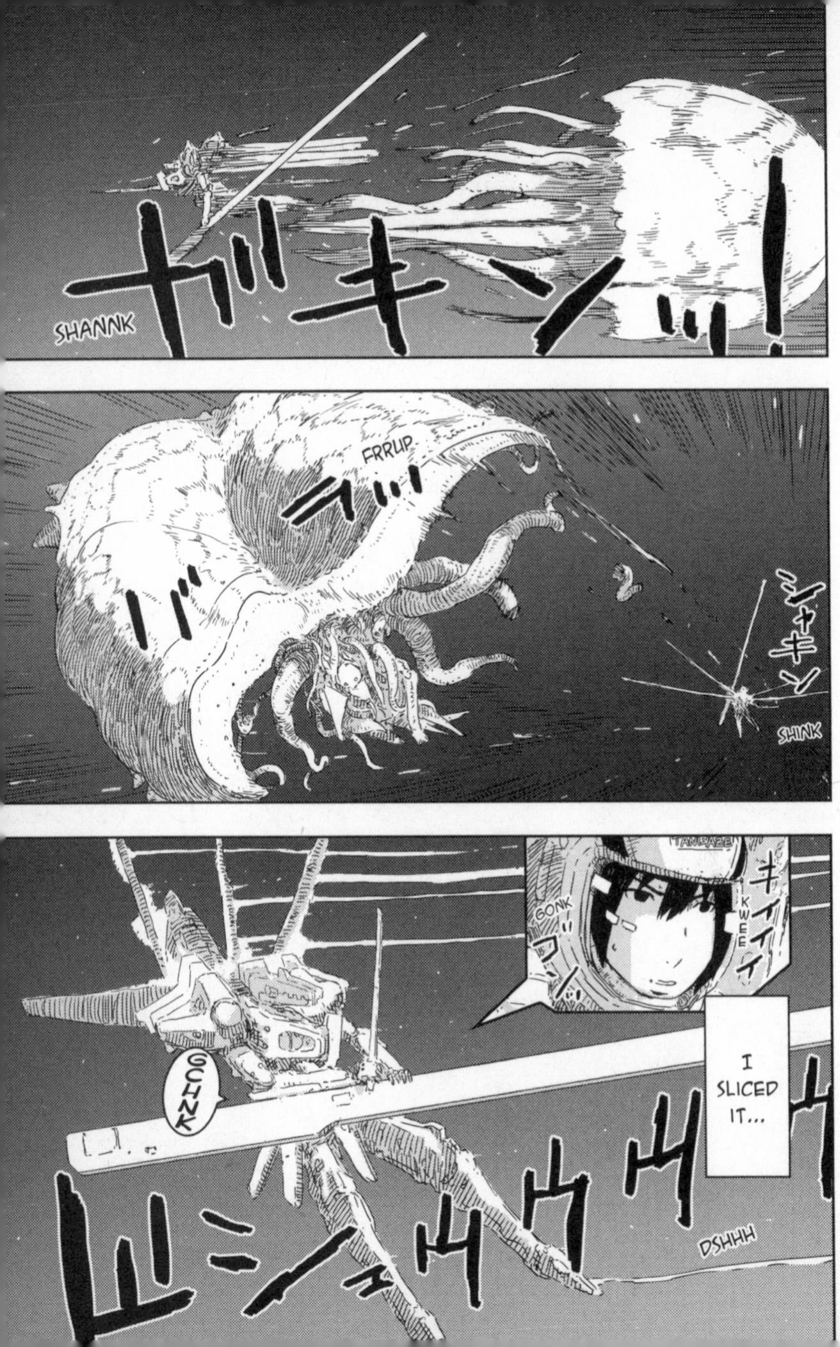
SHANNK
FRRUP
SHINK
KWEEE
GONK
I SLICED IT...
GCHNK
DSHHH

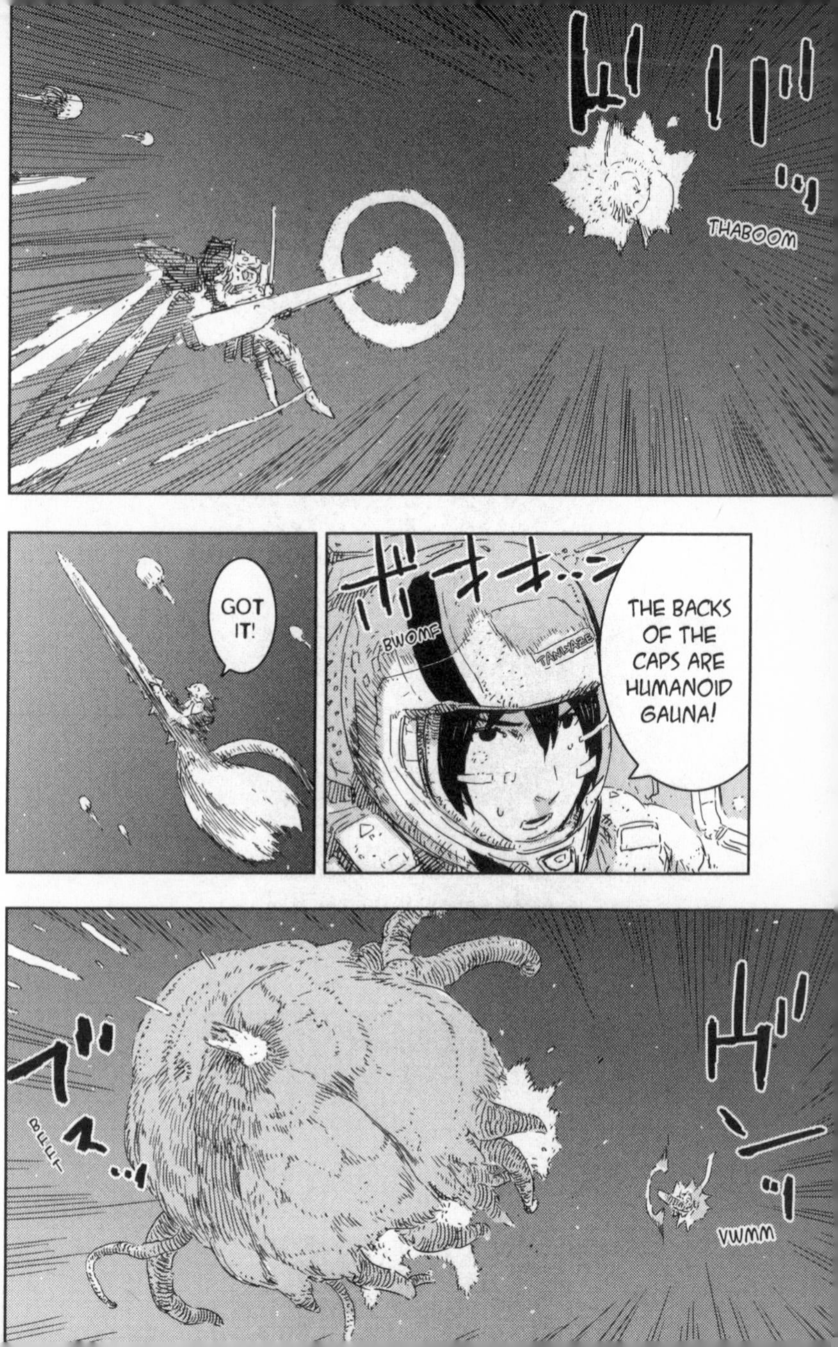
THABOOM
THE BACKS OF THE CAPS ARE HUMANOID GAUNA!
BWOMF
TANIKAZE
GOT IT!
VWMM

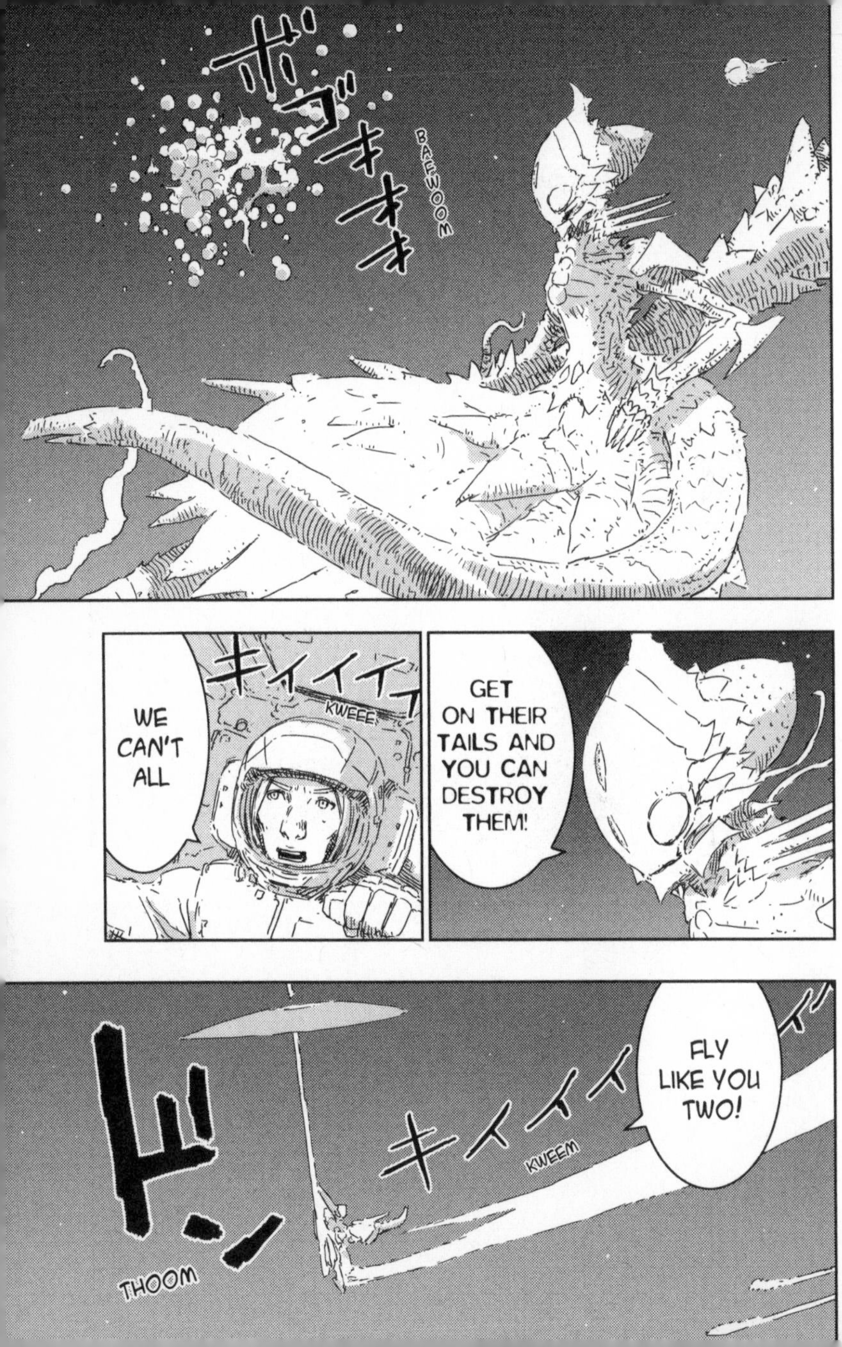
BAFWOOM
GET ON THEIR TAILS AND YOU CAN DESTROY THEM!
WE CAN'T ALL
キィイイ
KWEEE
FLY LIKE YOU TWO!
キィイイ
KWEEM
ドン
THOOM

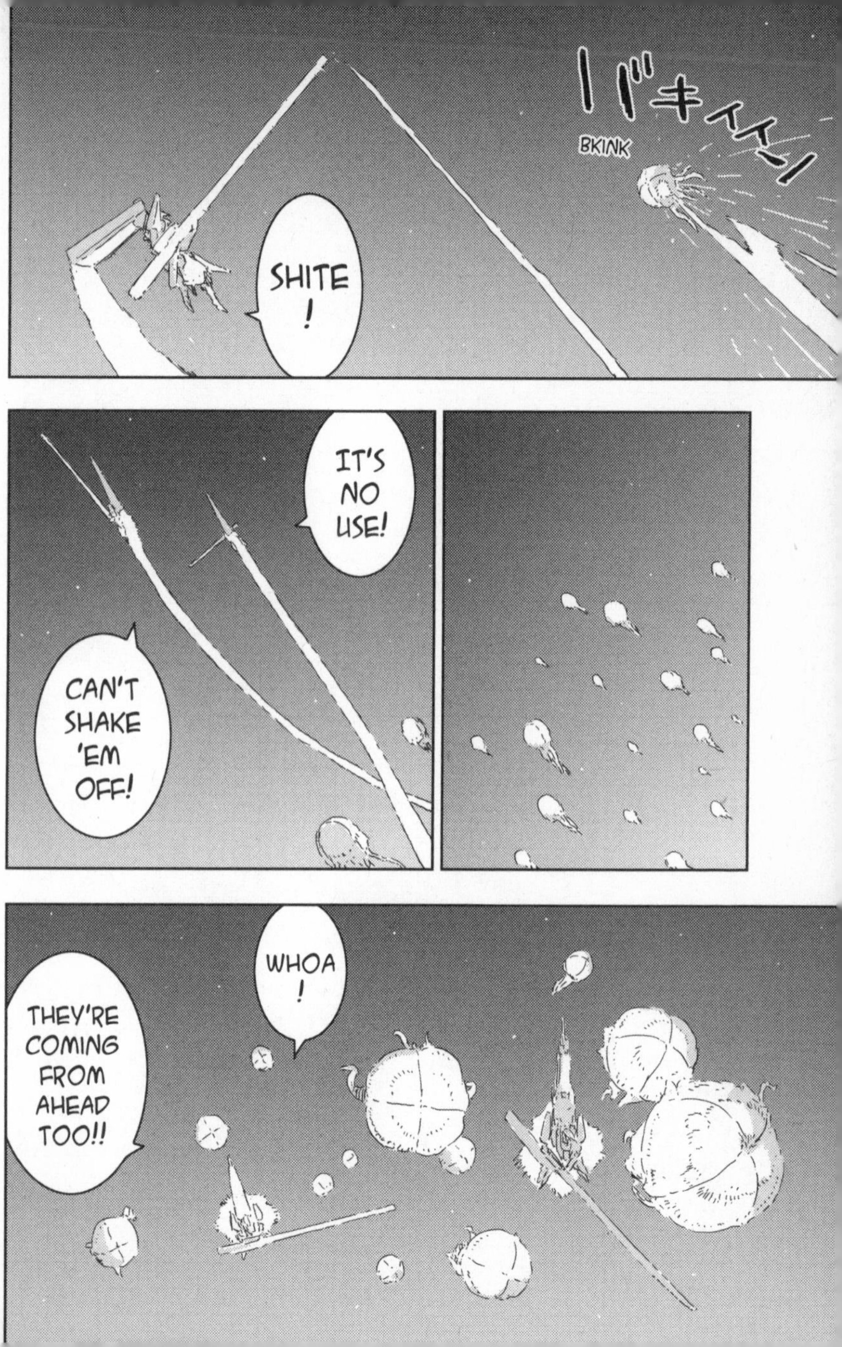
バキィーン
BKINK
SHITE!
IT'S NO USE!
CAN'T SHAKE 'EM OFF!
WHOA!
THEY'RE COMING FROM AHEAD TOO!!

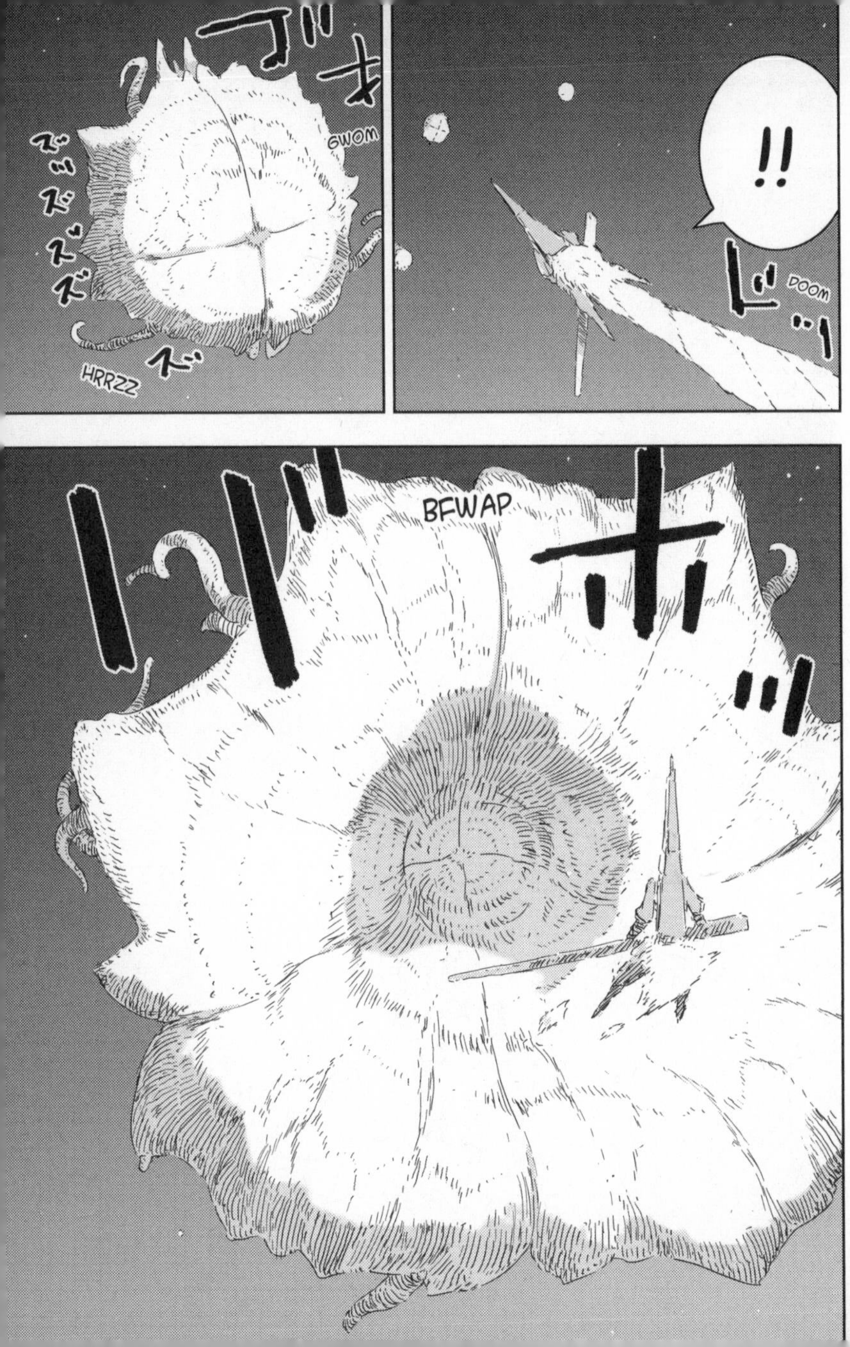
!!
DOOM
GWOM
HRRZZ
BFWAP

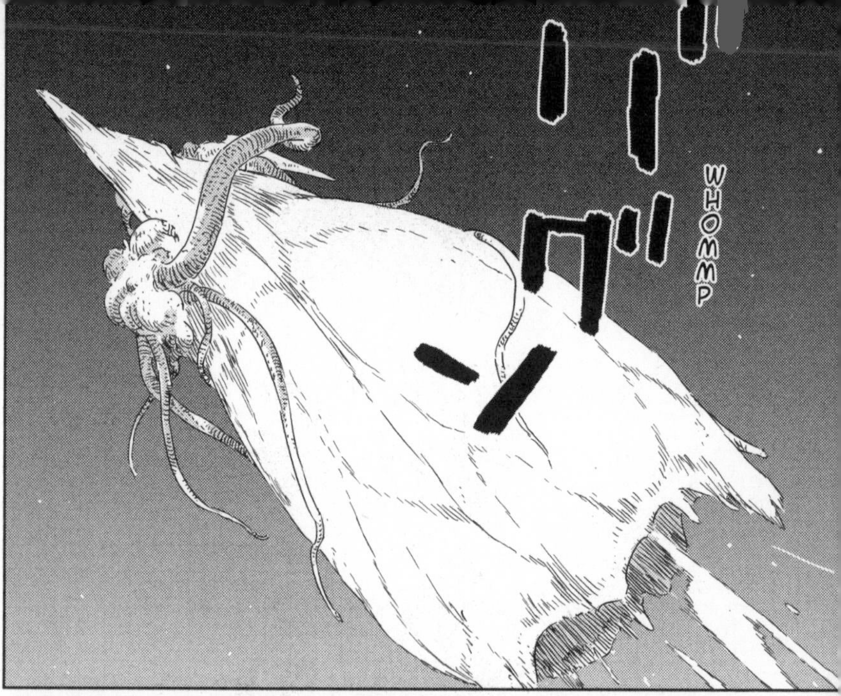
WHOMMP
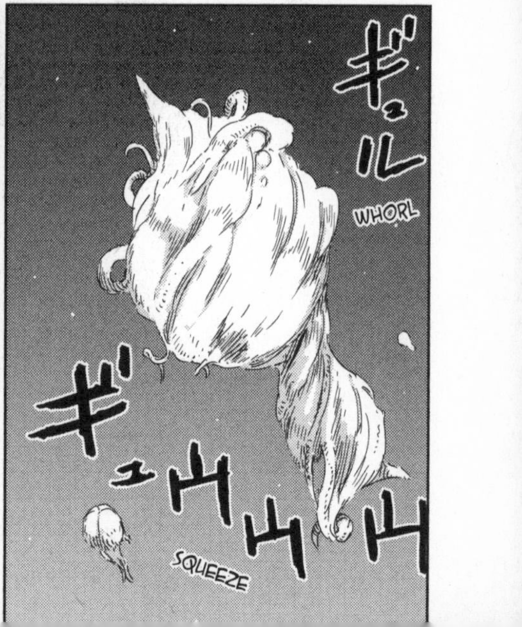
WHORL
SQUEEZE
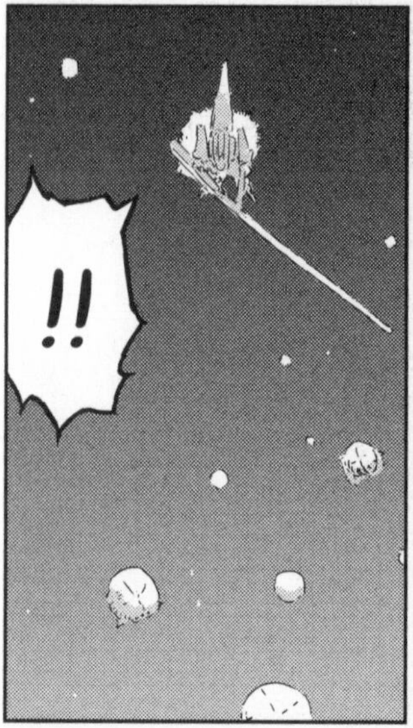
!!

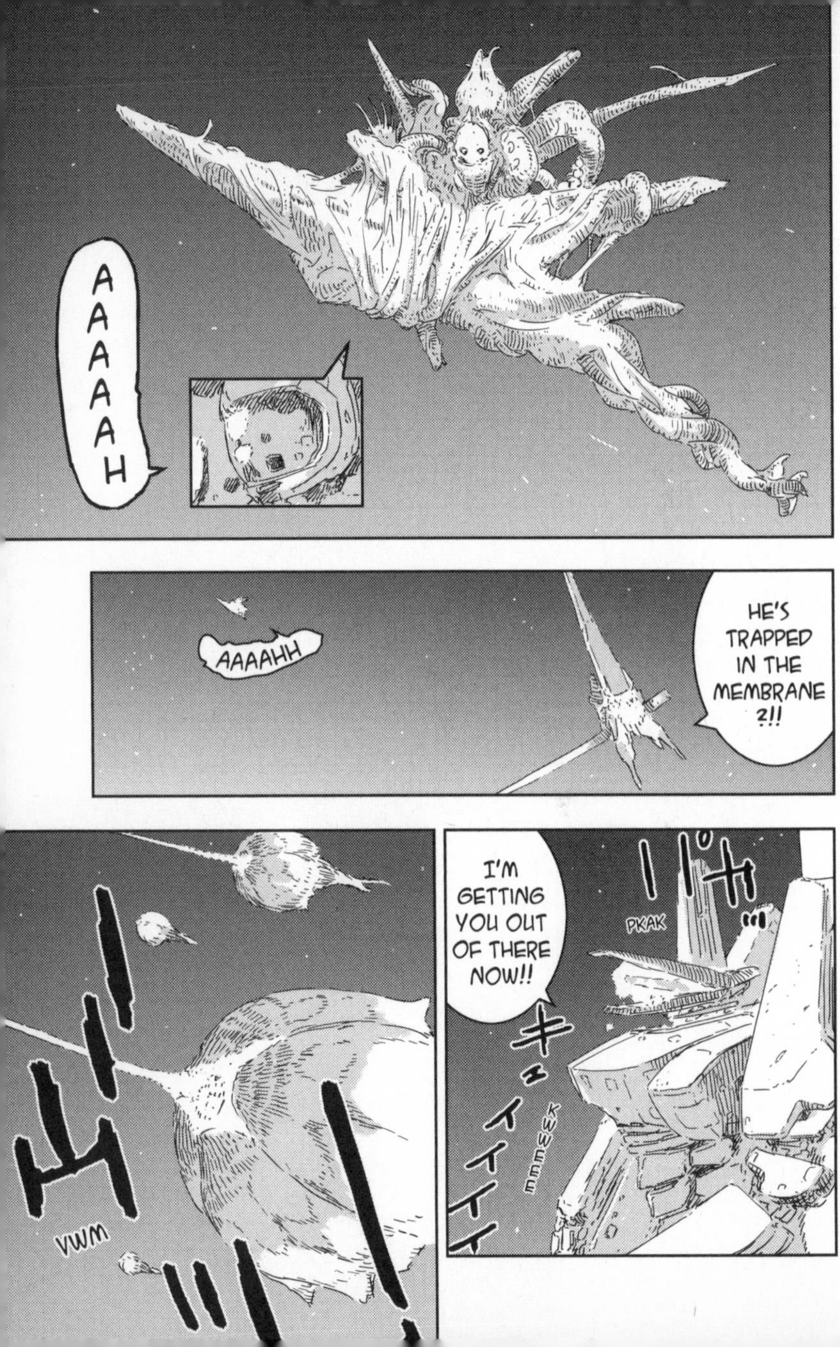
AAAAAAH
HE'S TRAPPED IN THE MEMBRANE?!!
AAAAHH
PKAK
I'M GETTING YOU OUT OF THERE NOW!!
KWEEEE
VWM

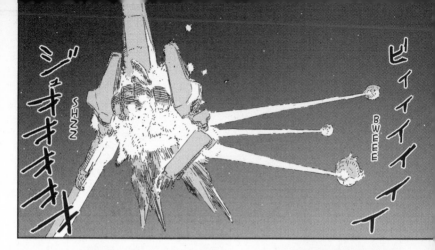

ビイイイイイ
BWEEE
ジュオオオオ
SHZZ
UNIT 8, MAJOR DAMAGE!! UNIT 7 TRAPPED BY A GAUNA !!
オオオー
SHZMM
READY HIGGS PARTICLE CANNON!!
ゴーン
KNNG
WE'LL CARVE OFF THE CLUSTER SHIP'S RIGHT FLANK!
FIRE !!

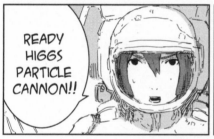

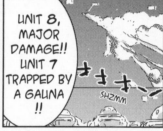

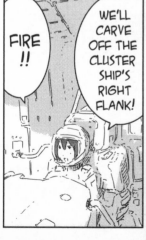

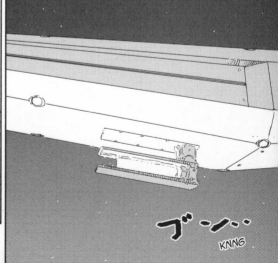

CANNON FIRE FROM CRUISER INCOMING!!

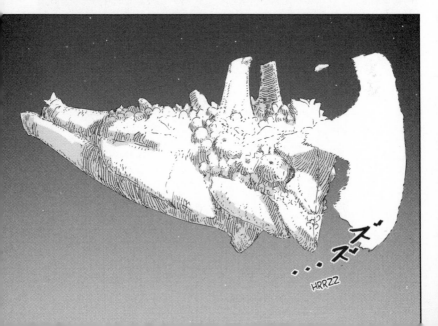

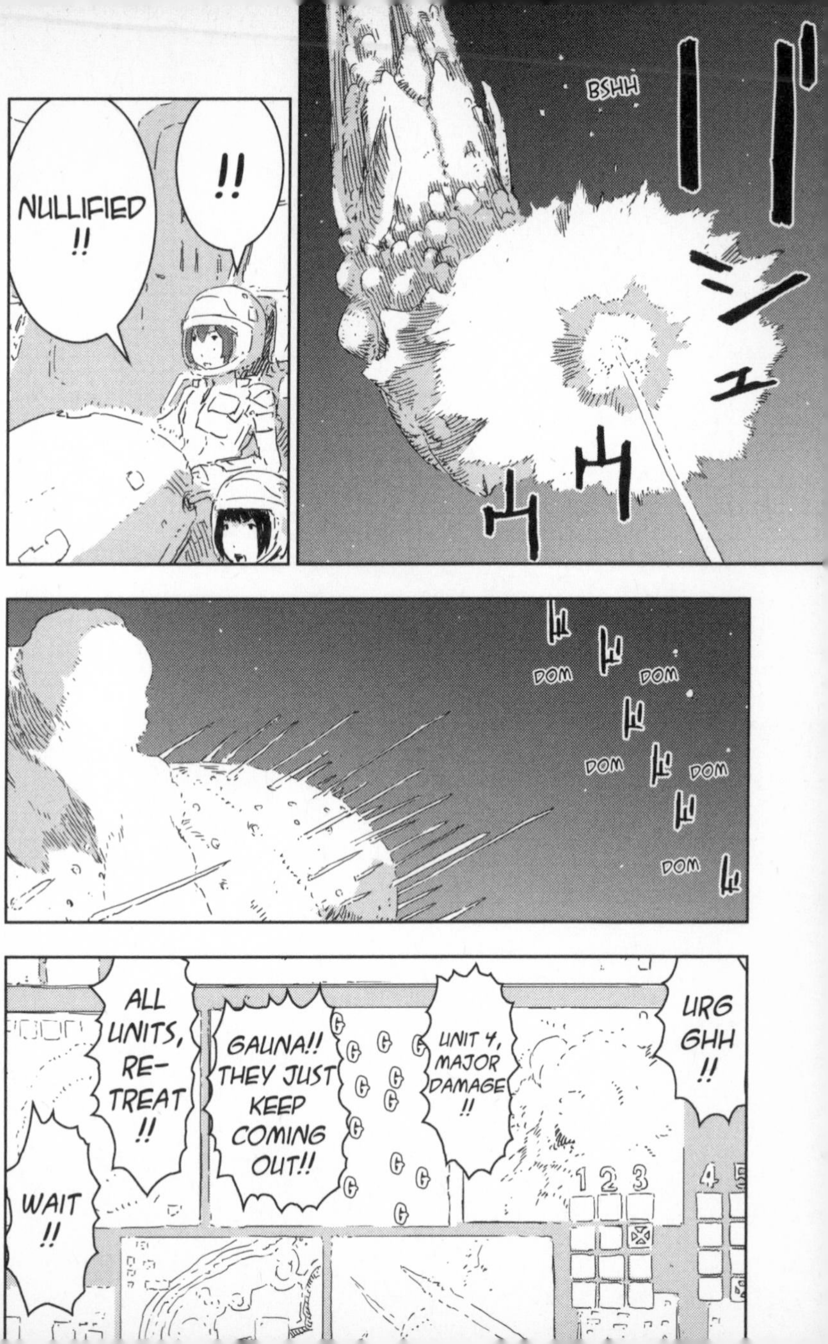
BSHH
!!
NULLIFIED !!
DOM
DOM
DOM
DOM
DOM
URGGHH !!
UNIT 4, MAJOR DAMAGE !!
GAUNA!! THEY JUST KEEP COMING OUT!!
ALL UNITS, RE-TREAT!!
WAIT !!

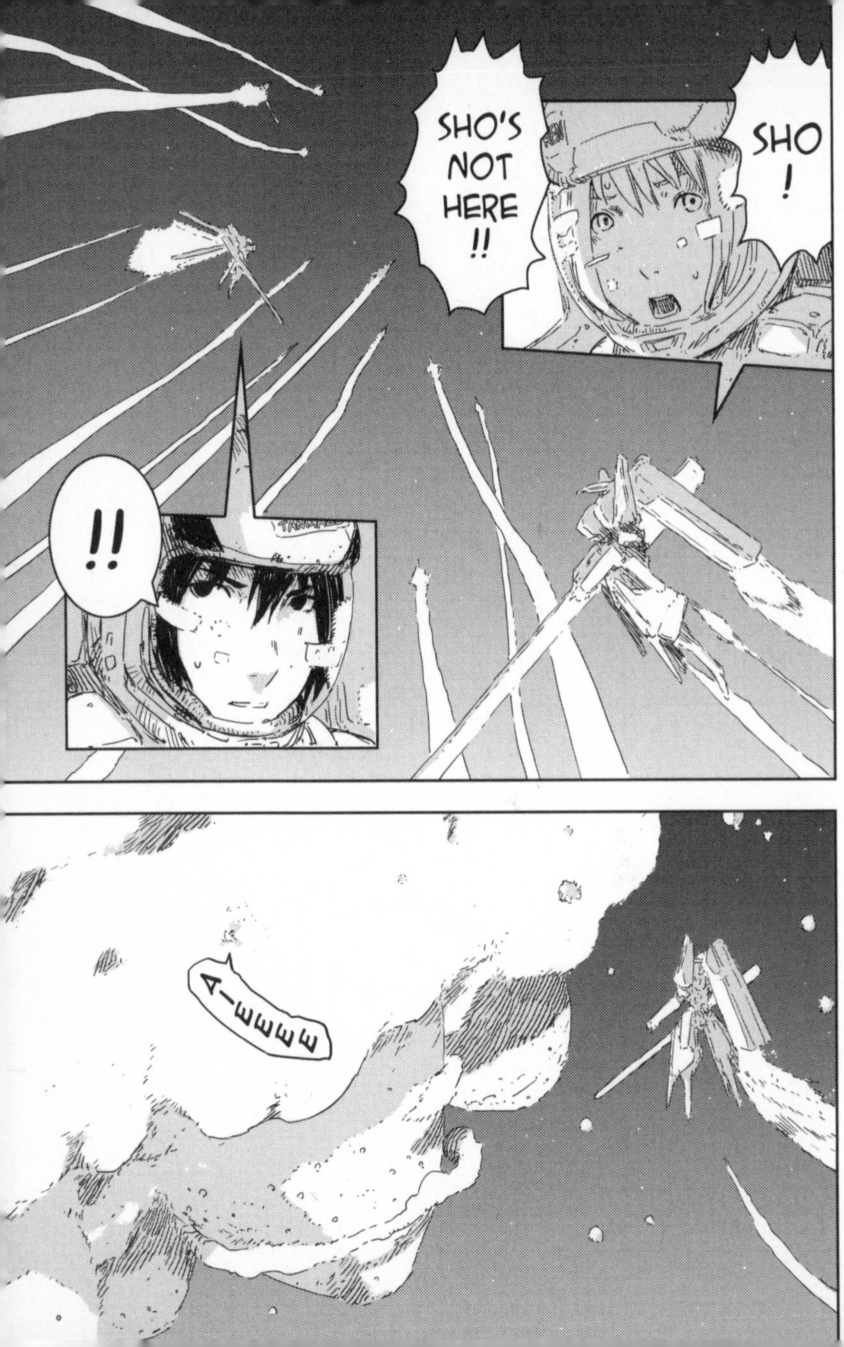
SHO!
SHO'S NOT HERE!!
!!
A-EEEE

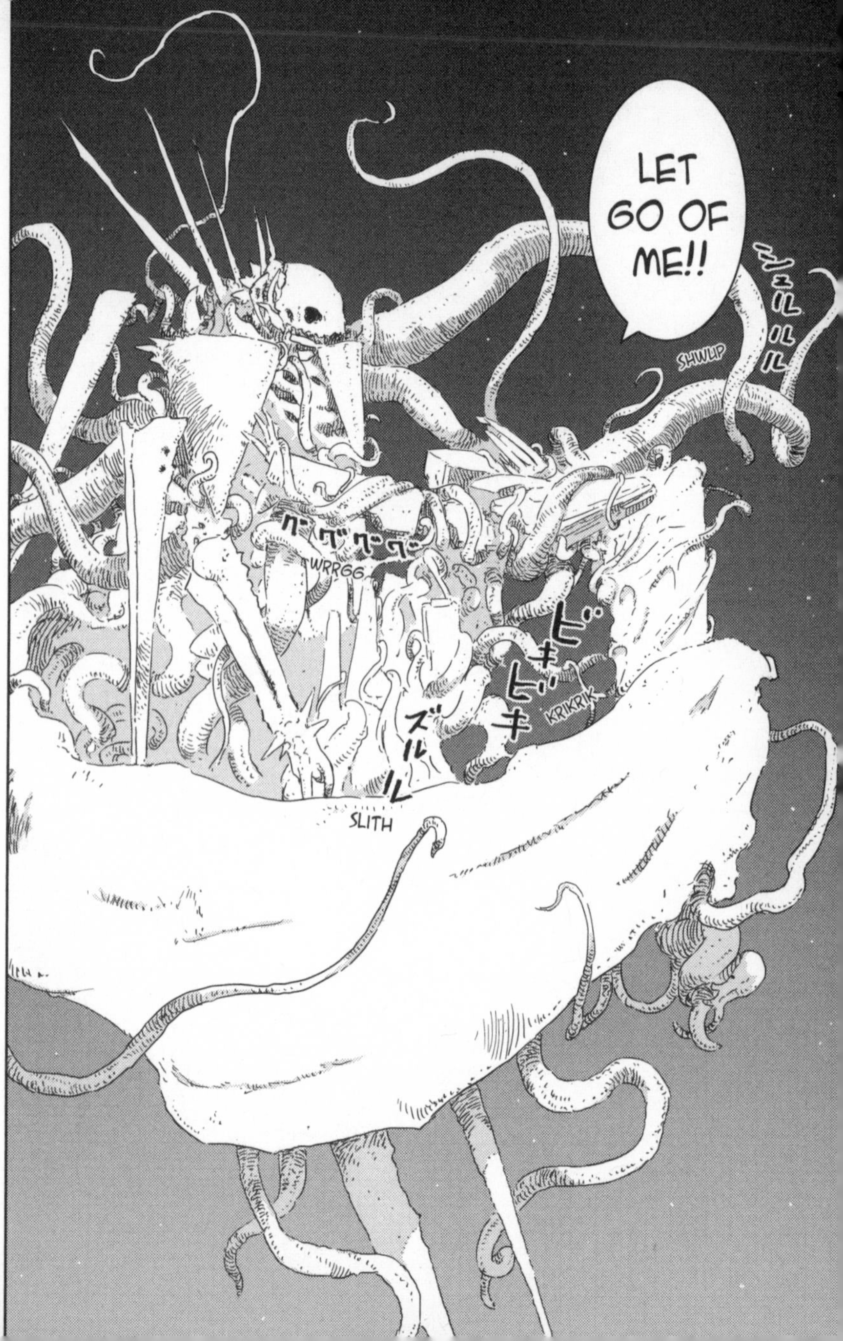
LET GO OF ME!!
シュルルル
SHWUP
ビキビキ
KRIKRIK
ググググ
WRRGG
ズルル
SLITH

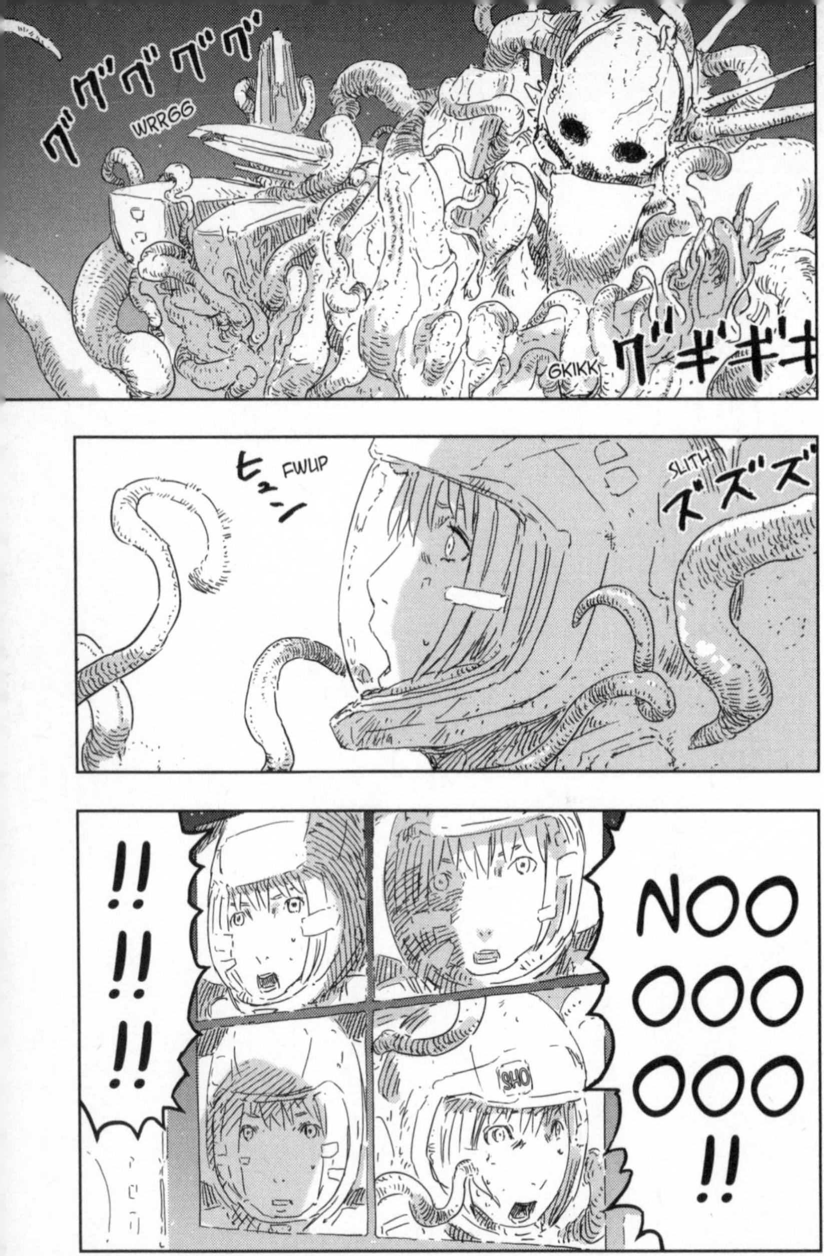
GKIKK
グギギギ
WRRGG
SLITH
ズズズ
ヒュン
FWUP
NOOOOOOOOO!!
!!!!!!

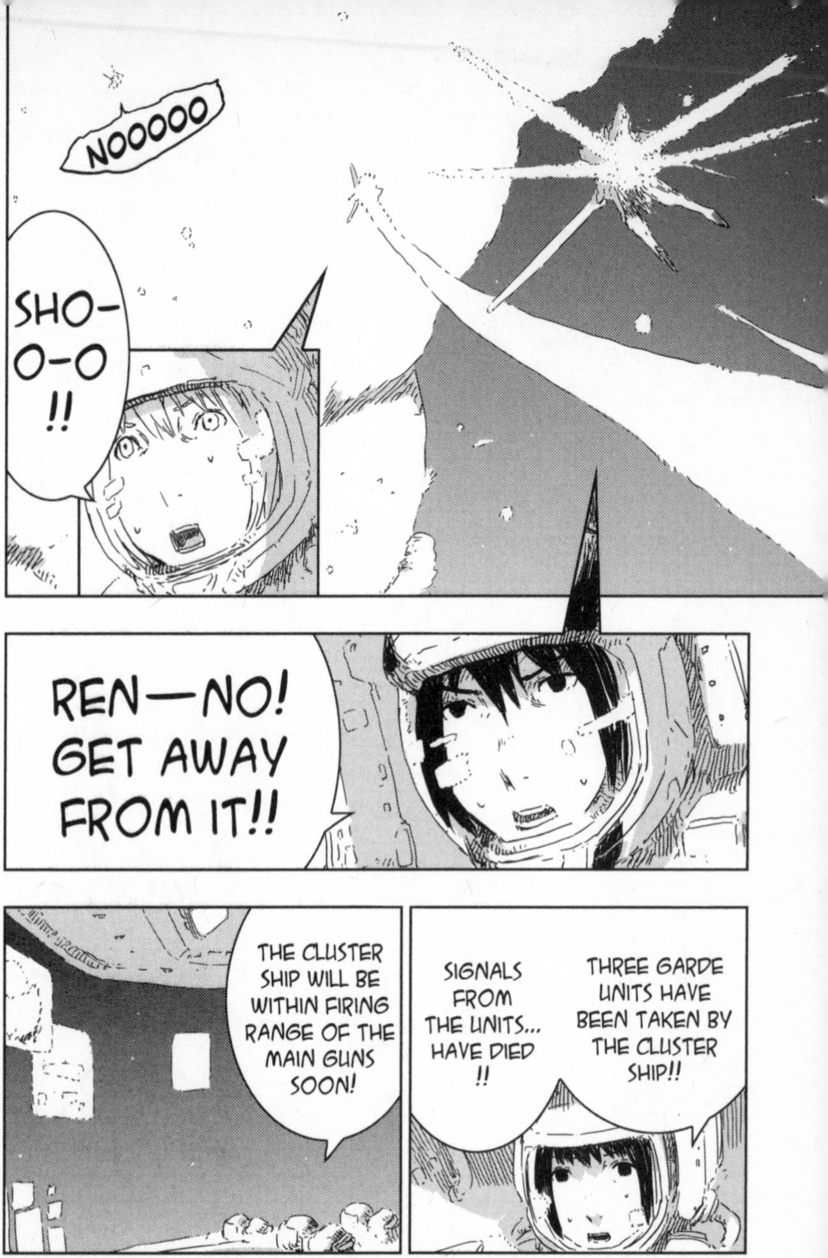
NOOOOO
SHO-O-O !!
REN—NO! GET AWAY FROM IT!!
THREE GARDE UNITS HAVE BEEN TAKEN BY THE CLUSTER SHIP!!
SIGNALS FROM THE UNITS... HAVE DIED !!
THE CLUSTER SHIP WILL BE WITHIN FIRING RANGE OF THE MAIN GUNS SOON!

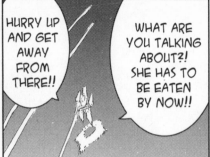

DON'T FIRE YET!!
EN
SHO IS IN THERE !!
WHAT ARE YOU TALKING ABOUT?! SHE HAS TO BE EATEN BY NOW!!
HURRY UP AND GET AWAY FROM THERE!!
LET GO OF ME, TANIKAZE !
THERE ARE TOO MANY GAUNA!
THERE'S NO WAY WE COULD RESCUE HER!
ブブブブブゴ
GWOOO
...
PREPARE TO FIRE MAIN CANNONS !!
KJINK

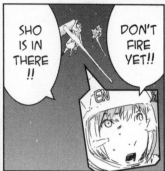

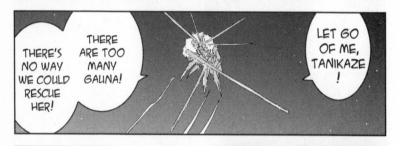

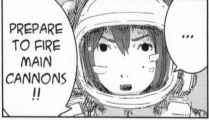

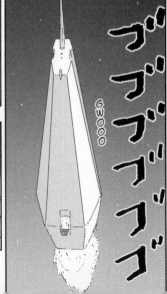

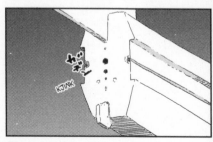

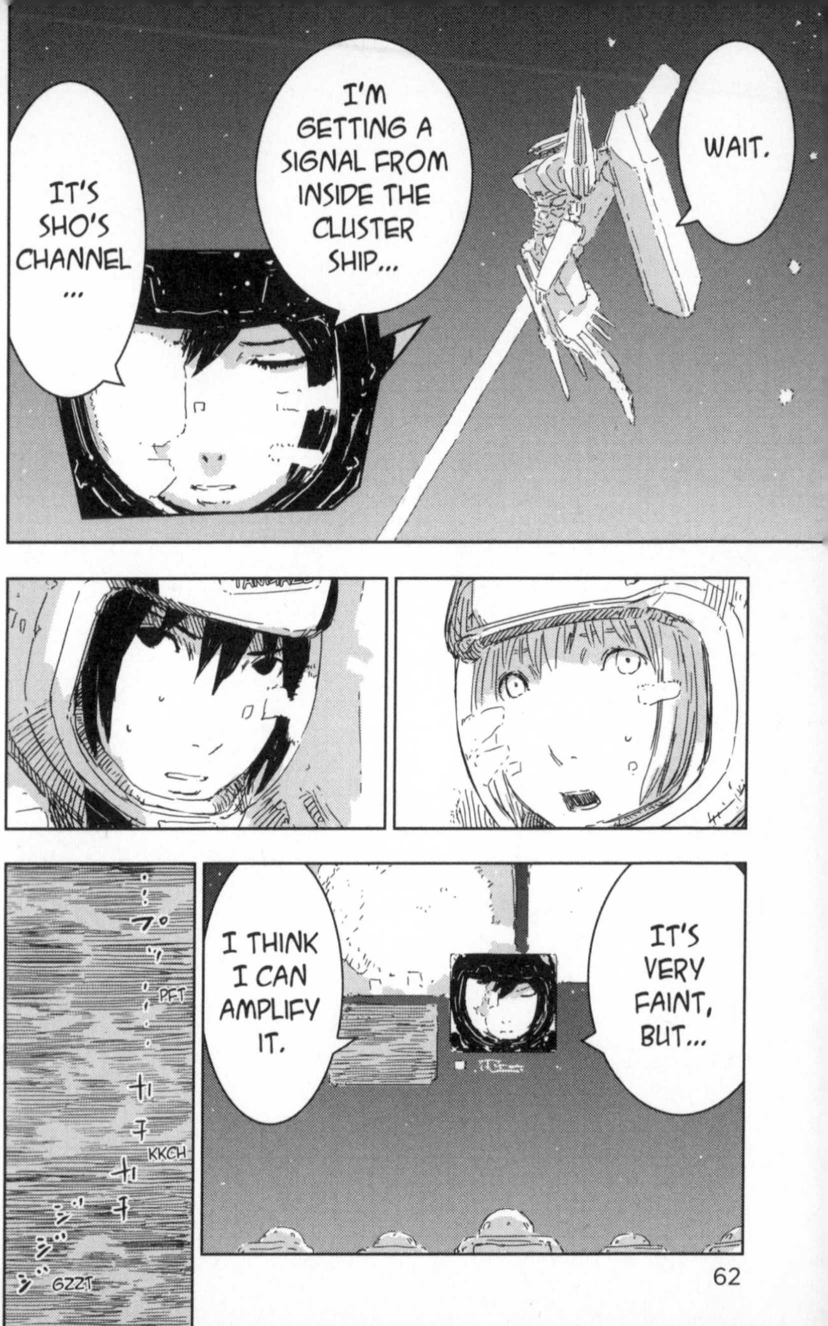
WAIT.
I'M GETTING A SIGNAL FROM INSIDE THE CLUSTER SHIP...
IT'S SHO'S CHANNEL...
IT'S VERY FAINT, BUT...
I THINK I CAN AMPLIFY IT.
PFT
KKCH
GZZT

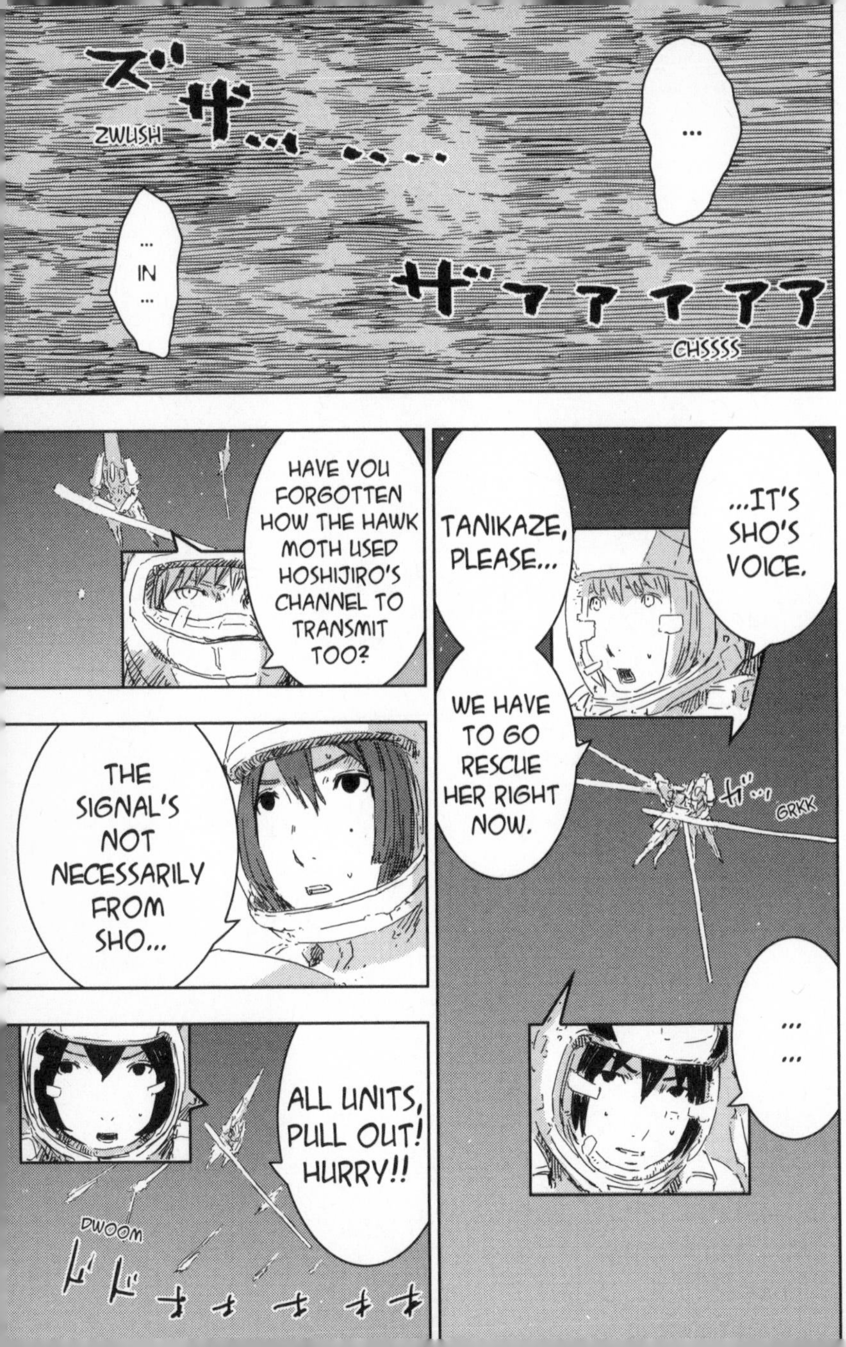
...
ZWLUSH
... IN ...
CHSSSS
...IT'S SHO'S VOICE.
TANIKAZE, PLEASE...
WE HAVE TO GO RESCUE HER RIGHT NOW.
GRKK
HAVE YOU FORGOTTEN HOW THE HAWK MOTH USED HOSHIJIRO'S CHANNEL TO TRANSMIT TOO?
THE SIGNAL'S NOT NECESSARILY FROM SHO...
... ...
ALL UNITS, PULL OUT! HURRY!!
DWOOM

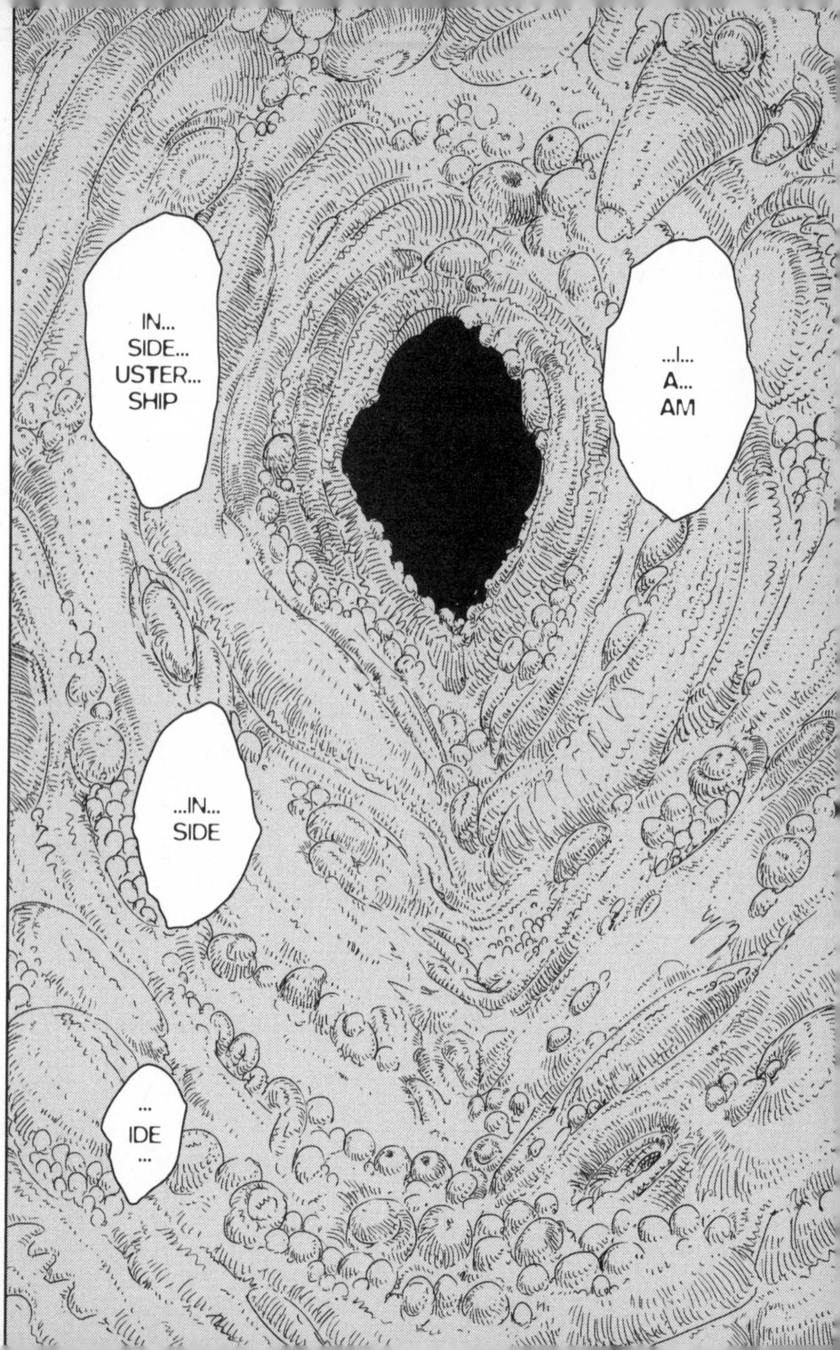
...I... A... AM
IN... SIDE... USTER... SHIP
...IN... SIDE
... IDE ...

Chapter 56: END

Chapter 57: Sho Honoka's Rescue

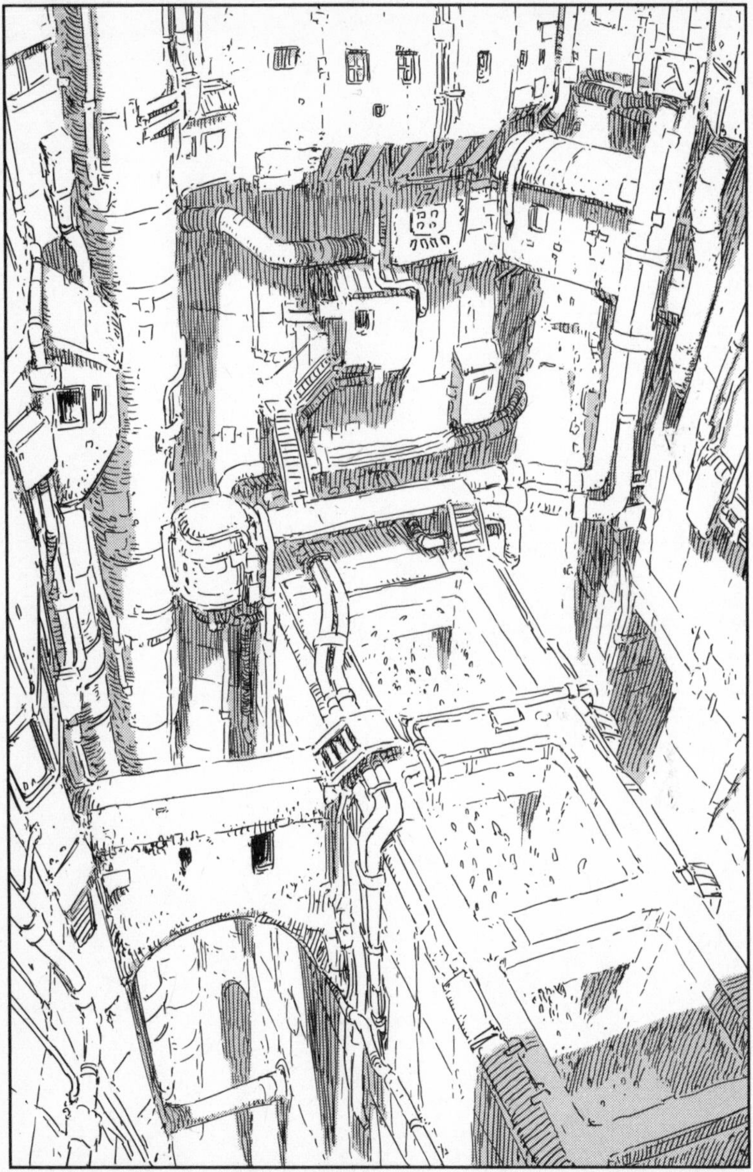

One Hundred Sights of Sidonia Part Forty-Three: Fish Nursery

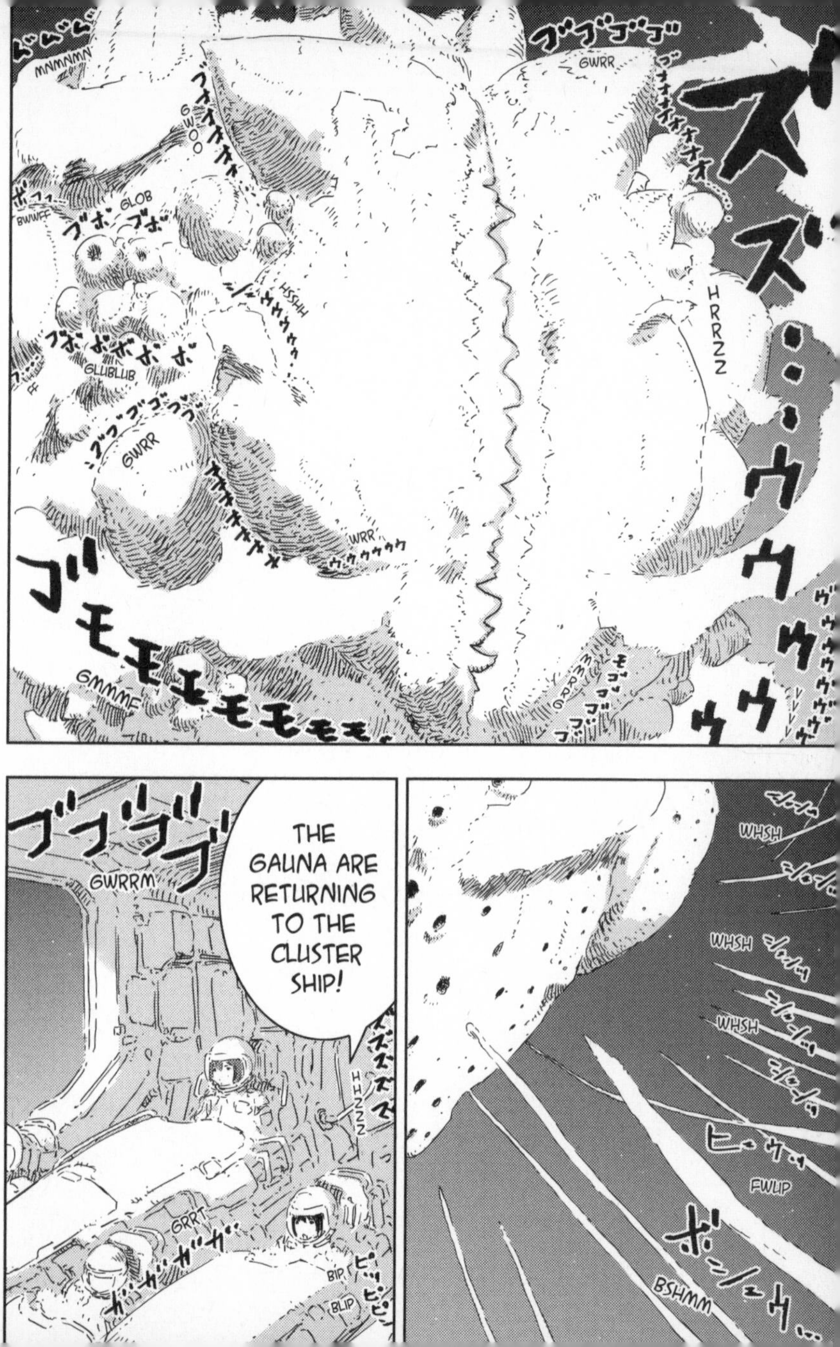
GWRR
HRRZZ
MNMNMN
GWOO
GLOB
BWWFF
HSSHH
GLUBLUB
FF
GWRR
WRR
GRRZZ
GMMME
WHSH
WHSH
WHSH
FWLIP
BSHMM
GWRRM
THE GAUNA ARE RETURNING TO THE CLUSTER SHIP!
HHZZZ
GRRT
BIP
BLIP

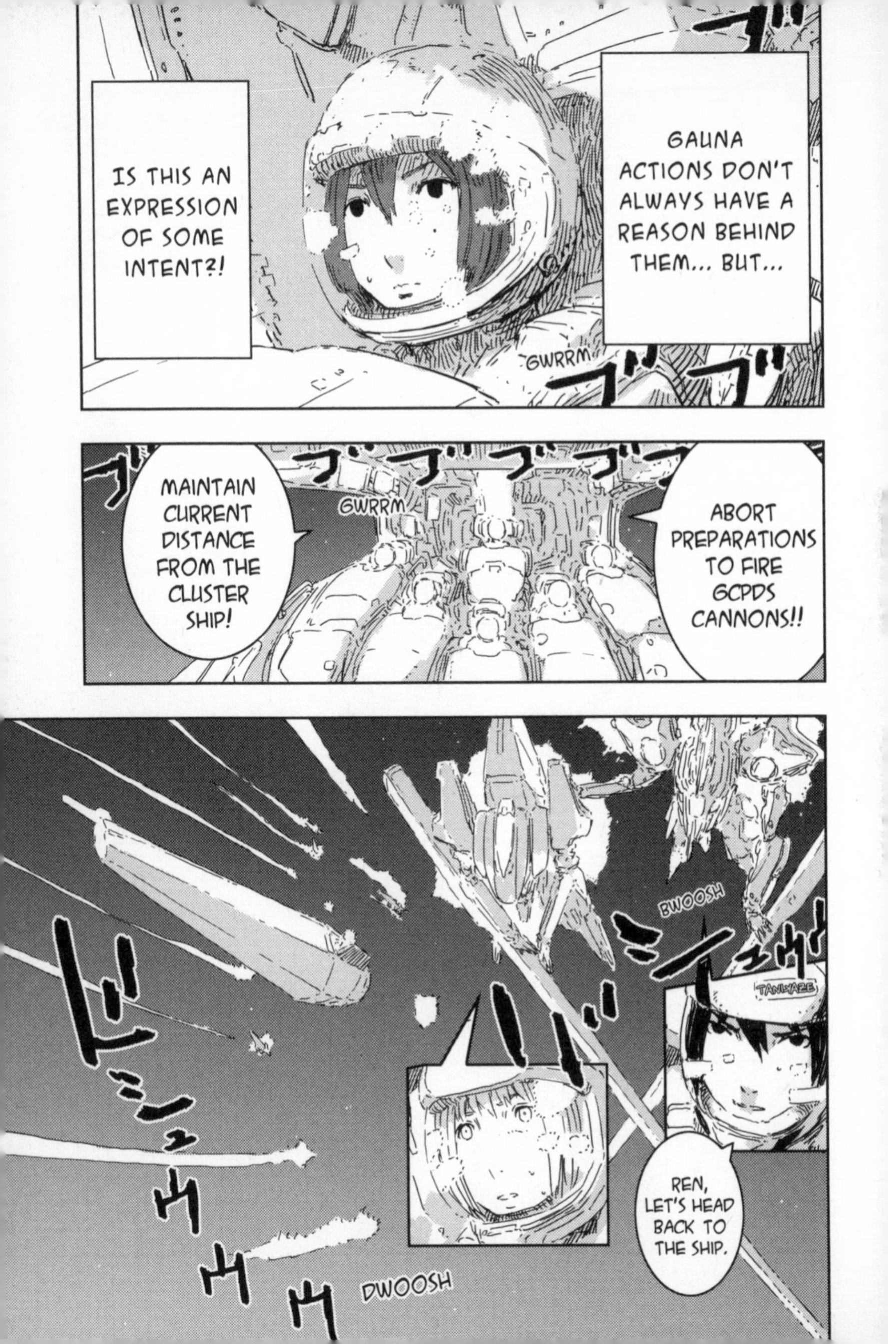
GAUNA ACTIONS DON'T ALWAYS HAVE A REASON BEHIND THEM... BUT...
IS THIS AN EXPRESSION OF SOME INTENT?!
GWRRM
ABORT PREPARATIONS TO FIRE GCPDS CANNONS!!
MAINTAIN CURRENT DISTANCE FROM THE CLUSTER SHIP!
GWRRM
BWOOSH
TANIKAZE
REN, LET'S HEAD BACK TO THE SHIP.
DWOOSH

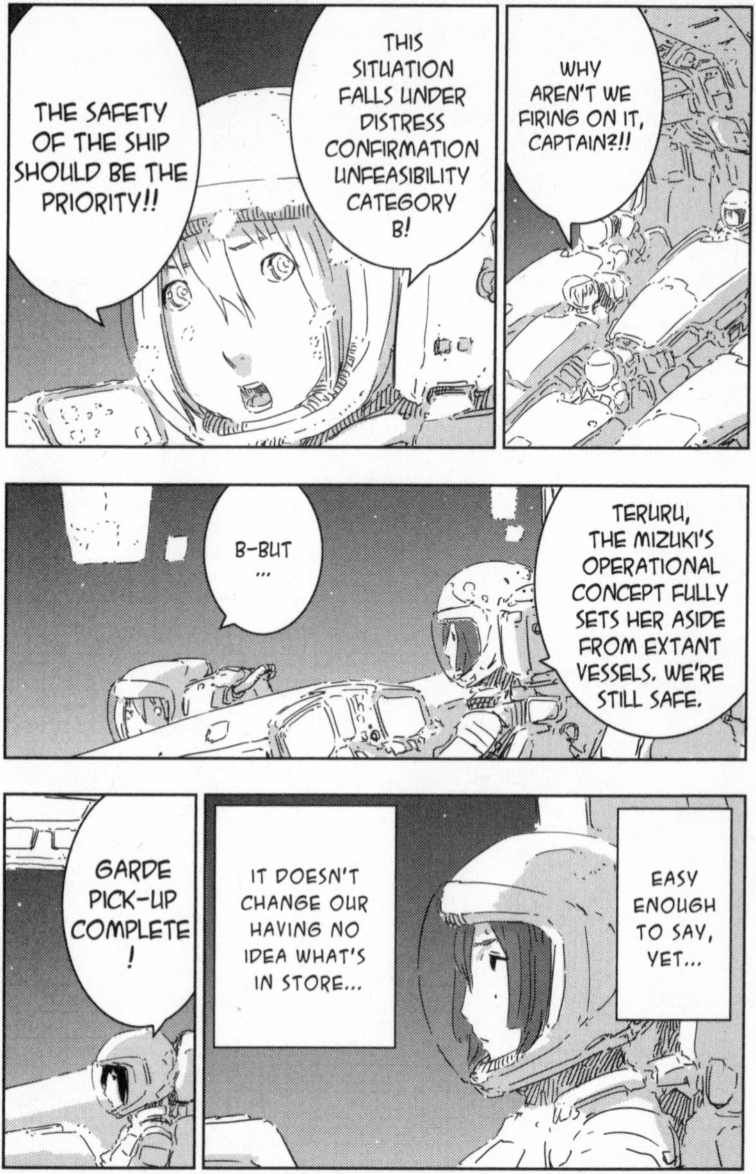
WHY AREN'T WE FIRING ON IT, CAPTAIN?!!
THIS SITUATION FALLS UNDER DISTRESS CONFIRMATION UNFEASIBILITY CATEGORY B!
THE SAFETY OF THE SHIP SHOULD BE THE PRIORITY!!
TERURU, THE MIZUKI'S OPERATIONAL CONCEPT FULLY SETS HER ASIDE FROM EXTANT VESSELS. WE'RE STILL SAFE.
B-BUT ...
EASY ENOUGH TO SAY, YET...
IT DOESN'T CHANGE OUR HAVING NO IDEA WHAT'S IN STORE...
GARDE PICK-UP COMPLETE!

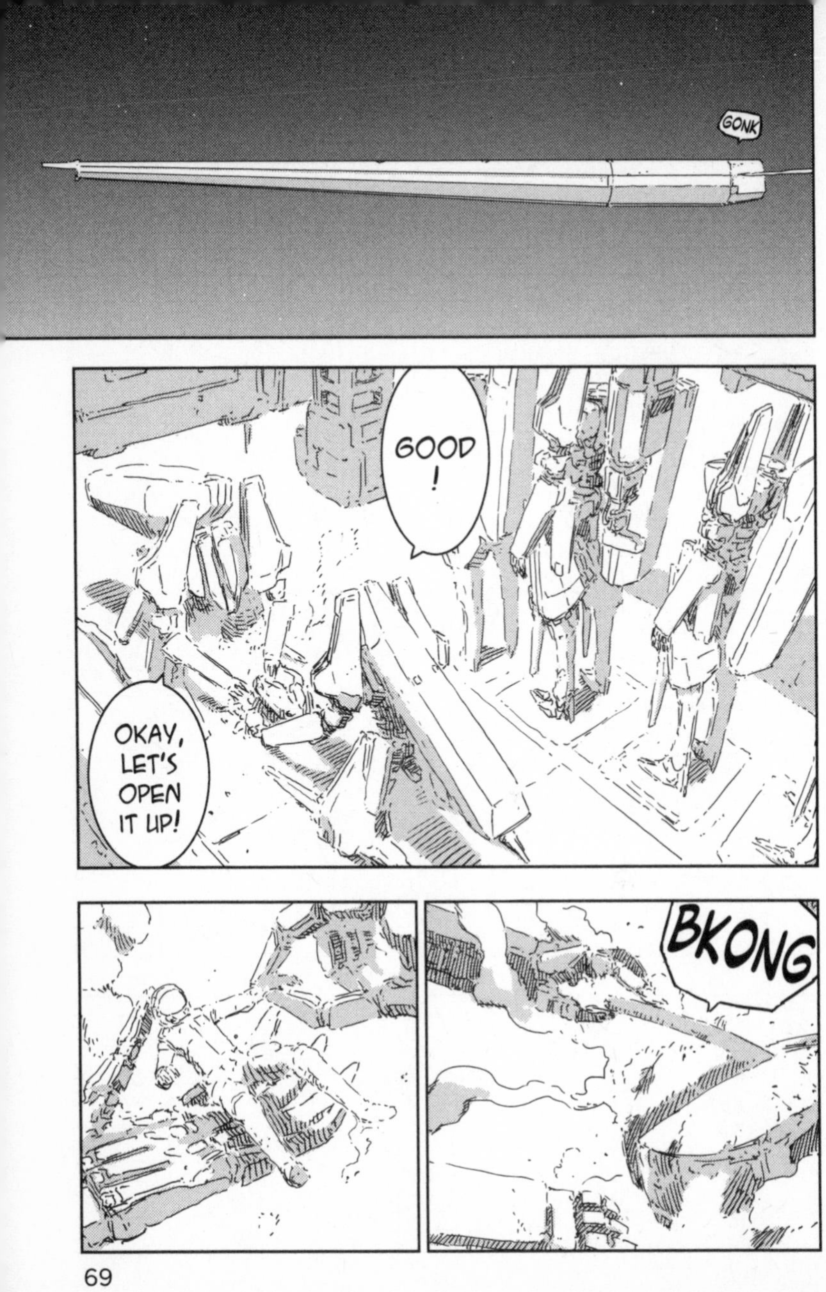
GONK
GOOD!
OKAY, LET'S OPEN IT UP!
BKONG

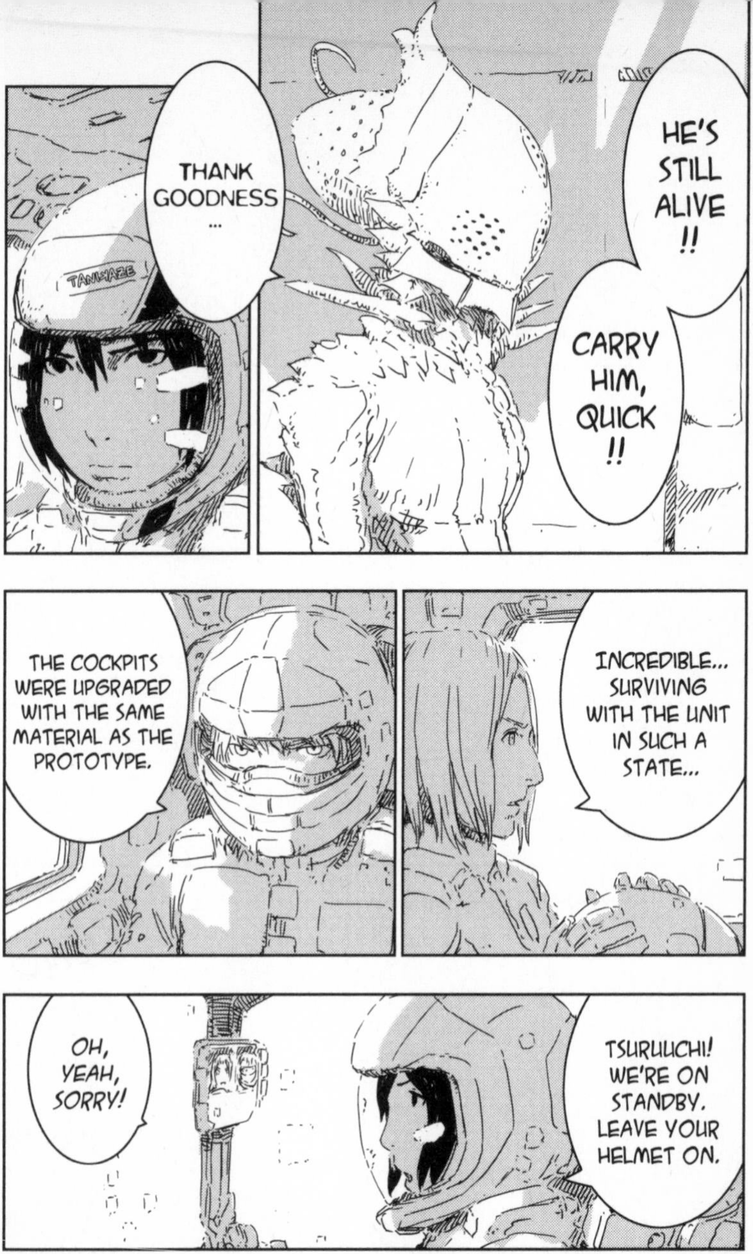
HE'S STILL ALIVE !!
CARRY HIM, QUICK !!
THANK GOODNESS ...
INCREDIBLE... SURVIVING WITH THE UNIT IN SUCH A STATE...
THE COCKPITS WERE UPGRADED WITH THE SAME MATERIAL AS THE PROTOTYPE.
TSURUUCHI! WE'RE ON STANDBY. LEAVE YOUR HELMET ON.
OH, YEAH, SORRY!

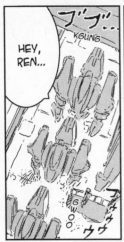

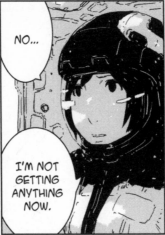

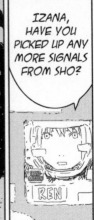

IZANA, HAVE YOU PICKED UP ANY MORE SIGNALS FROM SHO?
TRANS-MISSION
REN
NO...
I'M NOT GETTING ANYTHING NOW.
ブブ...
KGUNG
HEY, REN...
ブウウウ
GWOO
I'M SURE SHE'S ALIVE.
LET'S KEEP OUR HOPES UP AND WAIT FOR AN OPENING TO RESCUE HER.

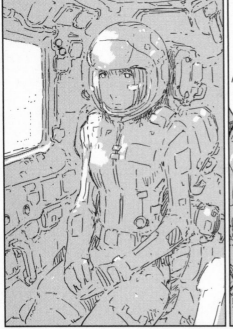

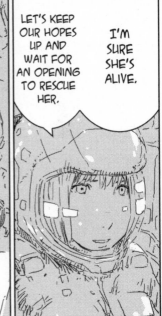

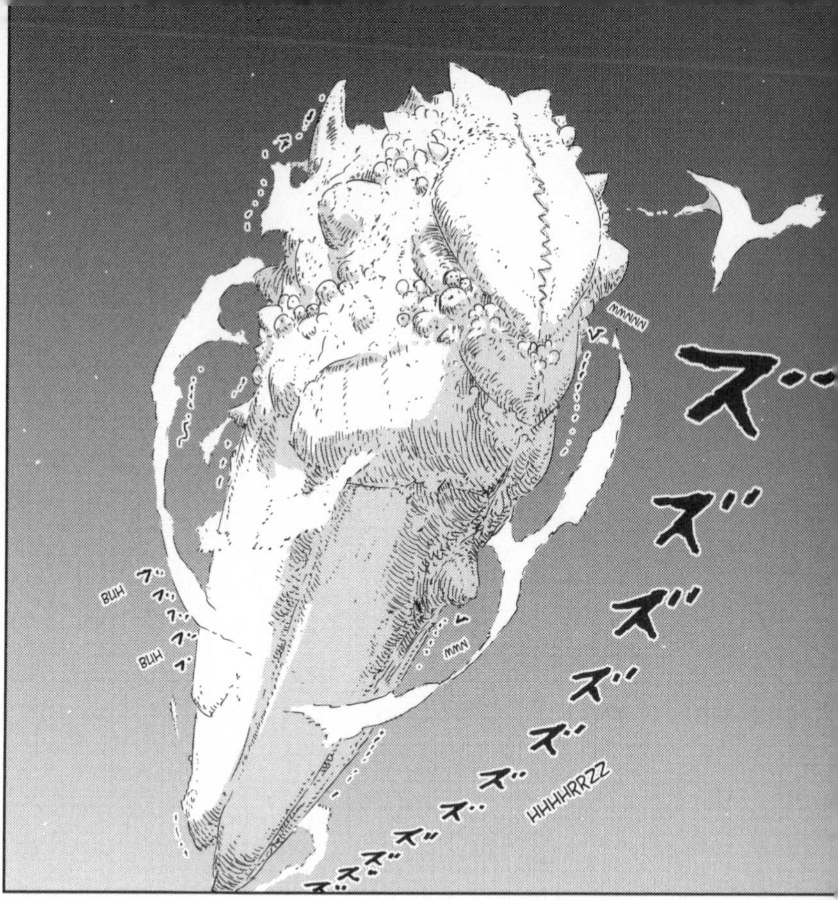
ズー
ズズズズズズズズズ
HHHHRRZZ
MMNNN
MMN
ブブブブブ
BUH
BUH
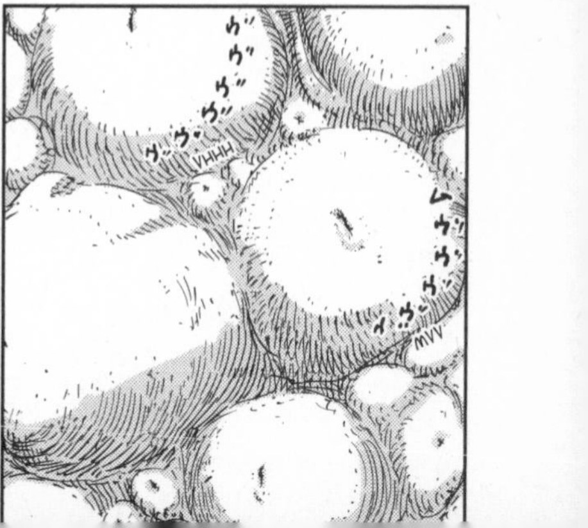
ヴヴヴヴヴ
VHHH
ムヴヴヴヴヴ
MVV
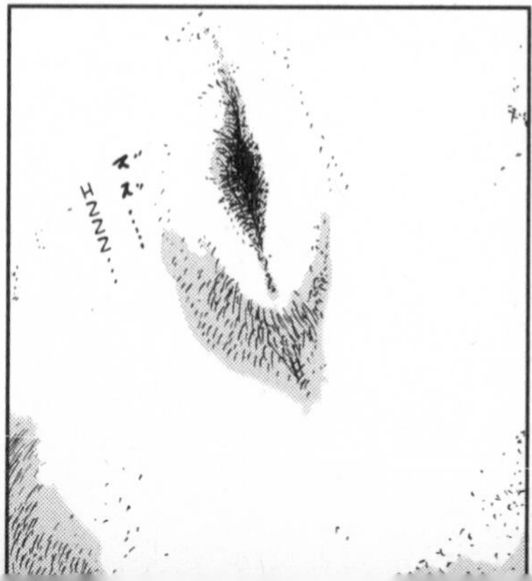
ズズ……
HZZZ…

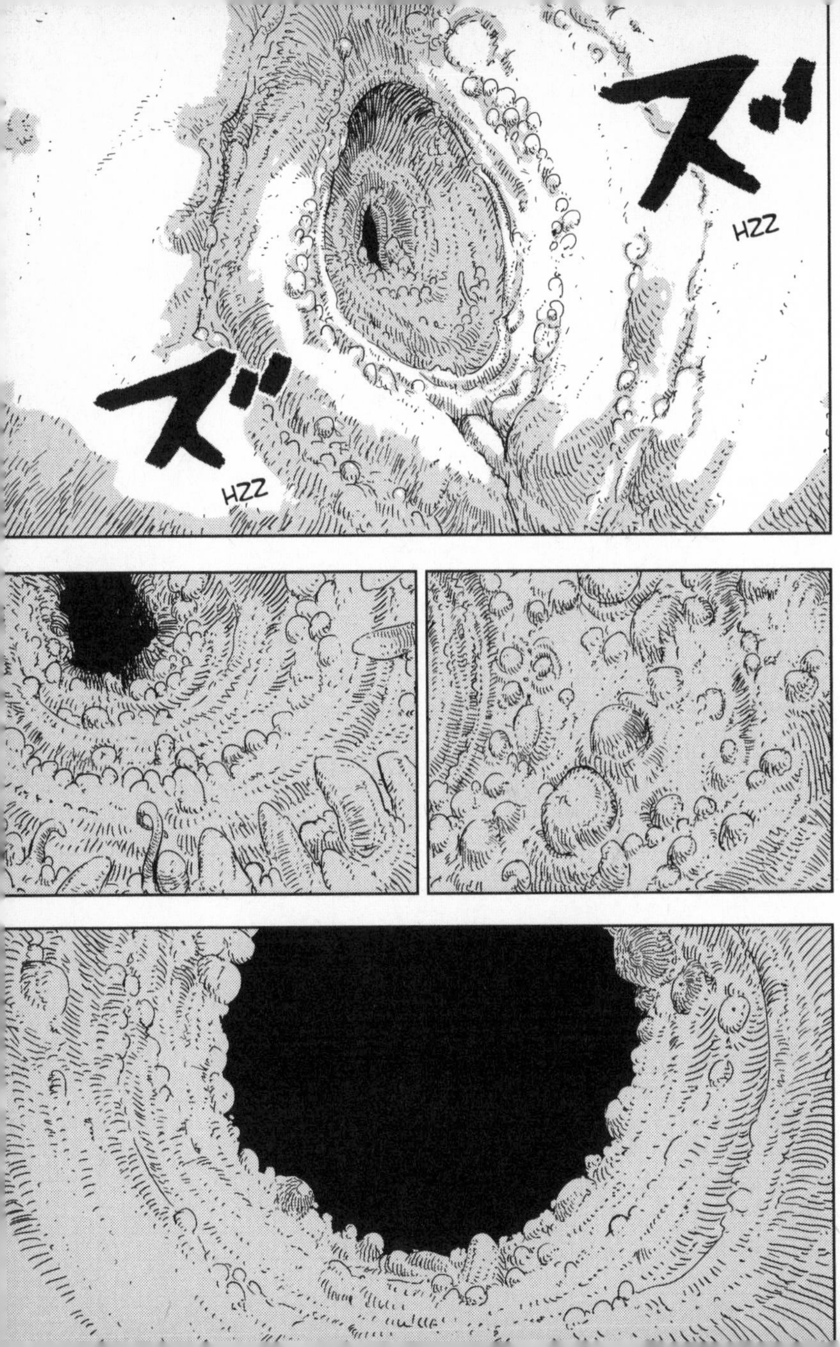
ズ
HZZ
ズ
HZZ

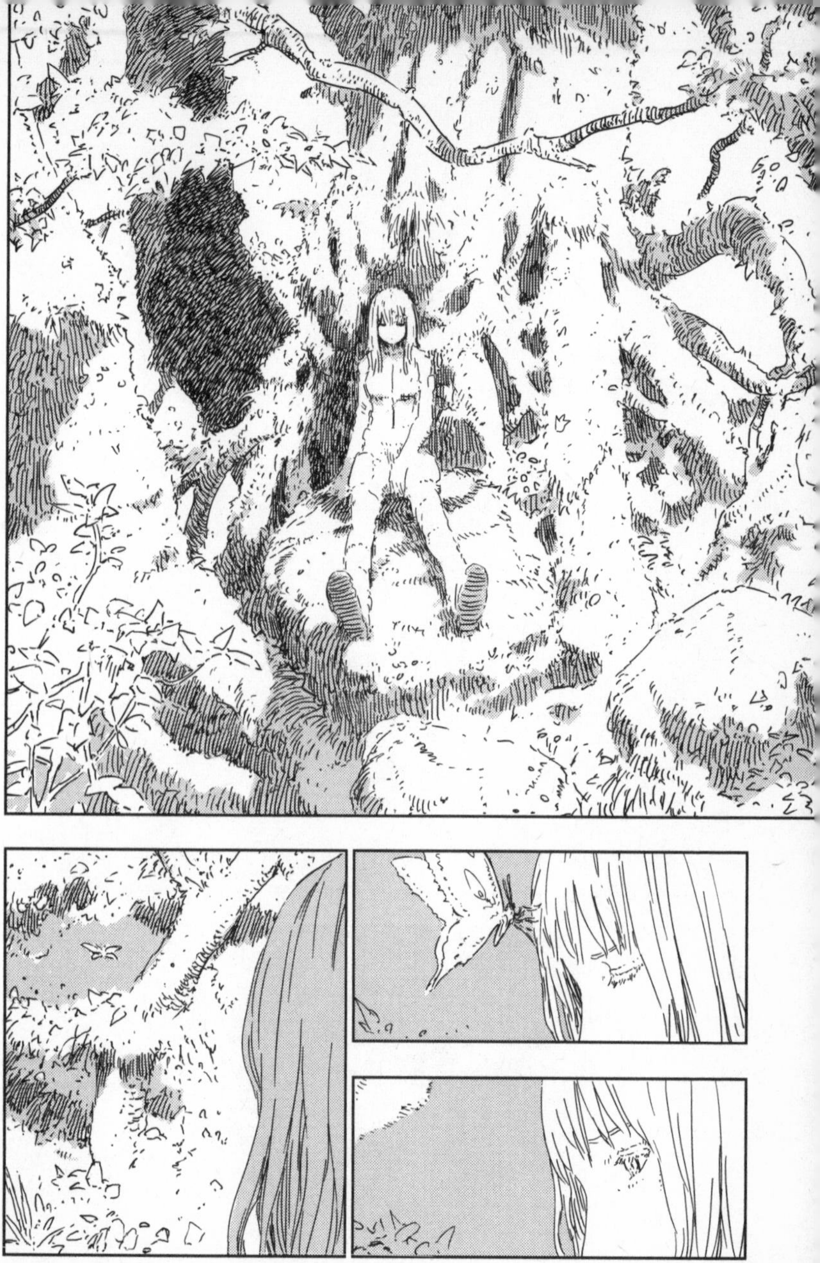

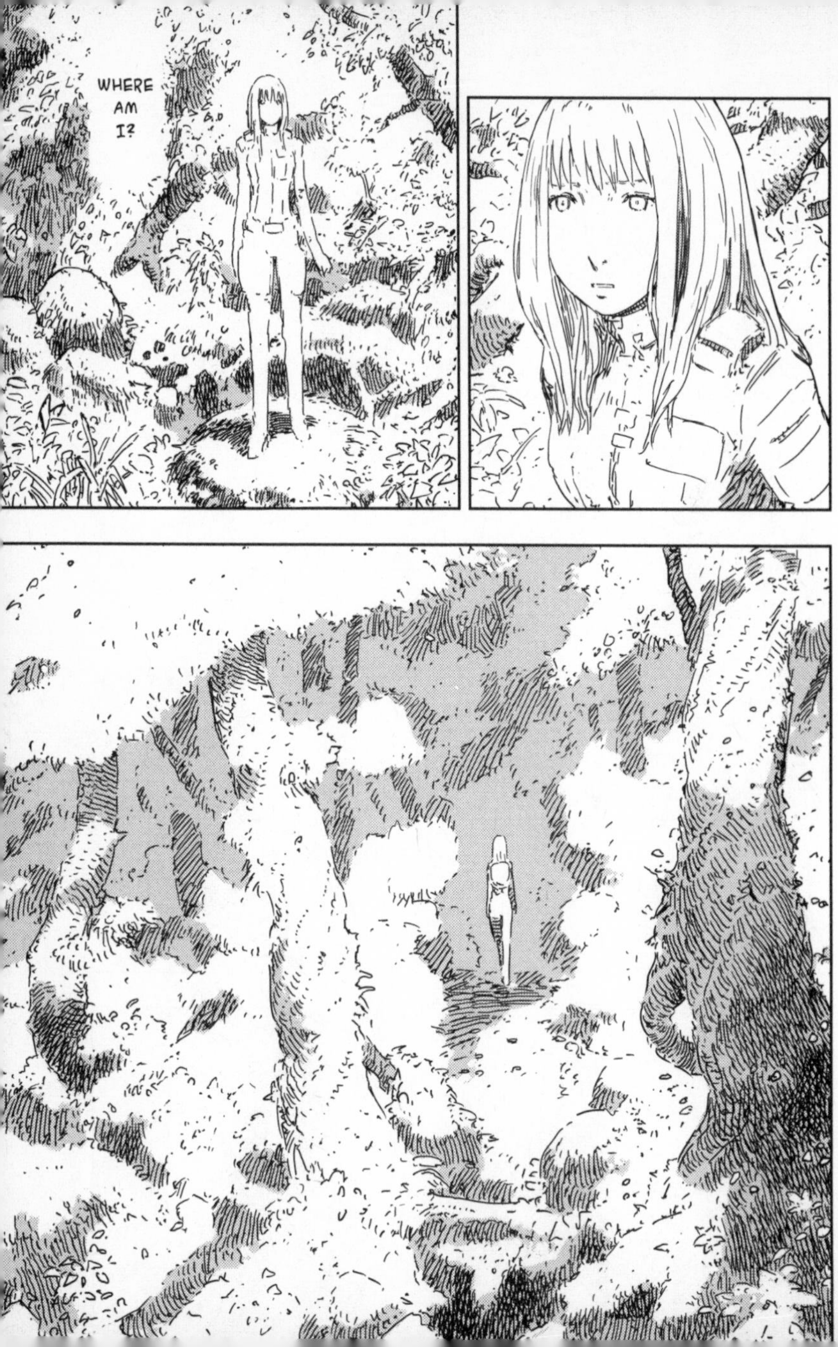
WHERE AM I?

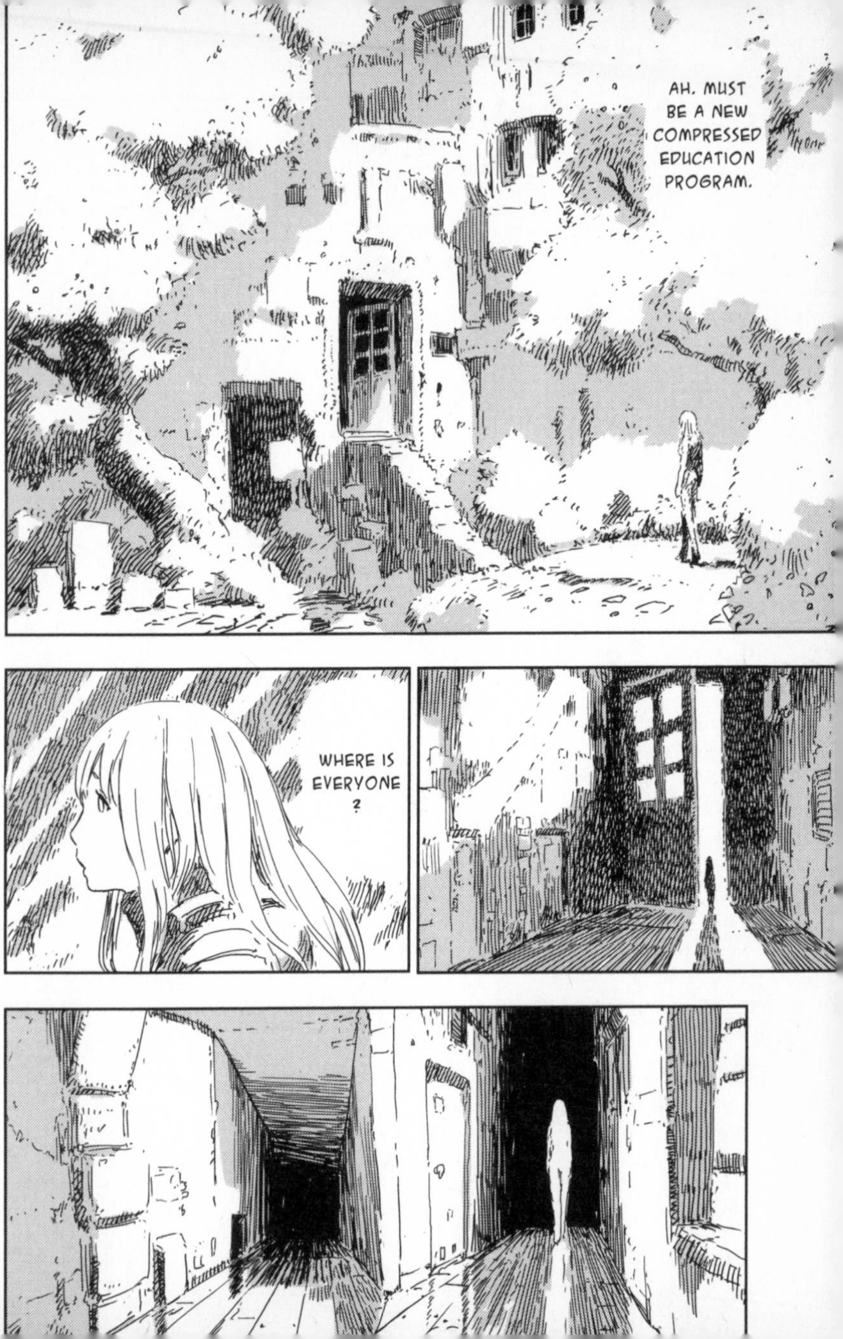
AH. MUST BE A NEW COMPRESSED EDUCATION PROGRAM.
WHERE IS EVERYONE?

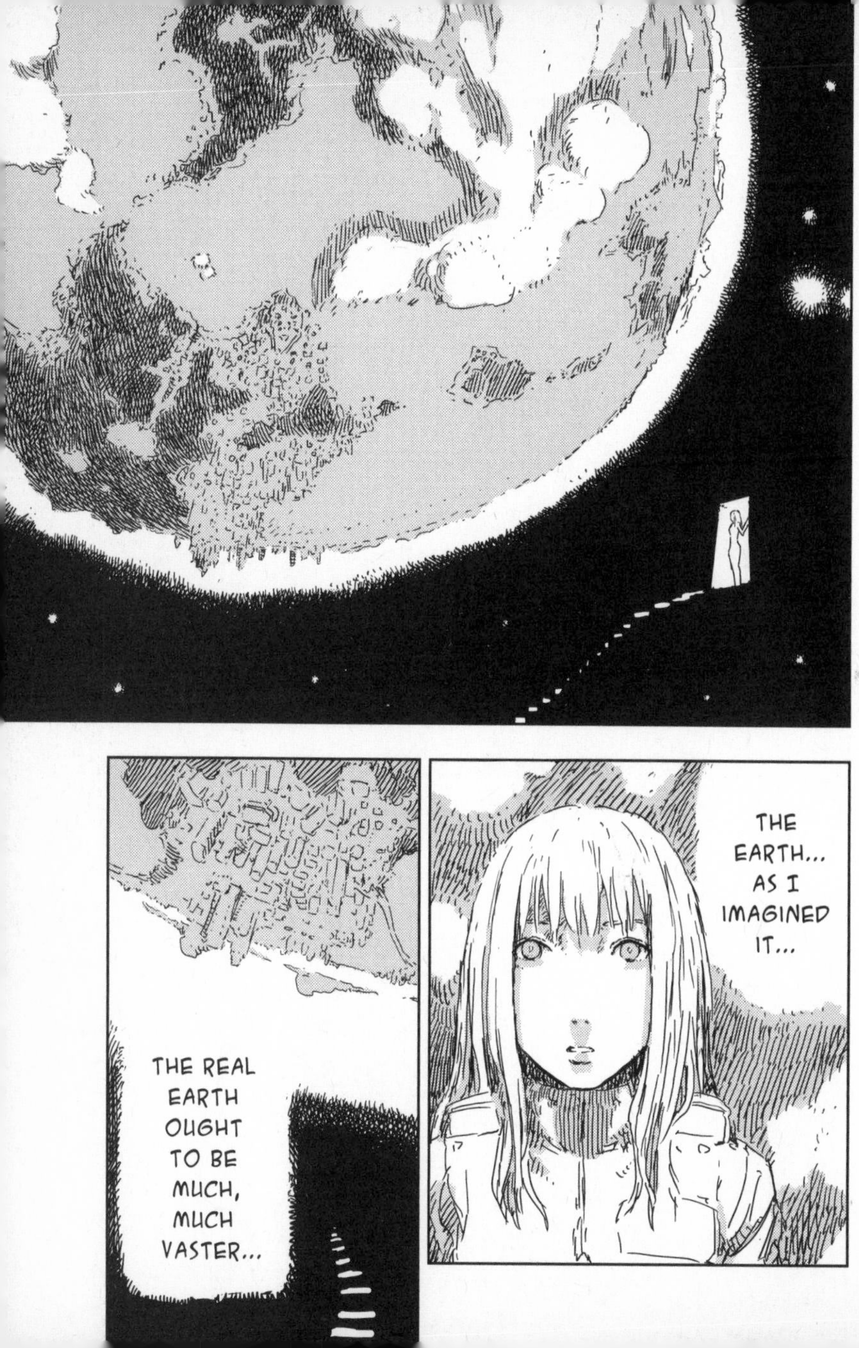
THE EARTH... AS I IMAGINED IT...
THE REAL EARTH OUGHT TO BE MUCH, MUCH VASTER...

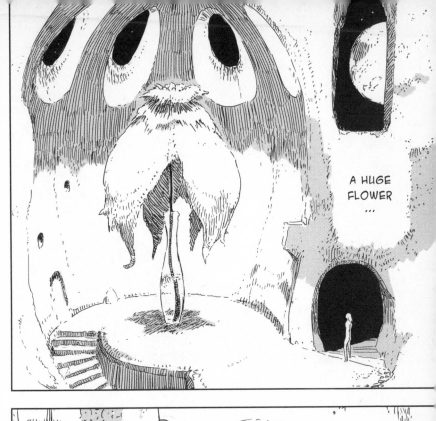

A HUGE
FLOWER
...

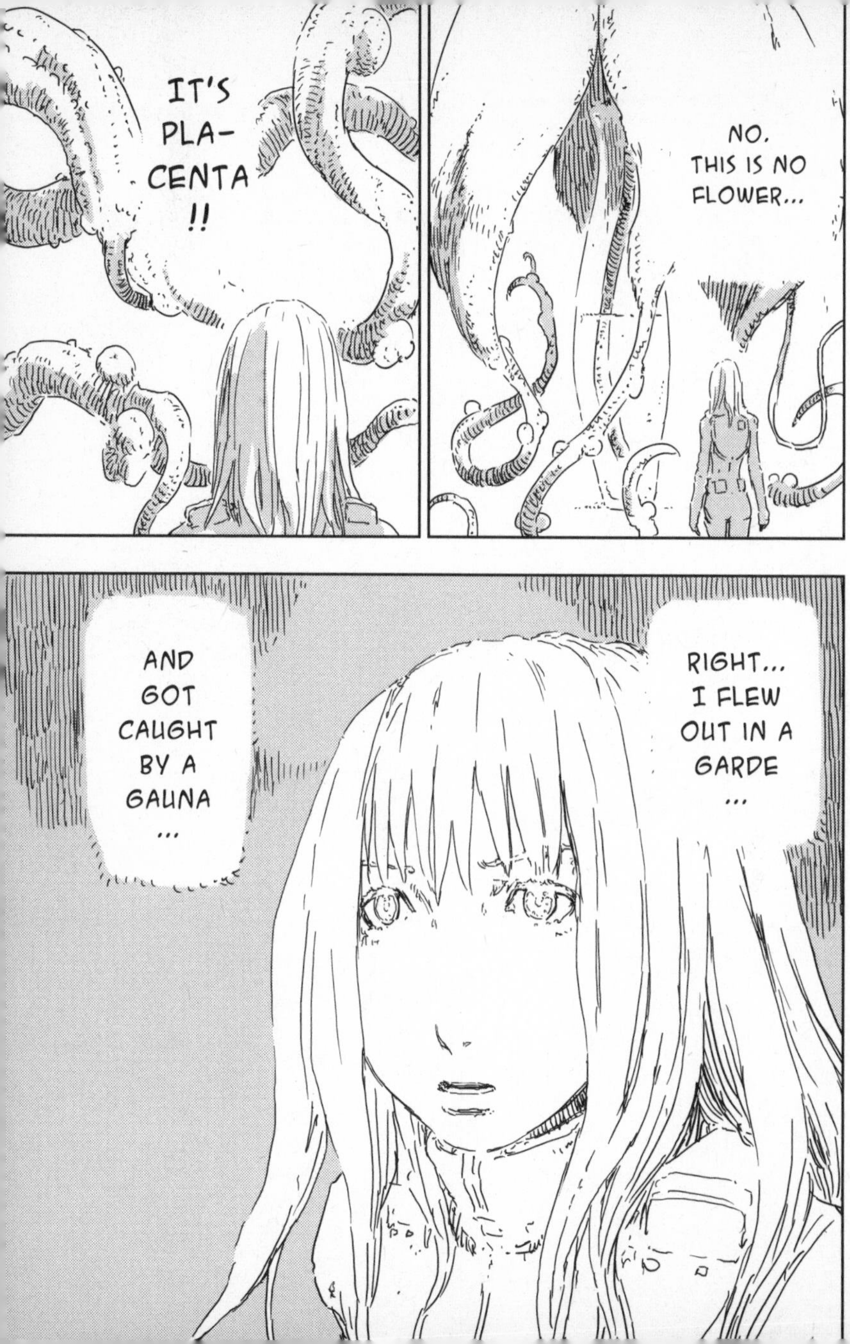
NO. THIS IS NO FLOWER...
IT'S PLA-CENTA!!
RIGHT... I FLEW OUT IN A GARDE...
AND GOT CAUGHT BY A GAUNA...

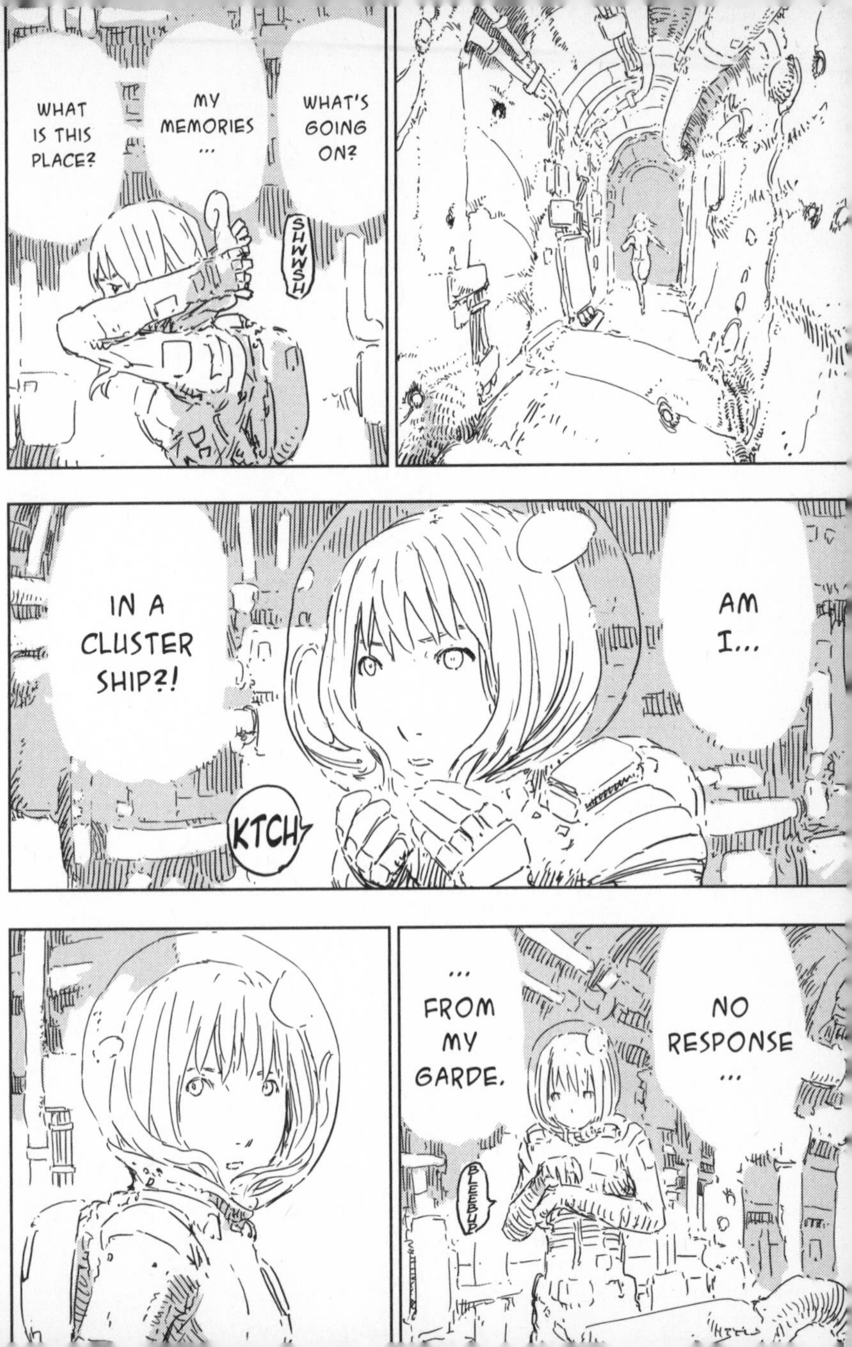
WHAT'S GOING ON?
MY MEMORIES ...
WHAT IS THIS PLACE?
SHWWSH
AM I...
IN A CLUSTER SHIP?!
KTCH
NO RESPONSE ...
... FROM MY GARDE.
BLEEBUP

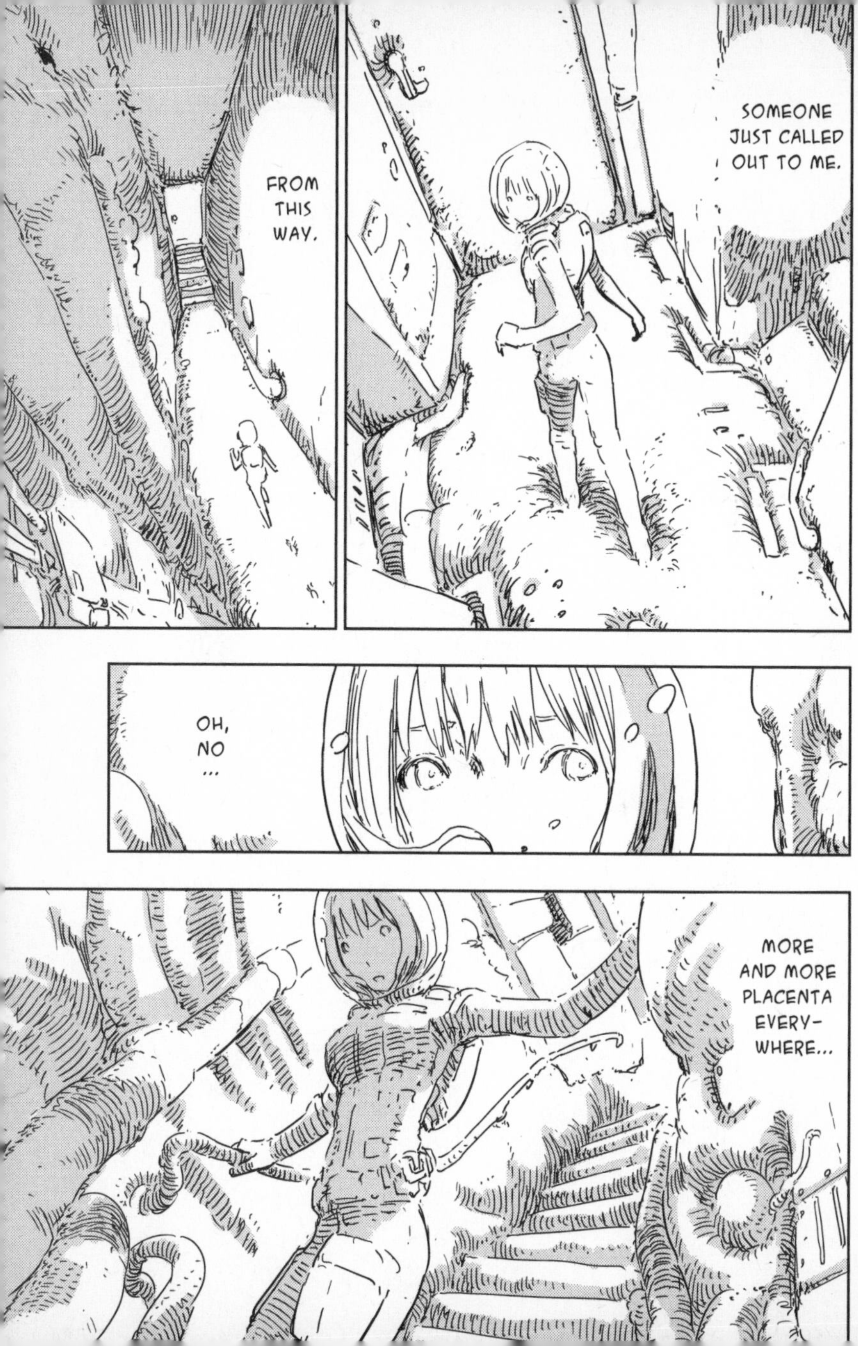
SOMEONE JUST CALLED OUT TO ME.
FROM THIS WAY.
OH, NO ...
MORE AND MORE PLACENTA EVERY-WHERE...

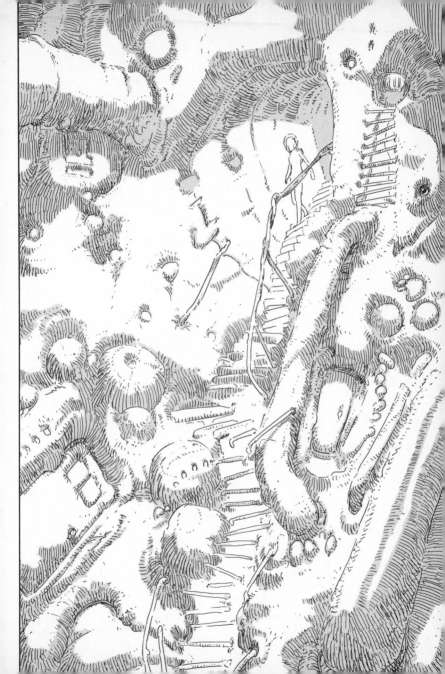

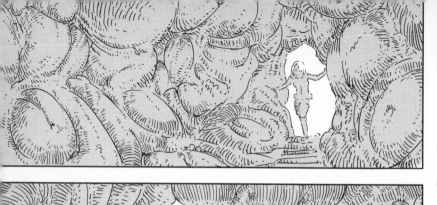

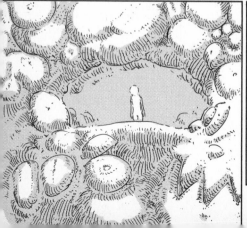

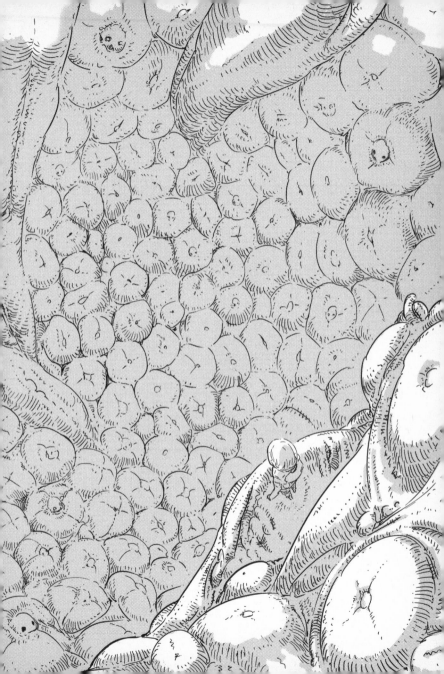

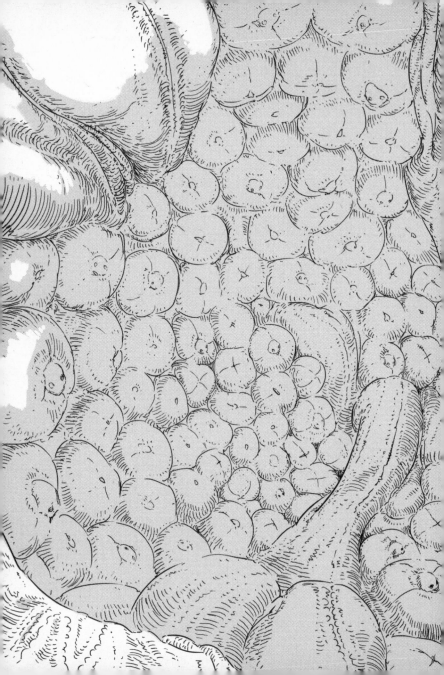

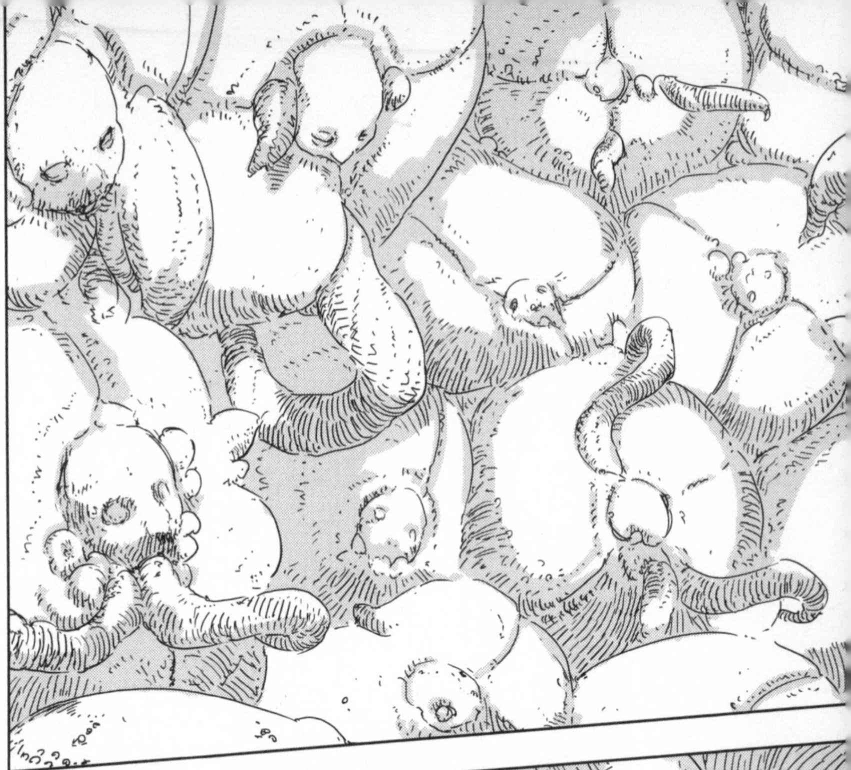
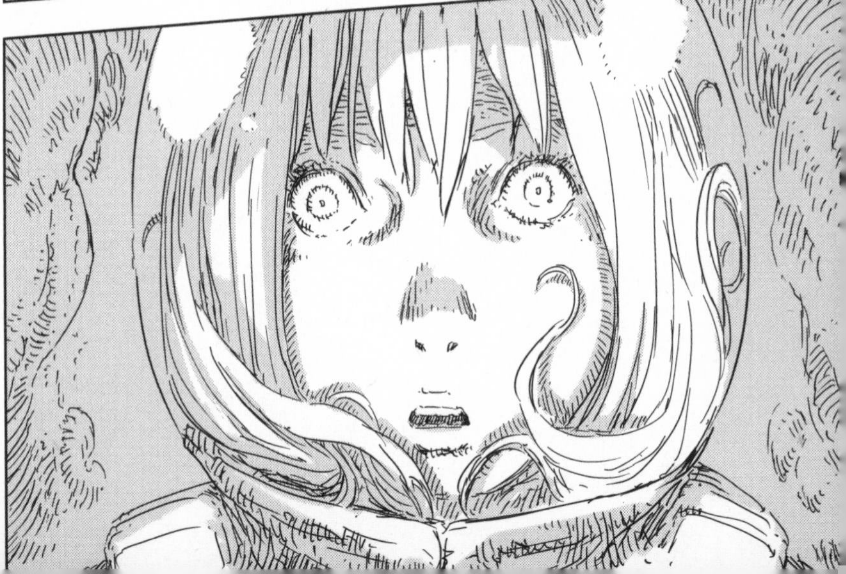

QUICKLY ...

I NEED
TO ESCAPE
...

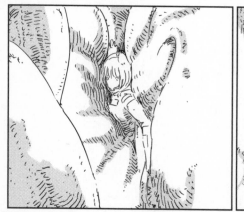

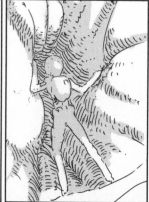

EVERY-
ONE
AGAIN...

I
WANNA
SEE

I
WANNA
GET OUT
OF HERE!!

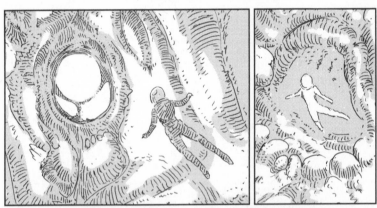

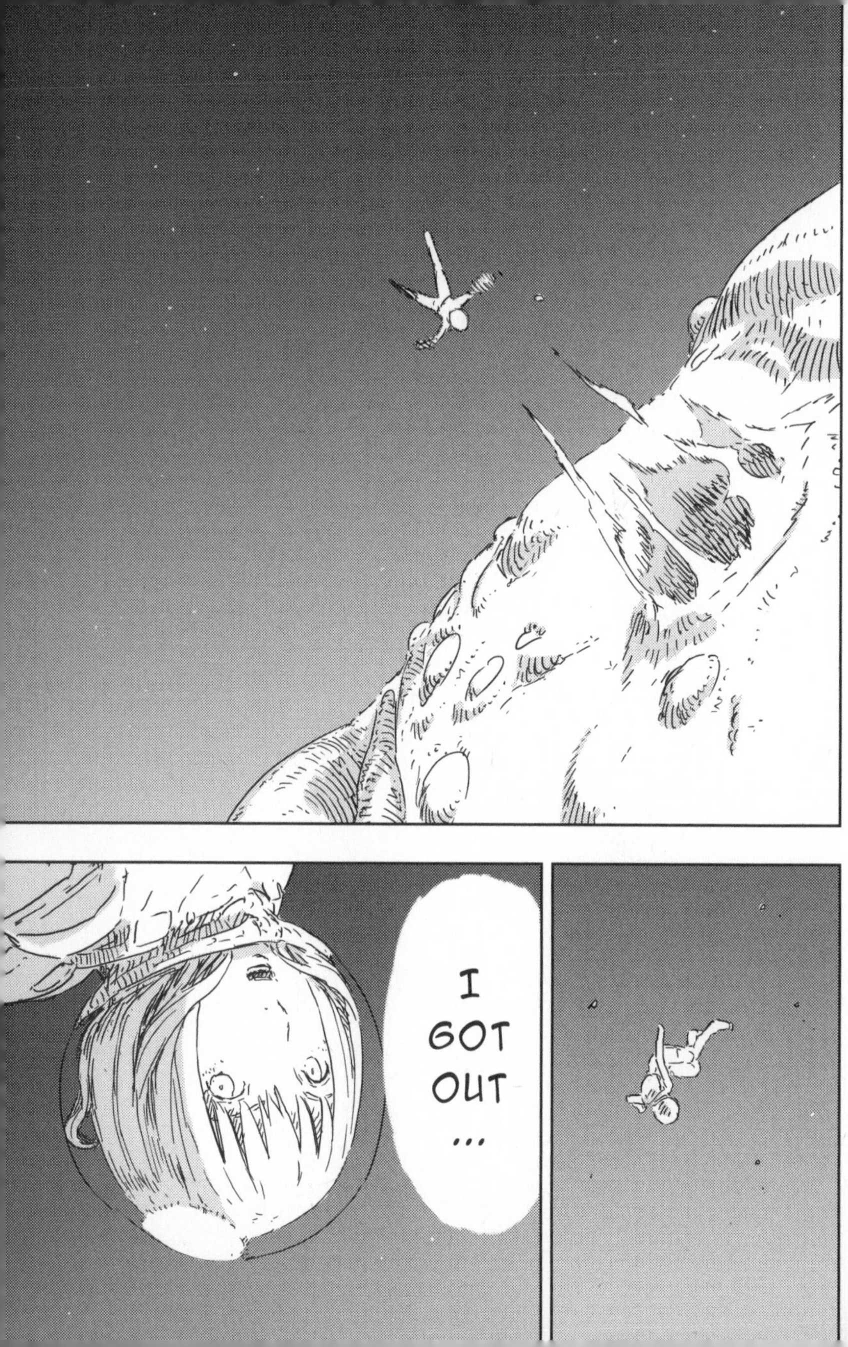
I GOT OUT ...

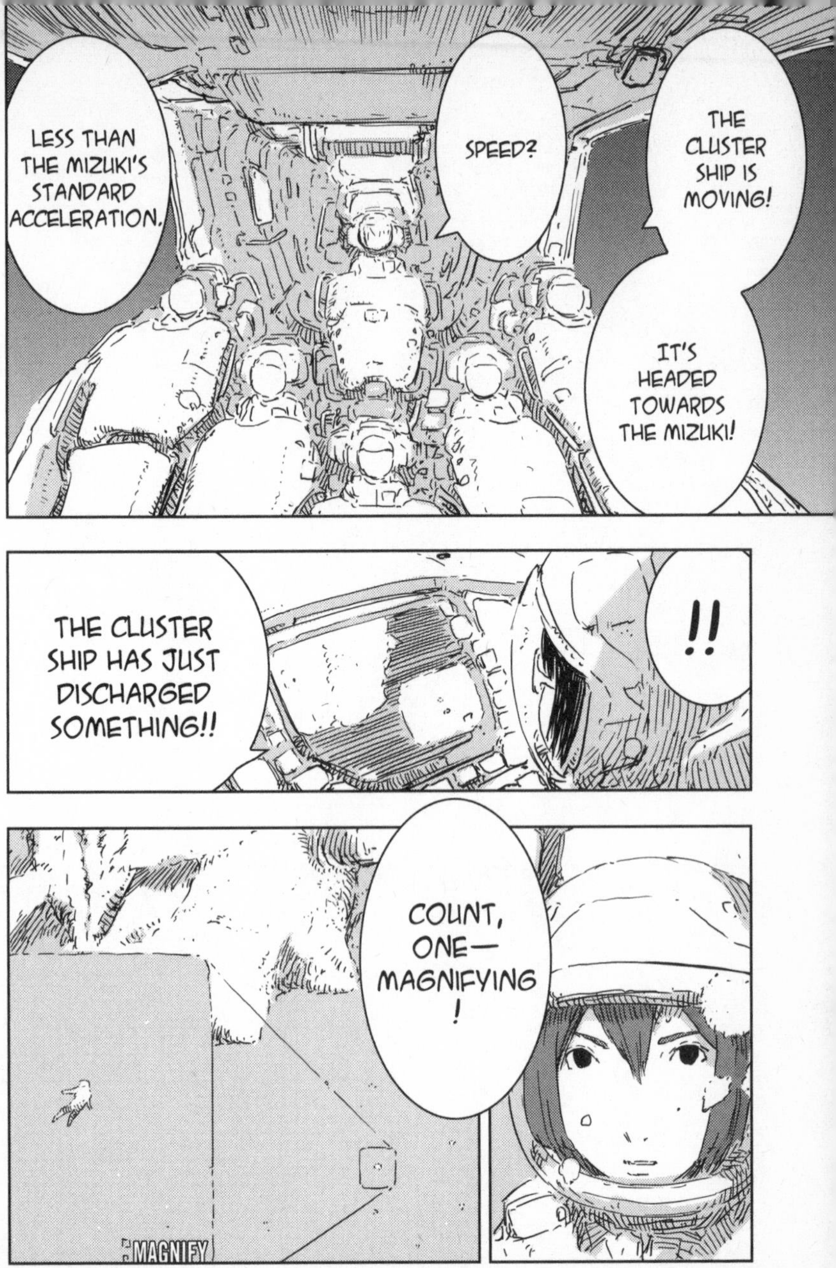
THE CLUSTER SHIP IS MOVING!
IT'S HEADED TOWARDS THE MIZUKI!
SPEED?
LESS THAN THE MIZUKI'S STANDARD ACCELERATION.
!!
THE CLUSTER SHIP HAS JUST DISCHARGED SOMETHING!!
COUNT, ONE—MAGNIFYING!
MAGNIFY

IS THAT ...

I–IT'S A PILOT!!

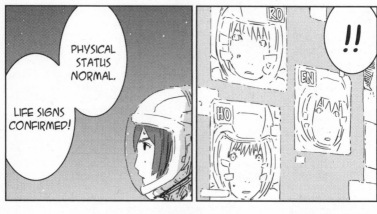

PHYSICAL STATUS NORMAL.

LIFE SIGNS CONFIRMED!

!!

ID-ING PILOT.

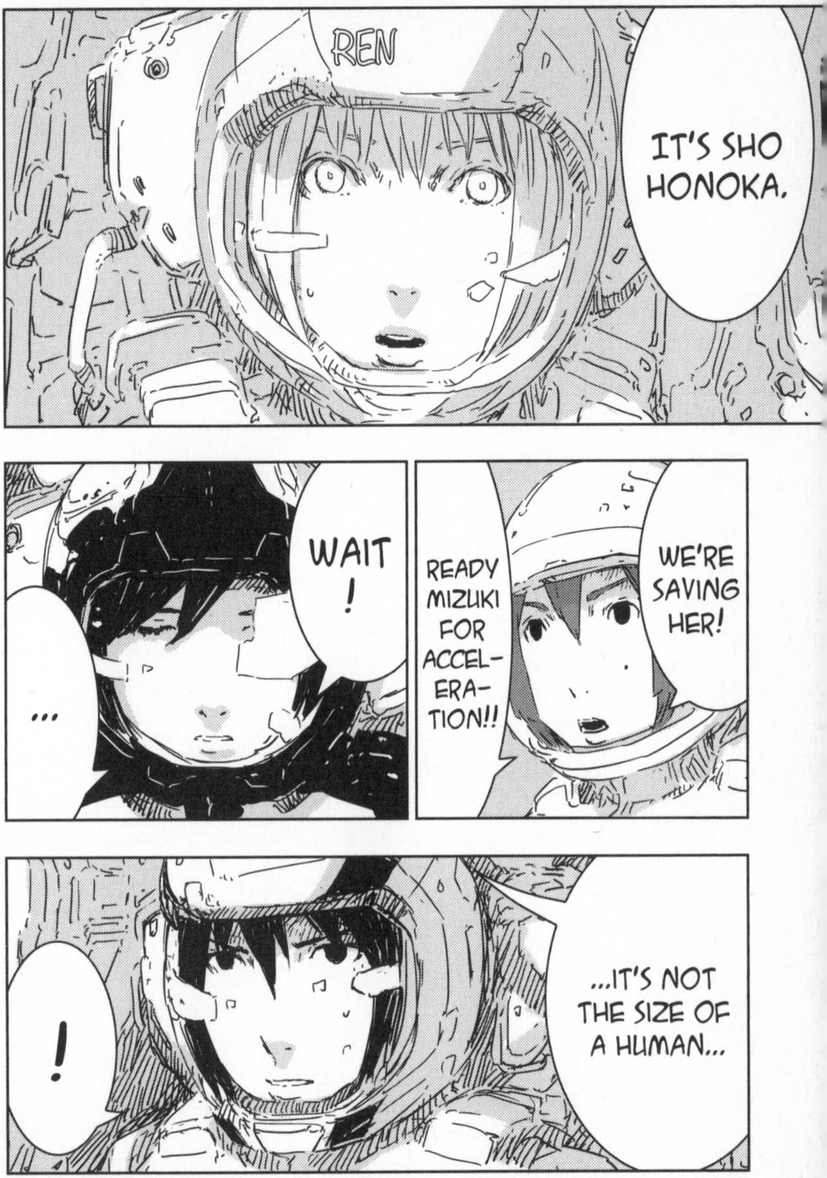
IT'S SHO HONOKA.
REN
WE'RE SAVING HER!
READY MIZUKI FOR ACCEL-ERA-TION!!
WAIT!
...
...IT'S NOT THE SIZE OF A HUMAN...
!

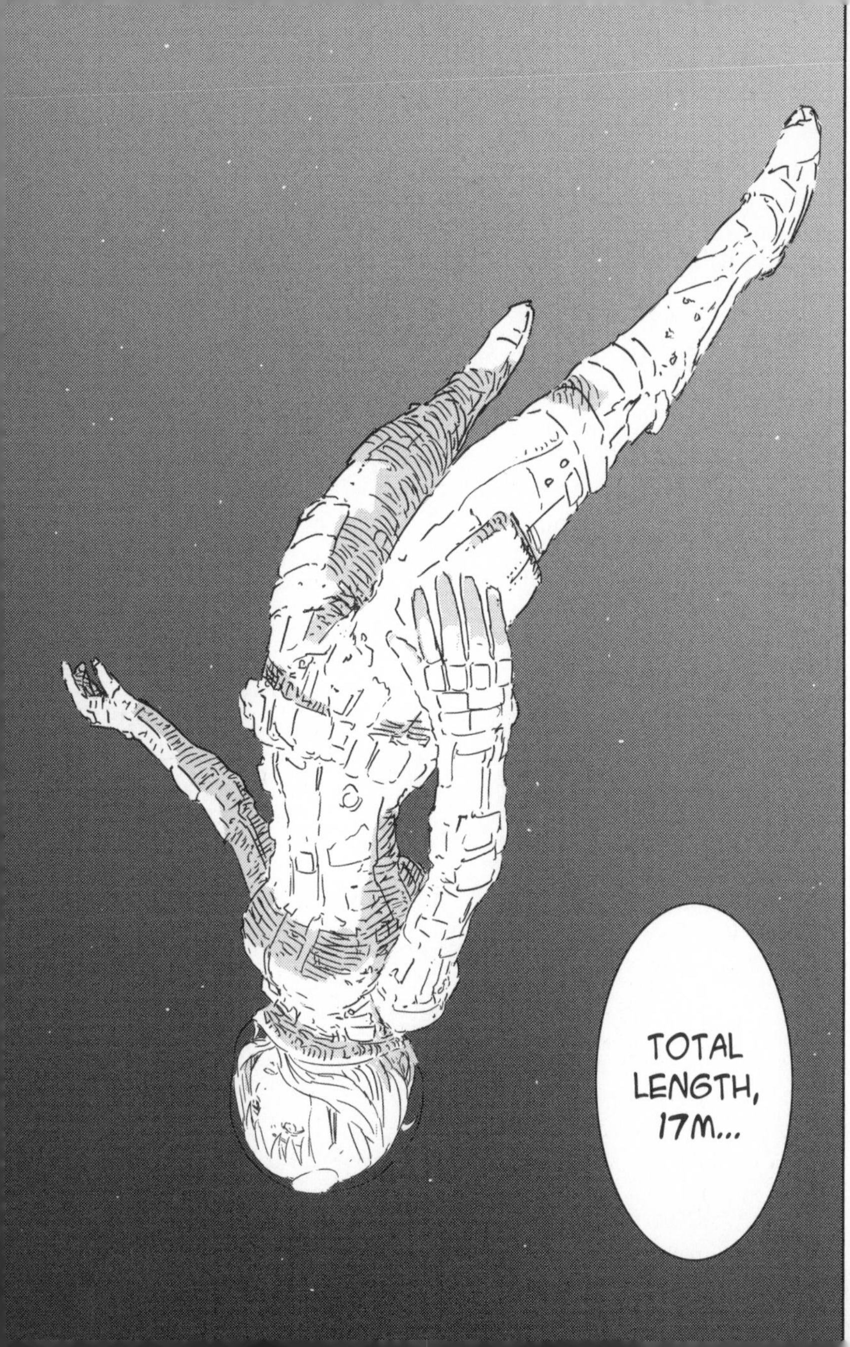
TOTAL LENGTH, 17M...

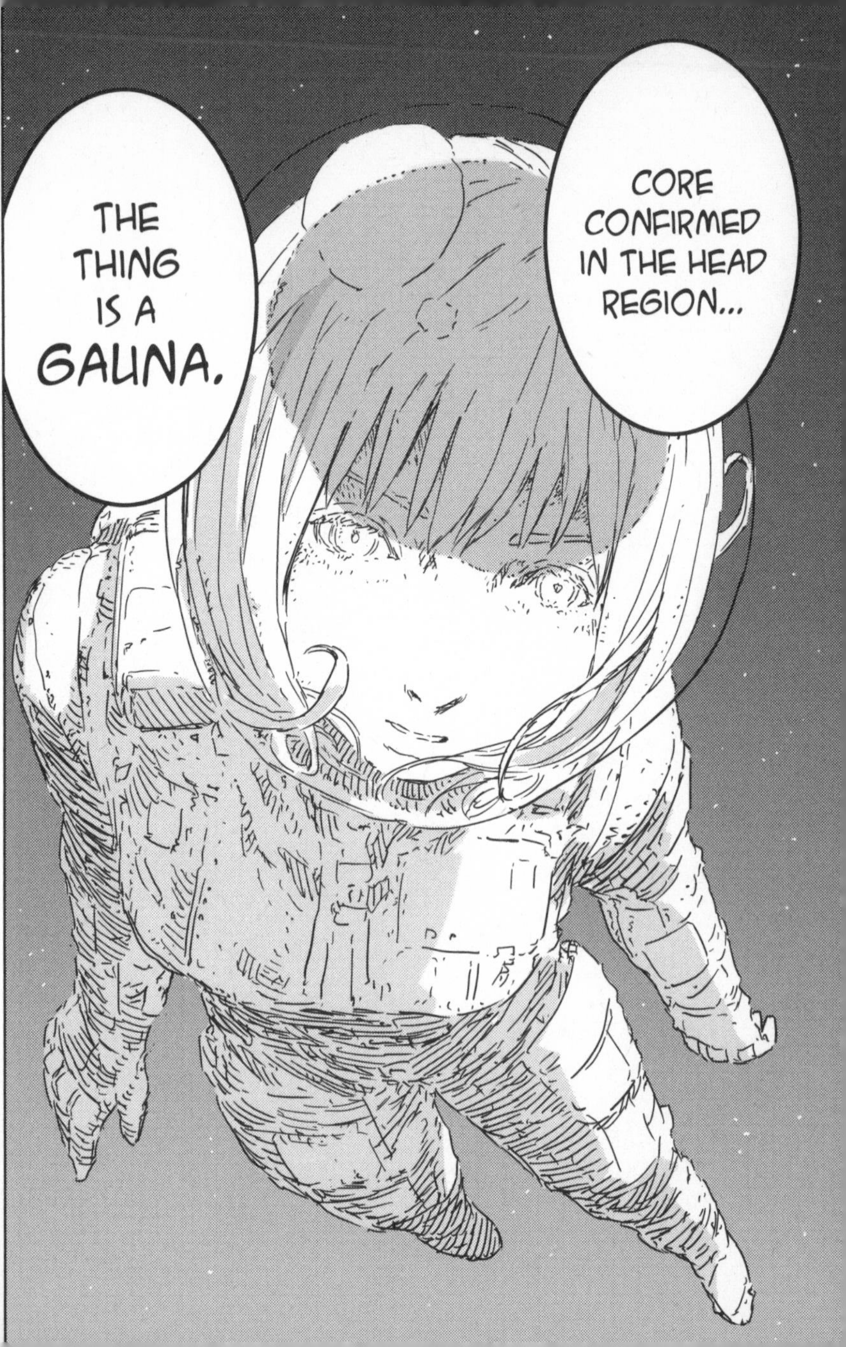
CORE CONFIRMED IN THE HEAD REGION...
THE THING IS A GAUNA.

Chapter 57: END

Chapter 58: The Mizuki's Capabilities

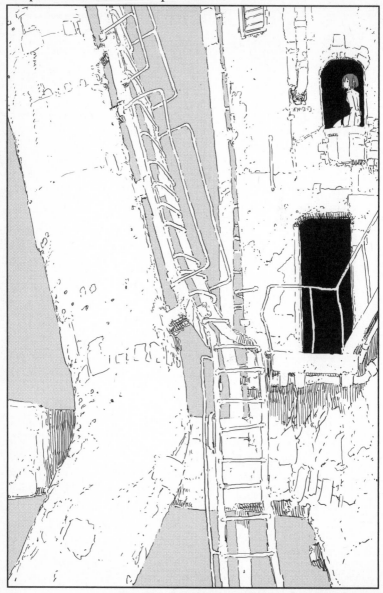

One Hundred Sights of Sidonia Part Forty-Four:
Tube Scheduled for Reconditioning

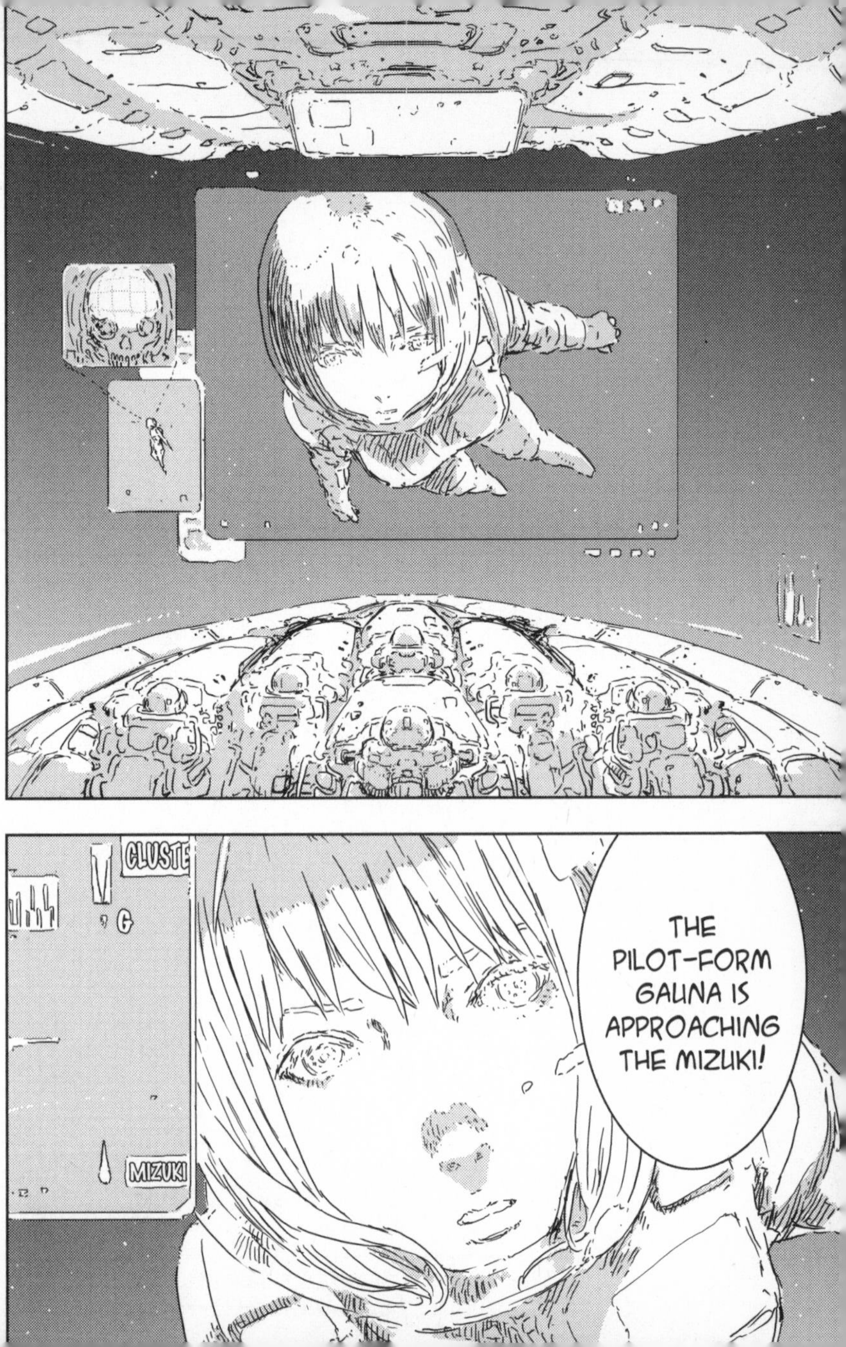
THE PILOT-FORM GAUNA IS APPROACHING THE MIZUKI!
CLUSTE
G
MIZUKI

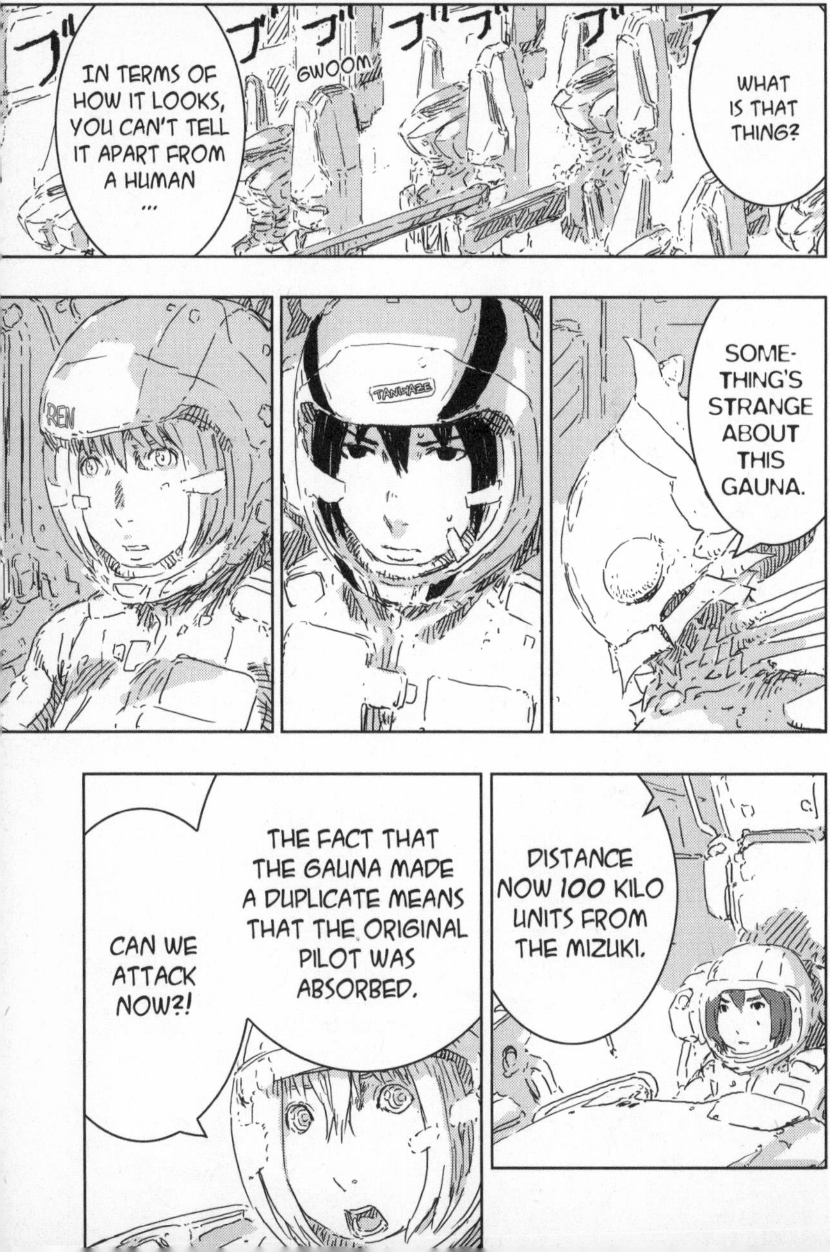
WHAT IS THAT THING?
GWOOM
IN TERMS OF HOW IT LOOKS, YOU CAN'T TELL IT APART FROM A HUMAN ...
SOME-THING'S STRANGE ABOUT THIS GAUNA.
TANIKAZE
REN
DISTANCE NOW 100 KILO UNITS FROM THE MIZUKI.
THE FACT THAT THE GAUNA MADE A DUPLICATE MEANS THAT THE ORIGINAL PILOT WAS ABSORBED.
CAN WE ATTACK NOW?!

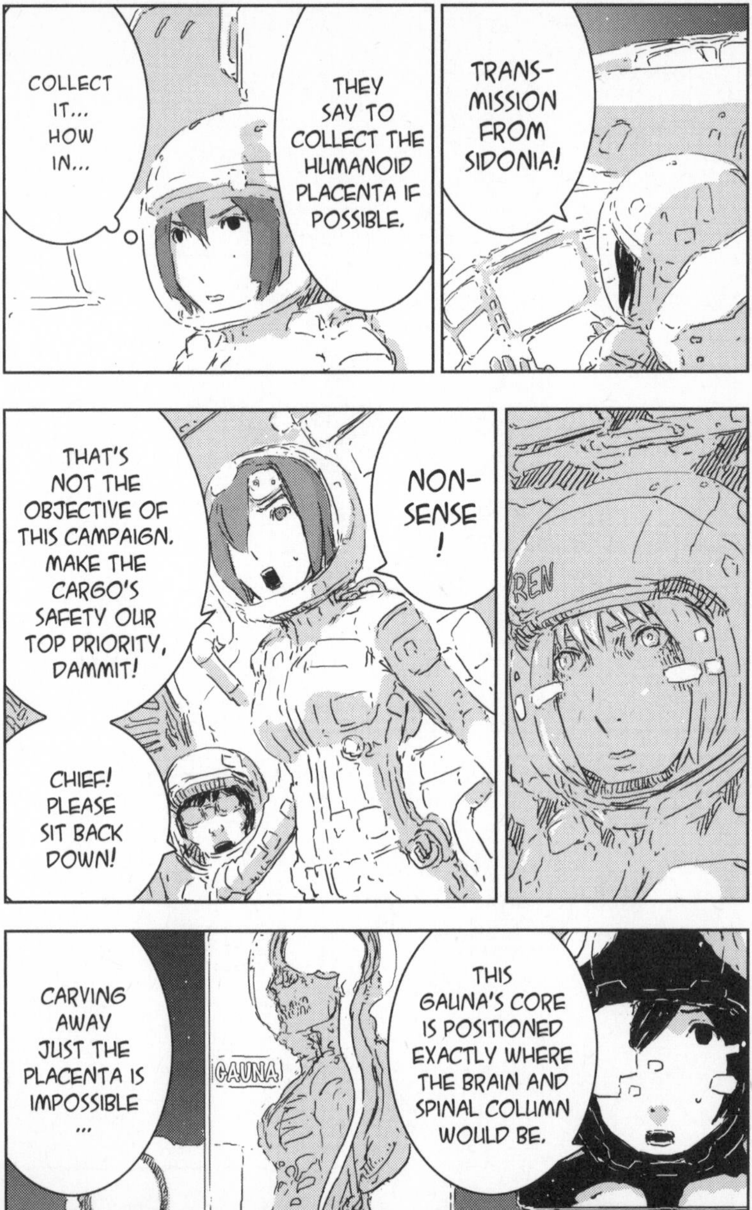
TRANS-MISSION FROM SIDONIA!
THEY SAY TO COLLECT THE HUMANOID PLACENTA IF POSSIBLE.
COLLECT IT... HOW IN...
NON-SENSE!
THAT'S NOT THE OBJECTIVE OF THIS CAMPAIGN. MAKE THE CARGO'S SAFETY OUR TOP PRIORITY, DAMMIT!
CHIEF! PLEASE SIT BACK DOWN!
THIS GAUNA'S CORE IS POSITIONED EXACTLY WHERE THE BRAIN AND SPINAL COLUMN WOULD BE.
GAUNA
CARVING AWAY JUST THE PLACENTA IS IMPOSSIBLE ...
REN

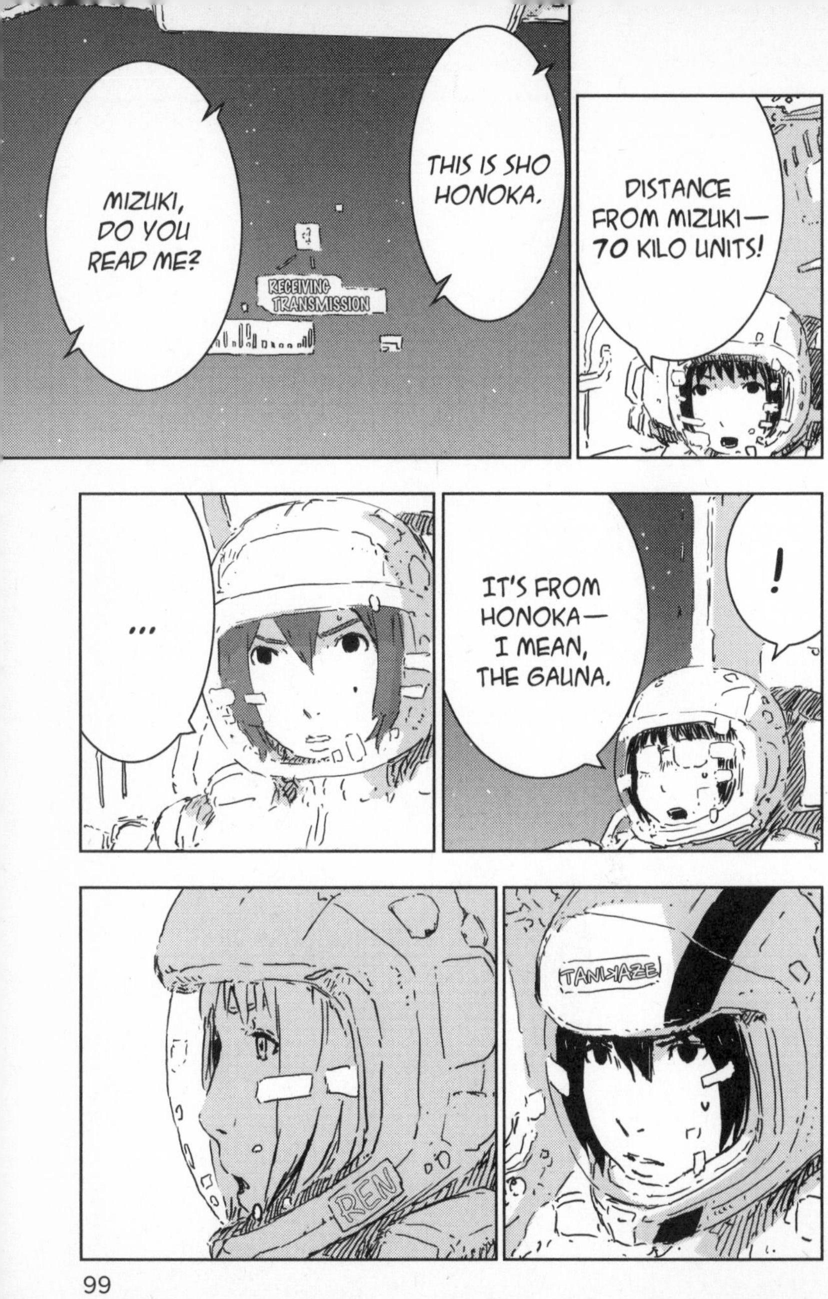

DISTANCE FROM MIZUKI— 70 KILO UNITS!
THIS IS SHO HONOKA.
MIZUKI, DO YOU READ ME?
RECEIVING TRANSMISSION
!
IT'S FROM HONOKA— I MEAN, THE GAUNA.
...
TANIKAZE
REN

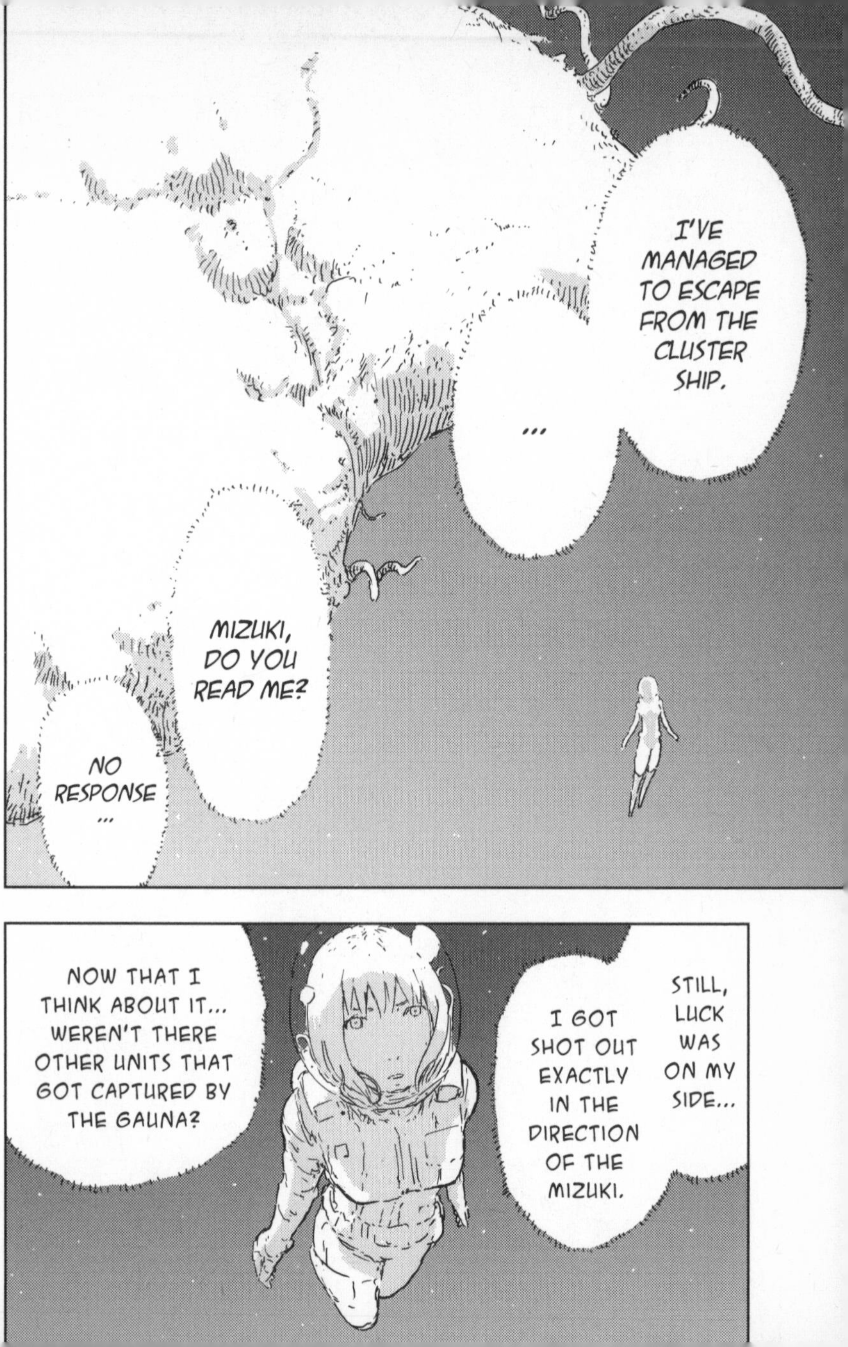
I'VE MANAGED TO ESCAPE FROM THE CLUSTER SHIP.
...
MIZUKI, DO YOU READ ME?
NO RESPONSE ...
STILL, LUCK WAS ON MY SIDE...
I GOT SHOT OUT EXACTLY IN THE DIRECTION OF THE MIZUKI.
NOW THAT I THINK ABOUT IT... WEREN'T THERE OTHER UNITS THAT GOT CAPTURED BY THE GAUNA?

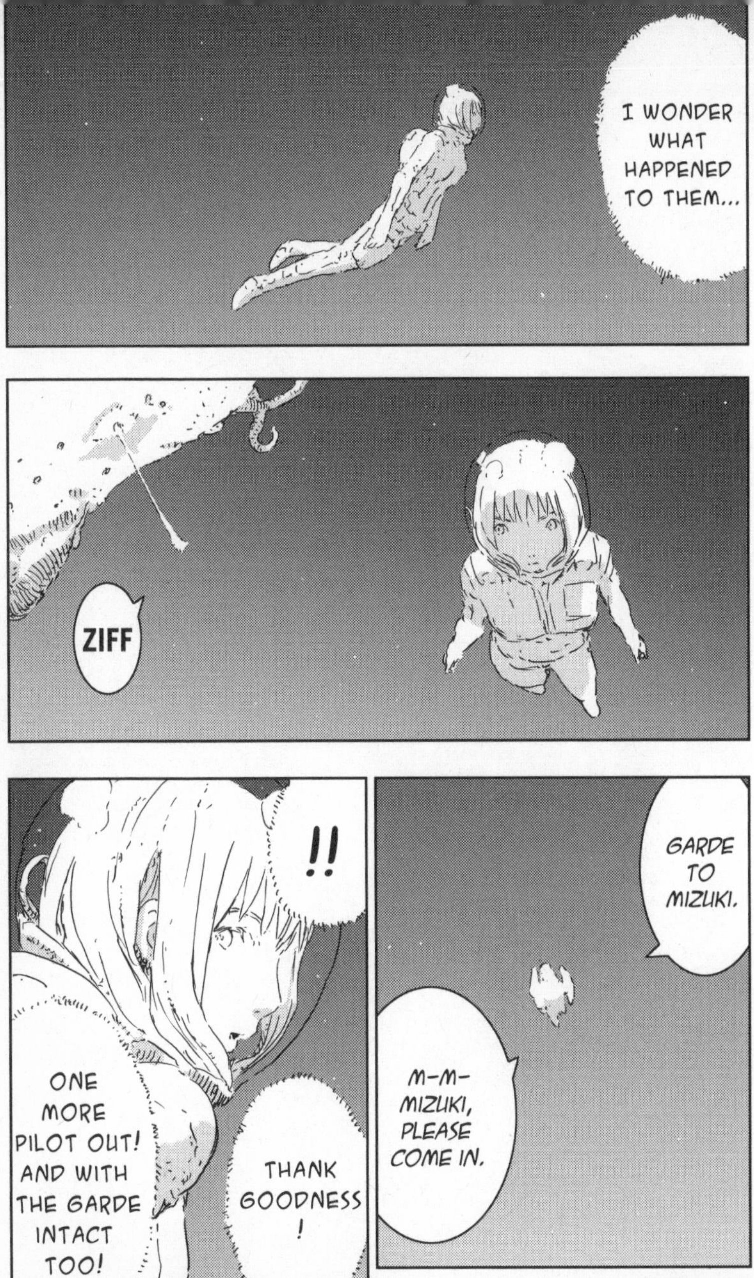
I WONDER WHAT HAPPENED TO THEM...
ZIFF
GARDE TO MIZUKI.
M-M-MIZUKI, PLEASE COME IN.
!!
THANK GOODNESS!
ONE MORE PILOT OUT! AND WITH THE GARDE INTACT TOO!

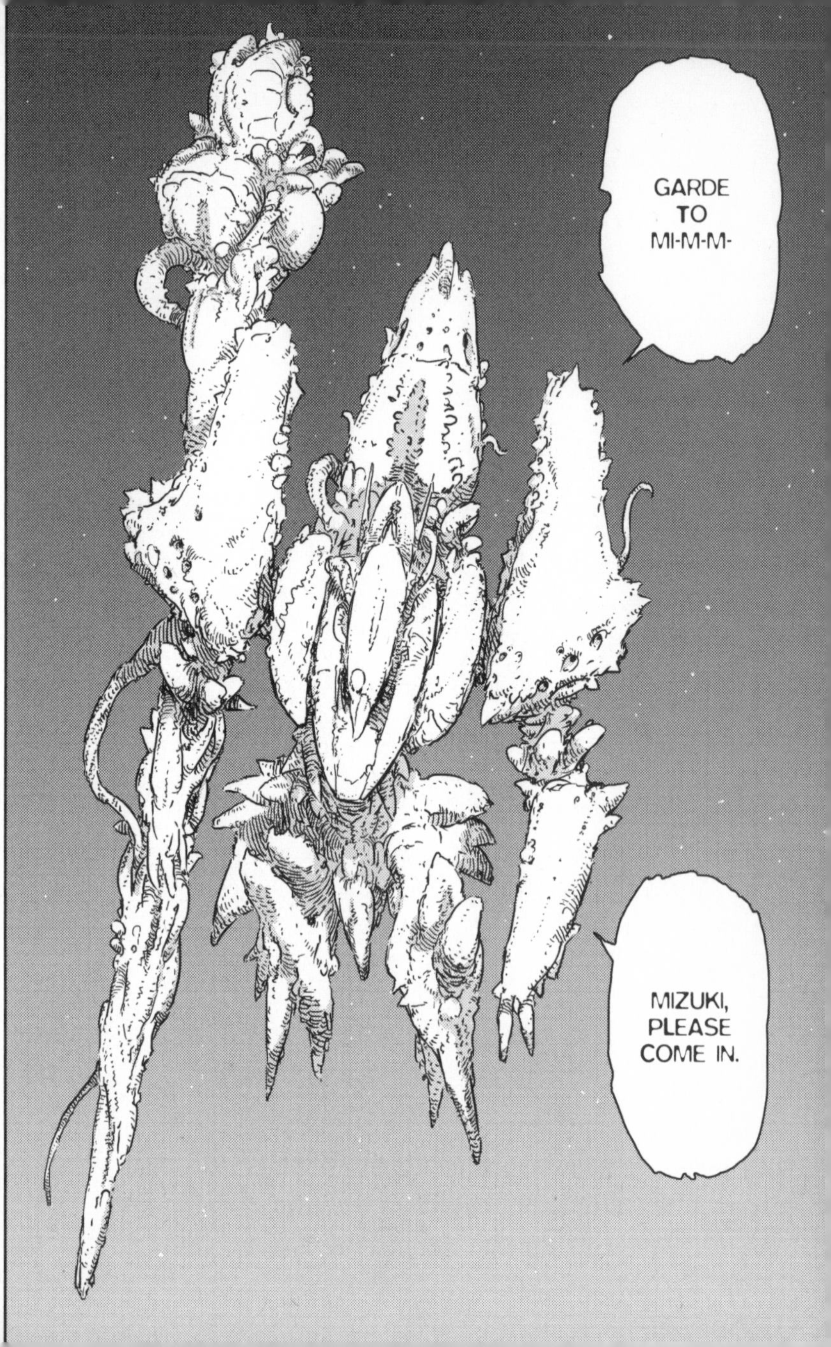
GARDE TO MI-M-M-
MIZUKI, PLEASE COME IN.

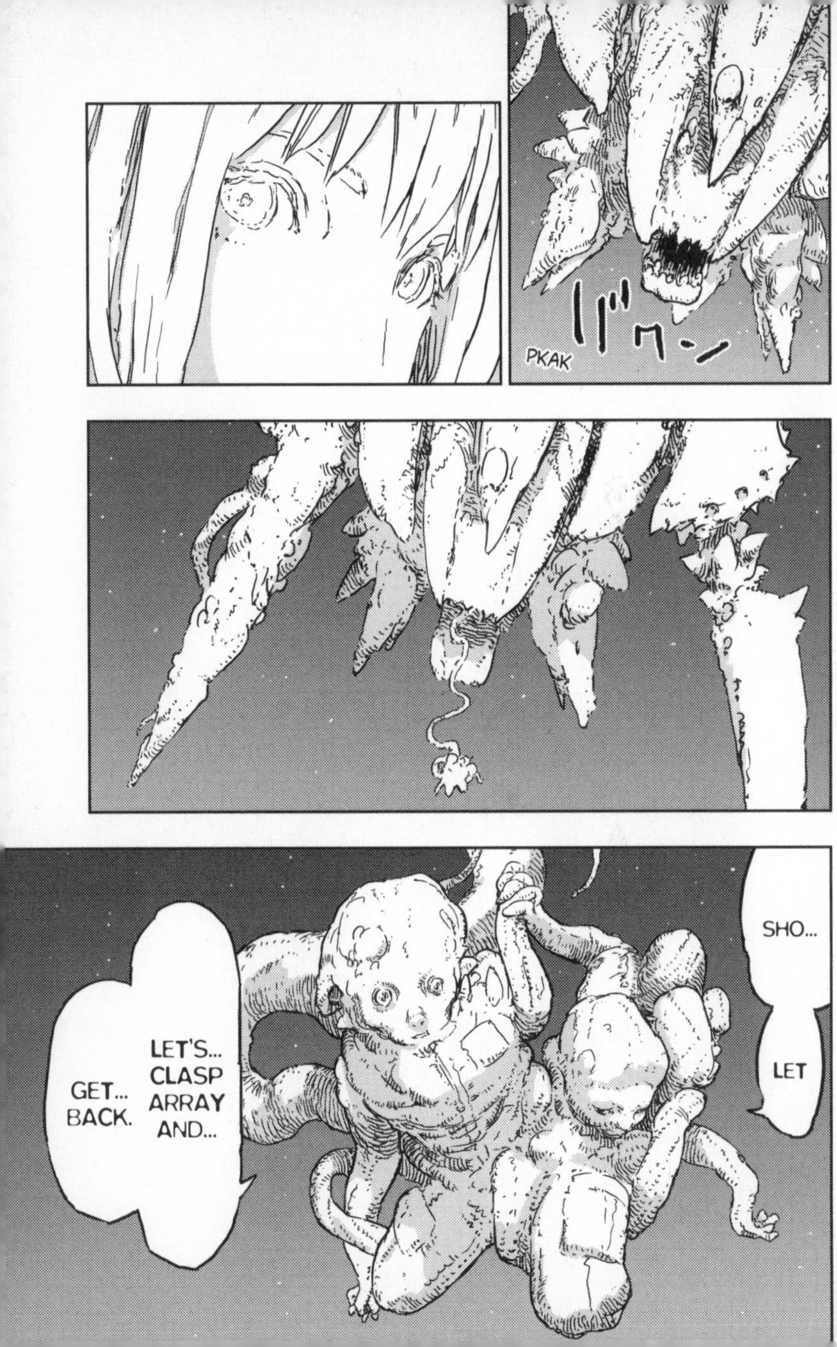
PKAK
SHO... LET
LET'S... CLASP ARRAY AND...
GET... BACK.

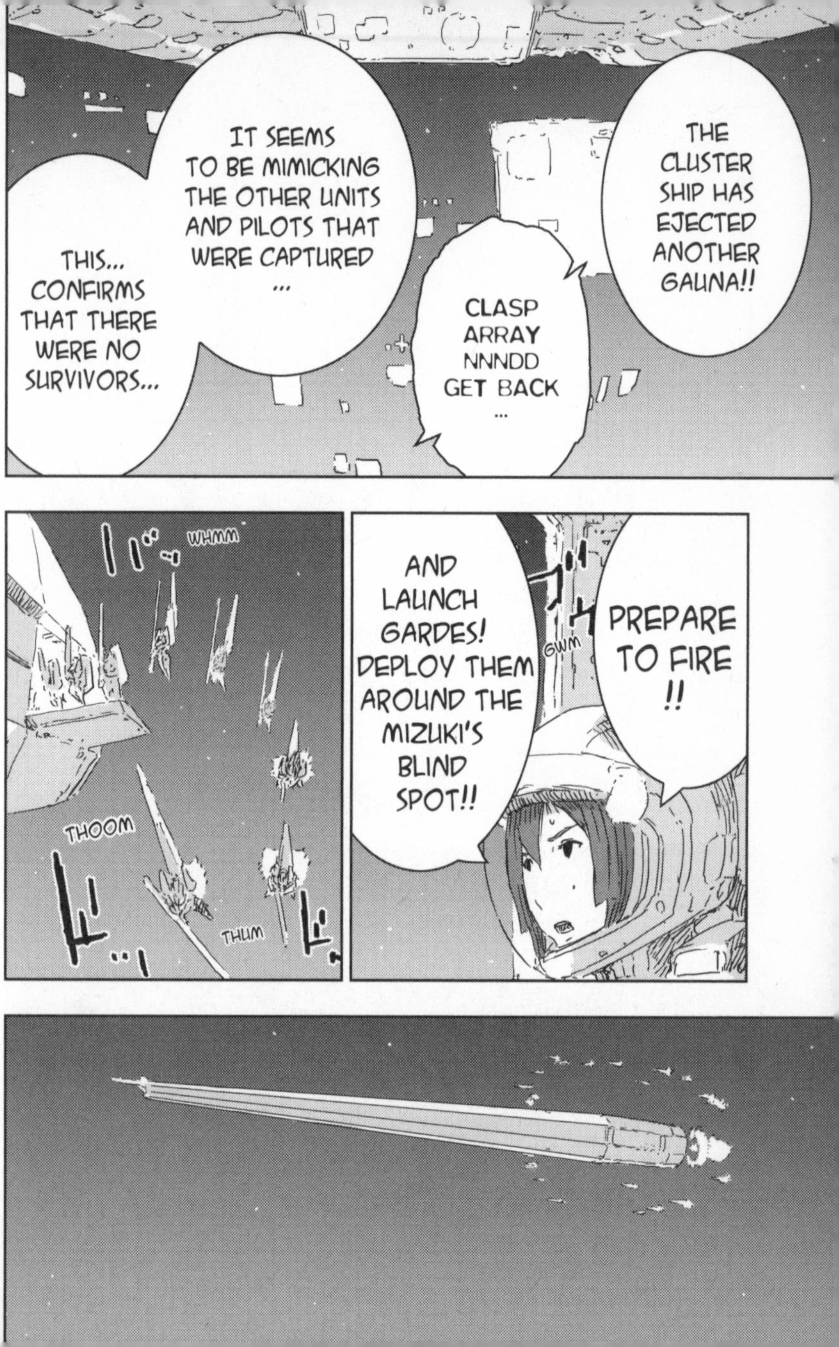

THE CLUSTER SHIP HAS EJECTED ANOTHER GAUNA!!
CLASP ARRAY NNNDD GET BACK ...
IT SEEMS TO BE MIMICKING THE OTHER UNITS AND PILOTS THAT WERE CAPTURED ...
THIS... CONFIRMS THAT THERE WERE NO SURVIVORS...
PREPARE TO FIRE !!
GWM
AND LAUNCH GARDES! DEPLOY THEM AROUND THE MIZUKI'S BLIND SPOT!!
WHMM
THOOM
THUM

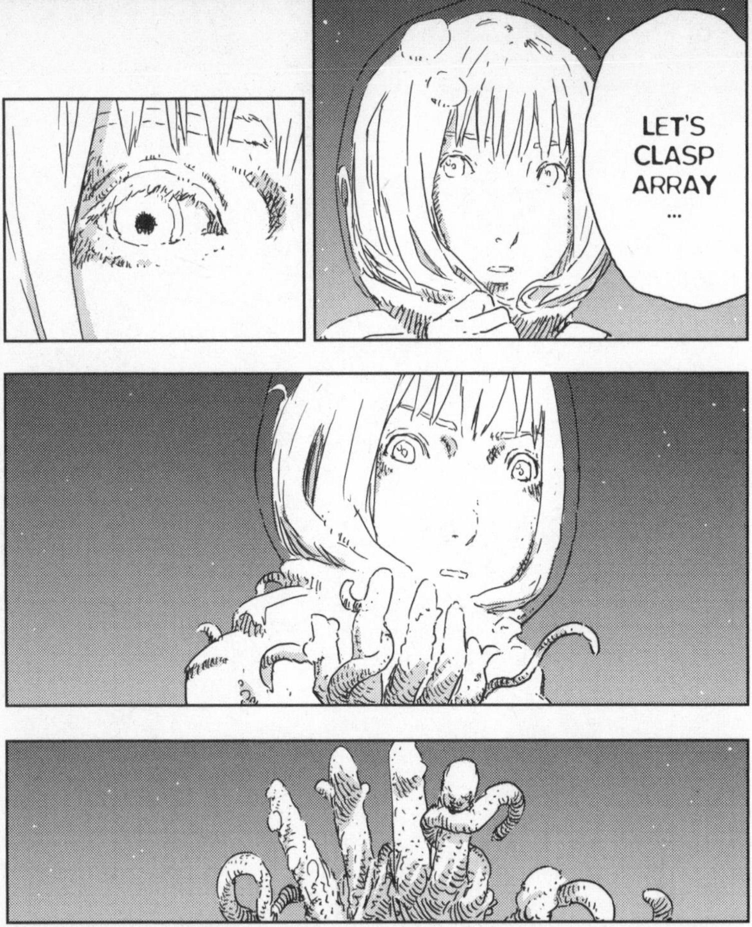
LET'S CLASP ARRAY ...

Gaunology

If a Gauna were to perfectly duplicate a human, that Gauna would have a personality utterly identical to that of the reproduced person.

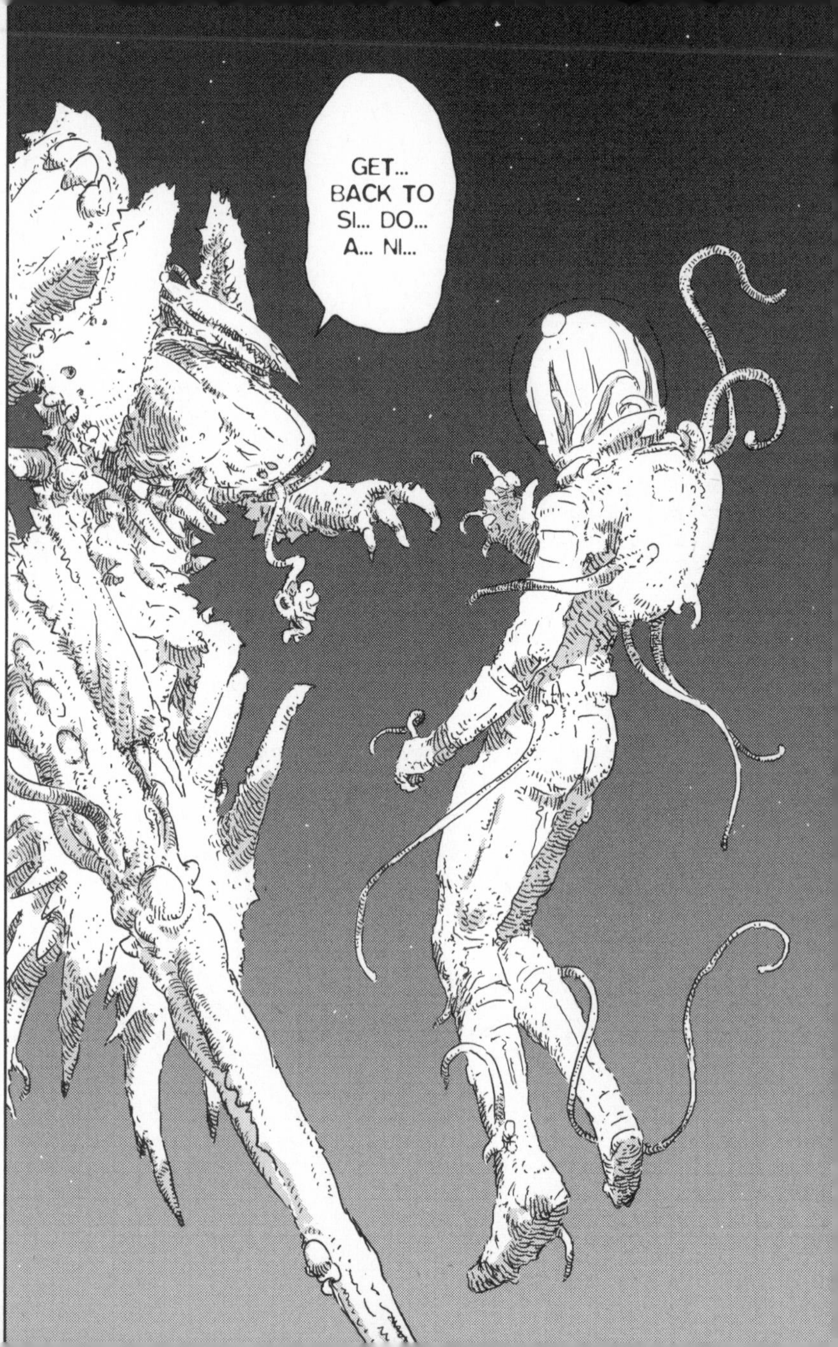
GET... BACK TO SI... DO... A... NI...

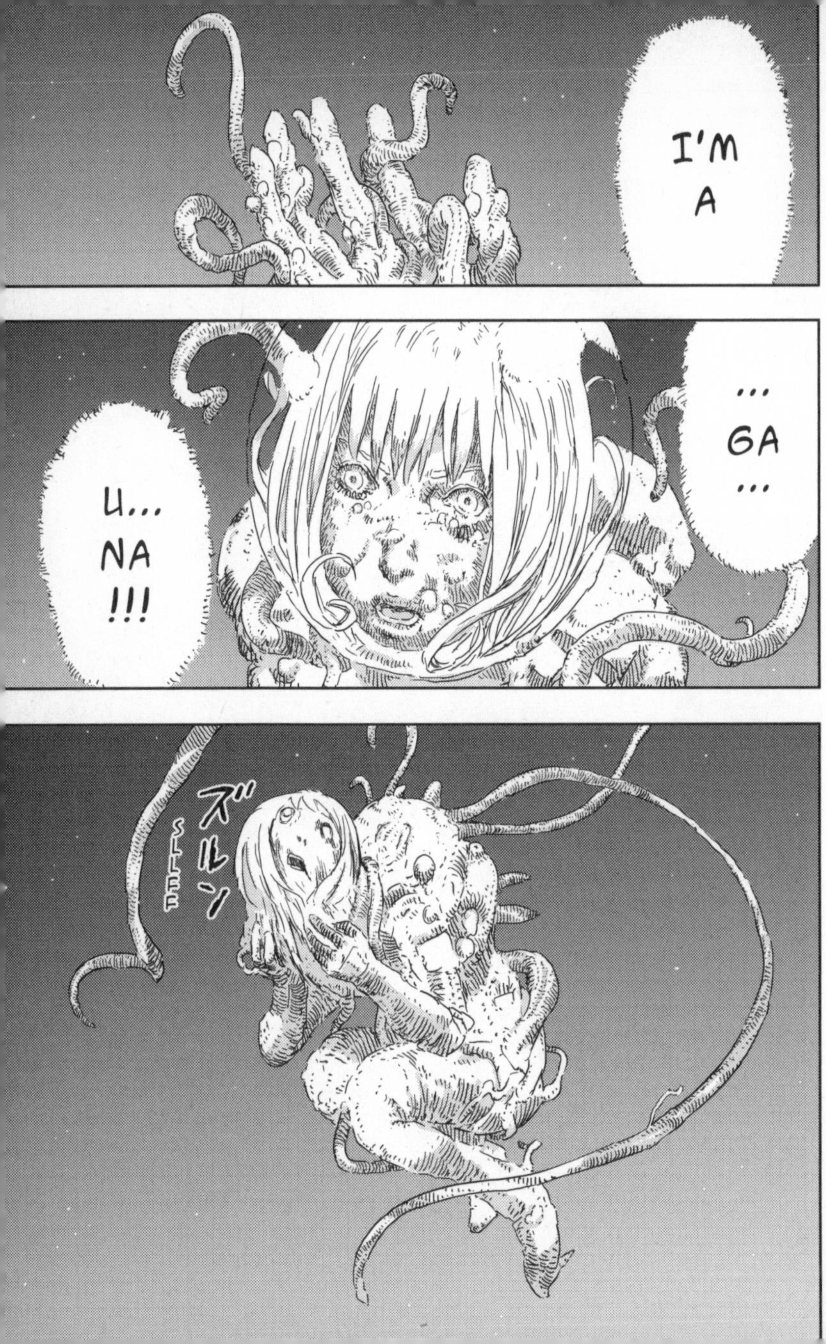
I'M A
... GA ...
U... NA !!!
ズルン

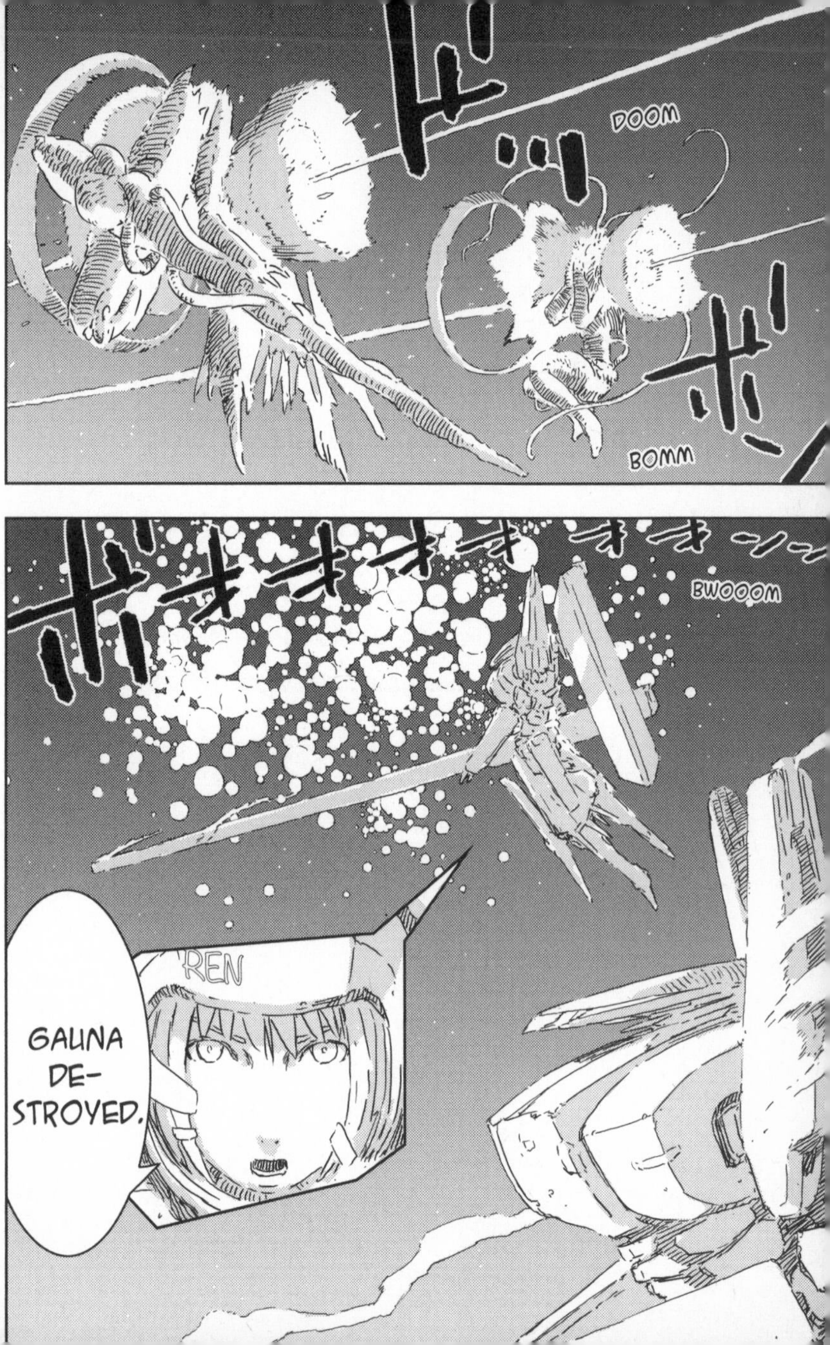
DOOM
BOMM
BWOOOM
REN
GAUNA DE-STROYED.

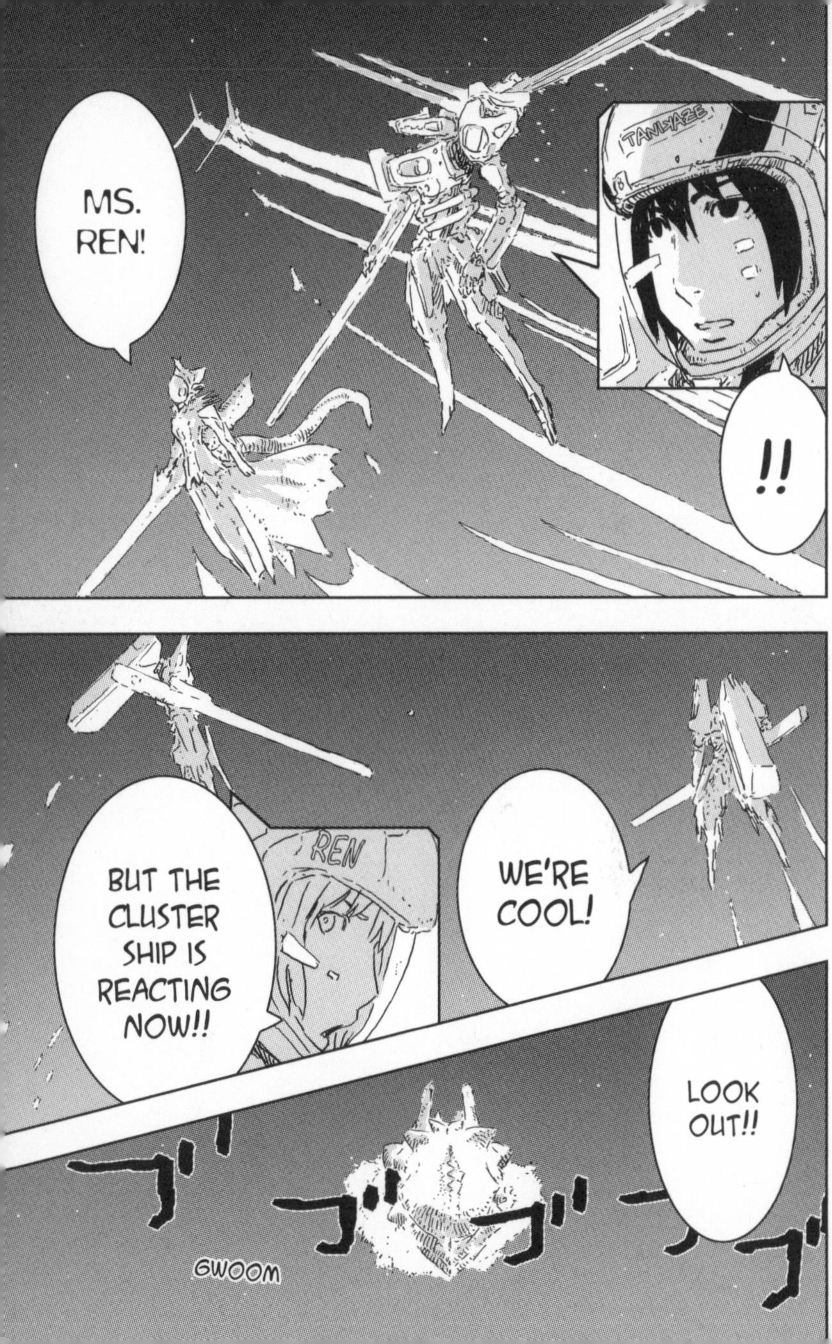
TANIKAZE
!!
MS. REN!
WE'RE COOL!
REN
BUT THE CLUSTER SHIP IS REACTING NOW!!
LOOK OUT!!
GWOOM

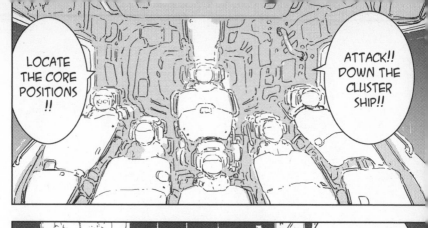

ATTACK!! DOWN THE CLUSTER SHIP!!
LOCATE THE CORE POSITIONS !!
THERE ARE THREE MAIN CORES! THE WAY THEY'RE POSITIONED, WE CAN'T TAKE AIM FROM HEAD ON!
MAIN CORE
1
2
3
GSHAKK
I'M TAKING THE HELM!

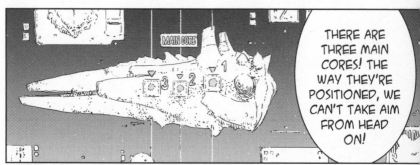

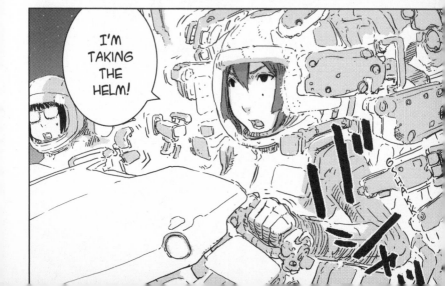

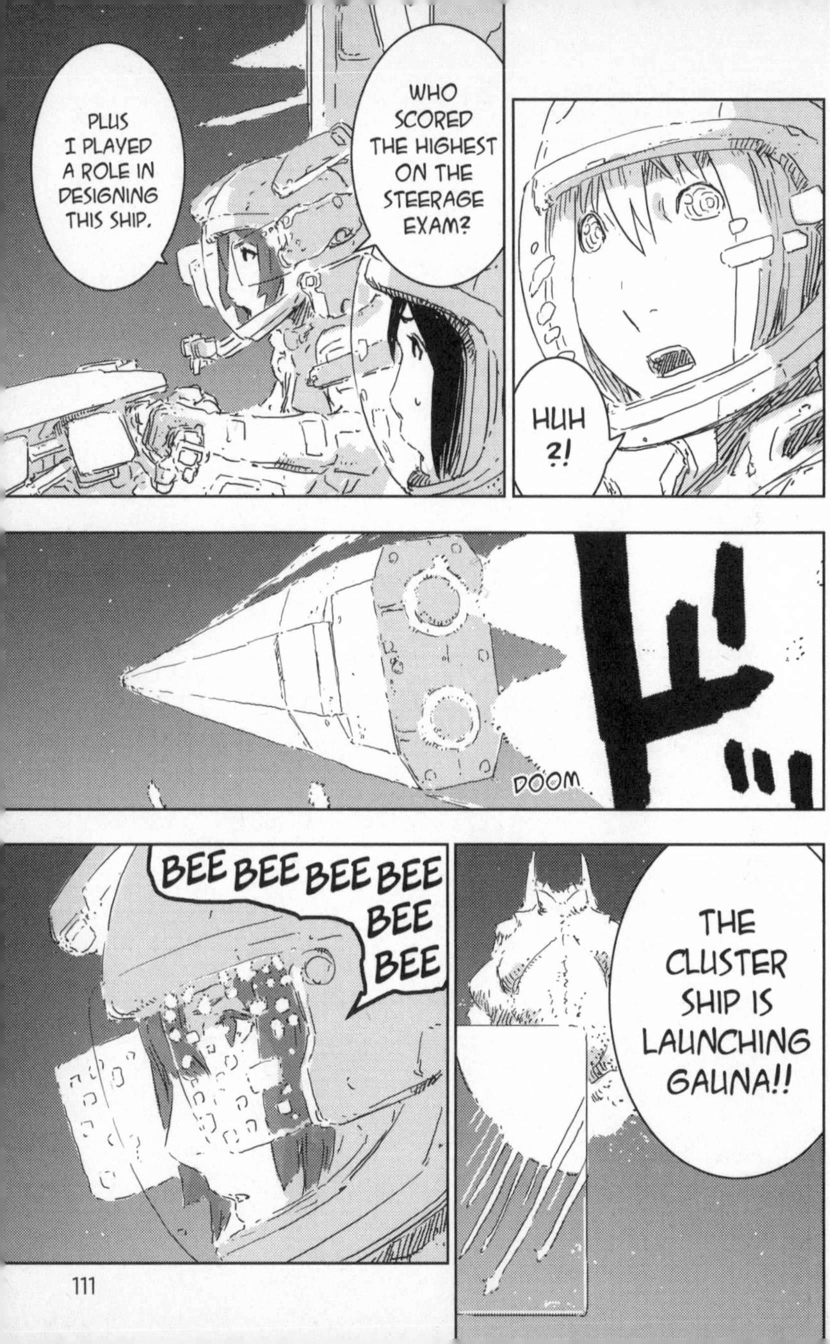
HUH ?!
WHO SCORED THE HIGHEST ON THE STEERAGE EXAM?
PLUS I PLAYED A ROLE IN DESIGNING THIS SHIP.
DOOM
THE CLUSTER SHIP IS LAUNCHING GAUNA!!
BEE BEE BEE BEE BEE BEE

GONK
GONK
GONK
GONK
GAGONK
GONK
GONK
GONK
GONK
VVN
BIBIP BIBIP BIBIP BIBIP BIP
KLIK
THOOM

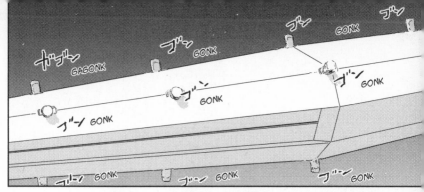

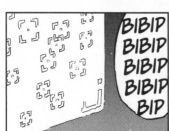

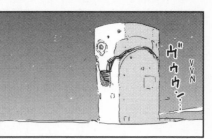

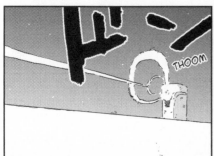

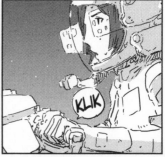

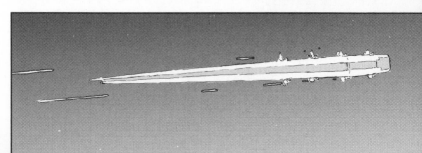

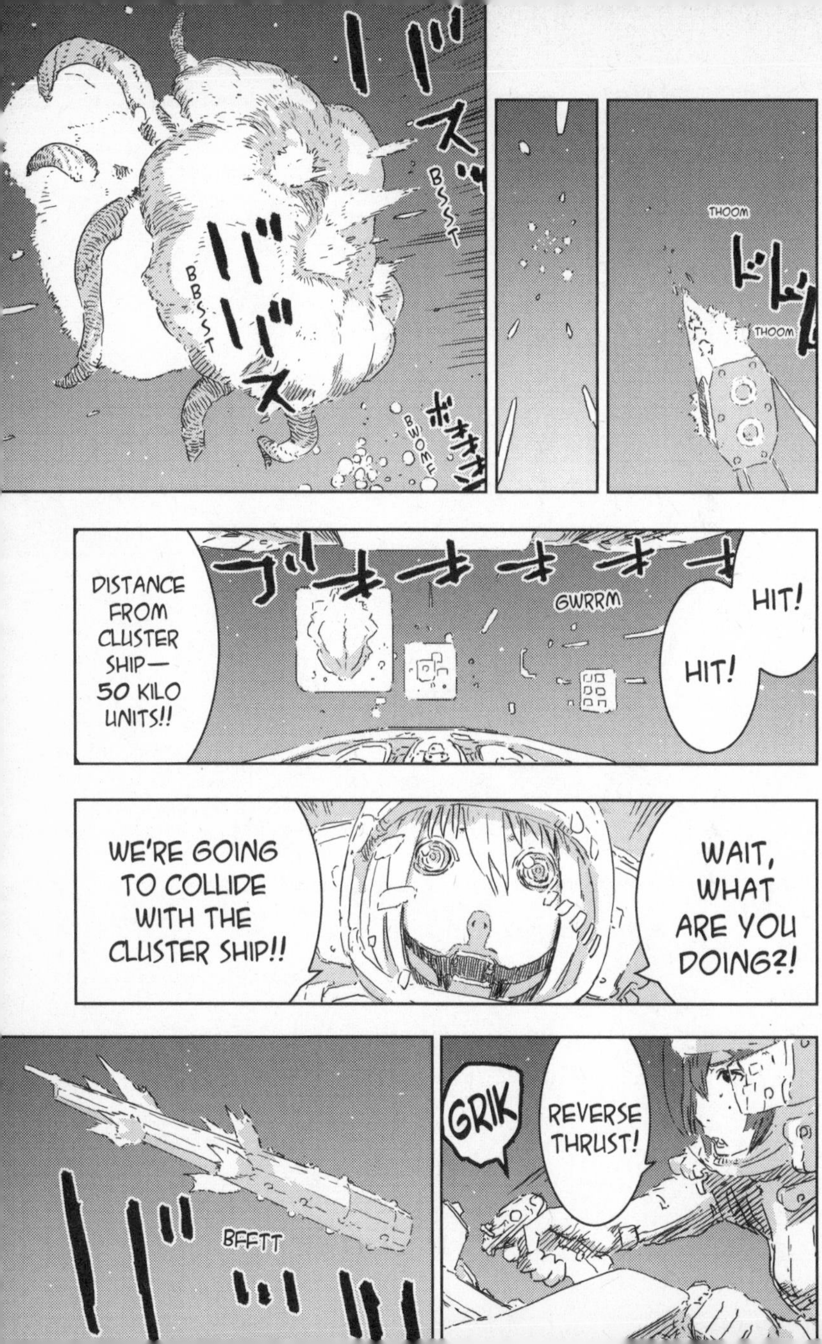
THOOM
THOOM
BSSST
BBSST
BWOMF
HIT!
HIT!
GWRRM
DISTANCE FROM CLUSTER SHIP— 50 KILO UNITS!!
WAIT, WHAT ARE YOU DOING?!
WE'RE GOING TO COLLIDE WITH THE CLUSTER SHIP!!
REVERSE THRUST!
GRIK
BFFTT

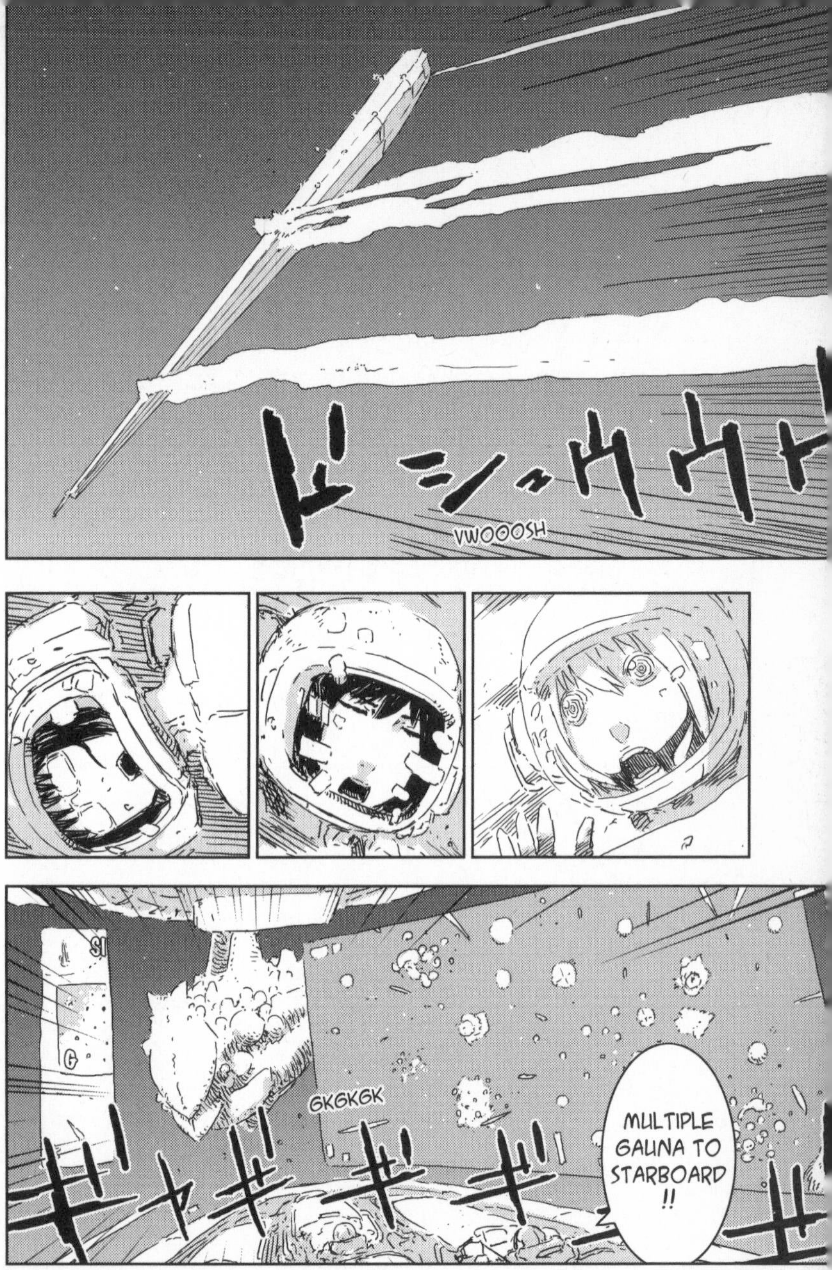
VWOOOSH
MULTIPLE GAUNA TO STARBOARD !!
GKGKGK

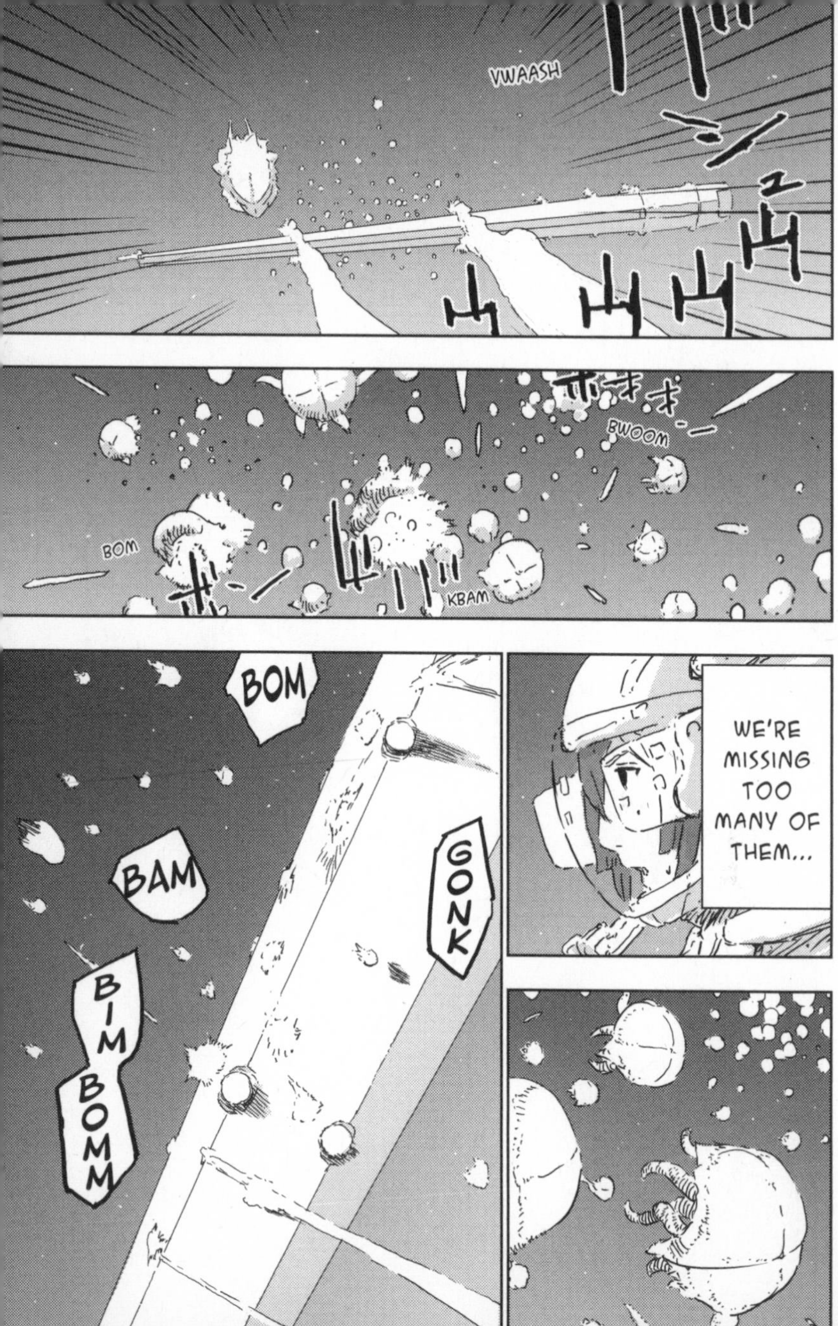
VWAASH
BWOOM
BOM
KBAM
WE'RE MISSING TOO MANY OF THEM...
BOM
GONK
BAM
BIM BOMM

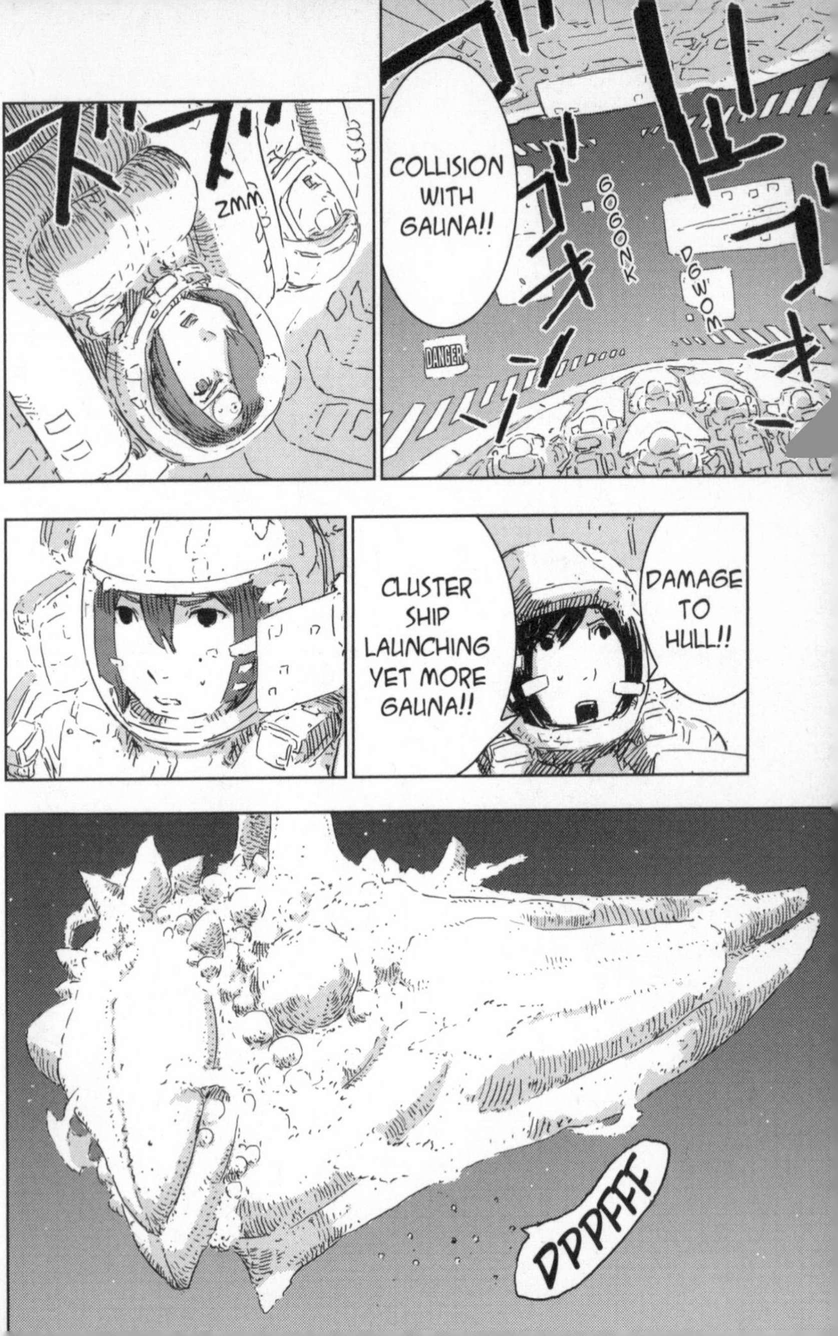
COLLISION WITH GAUNA!!
GOGONK
DGWOM
DANGER
ZMM
DAMAGE TO HULL!!
CLUSTER SHIP LAUNCHING YET MORE GAUNA!!
DPPFFF

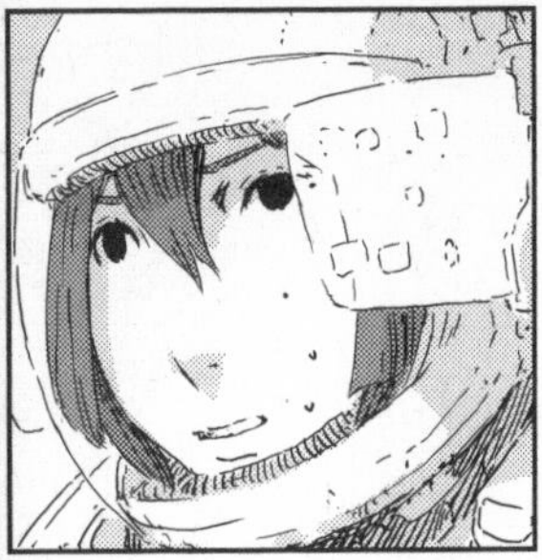
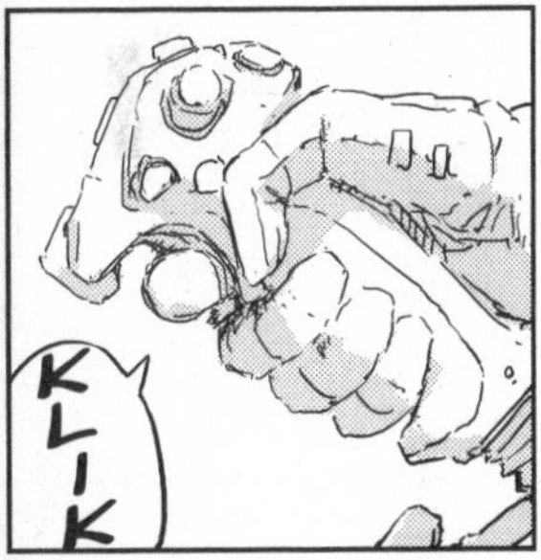
KLIK
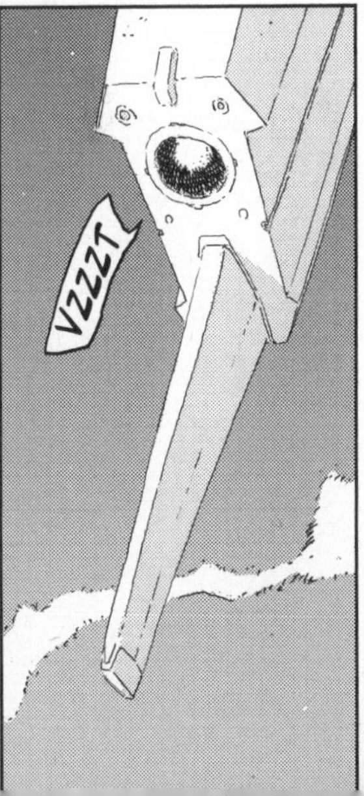
VZZZT
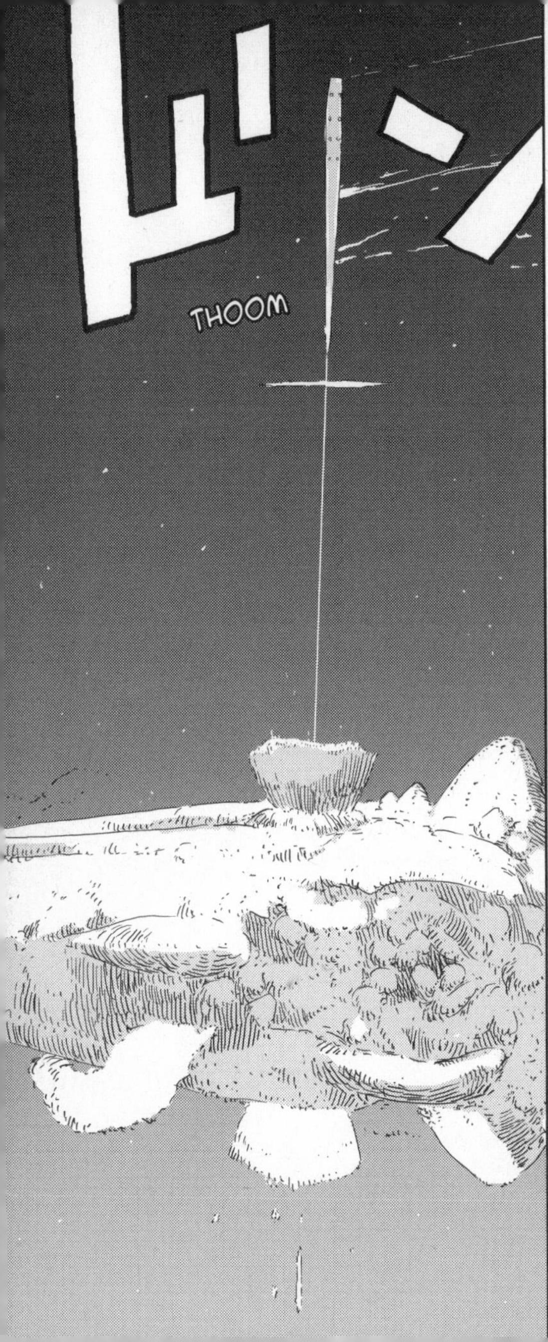
THOOM

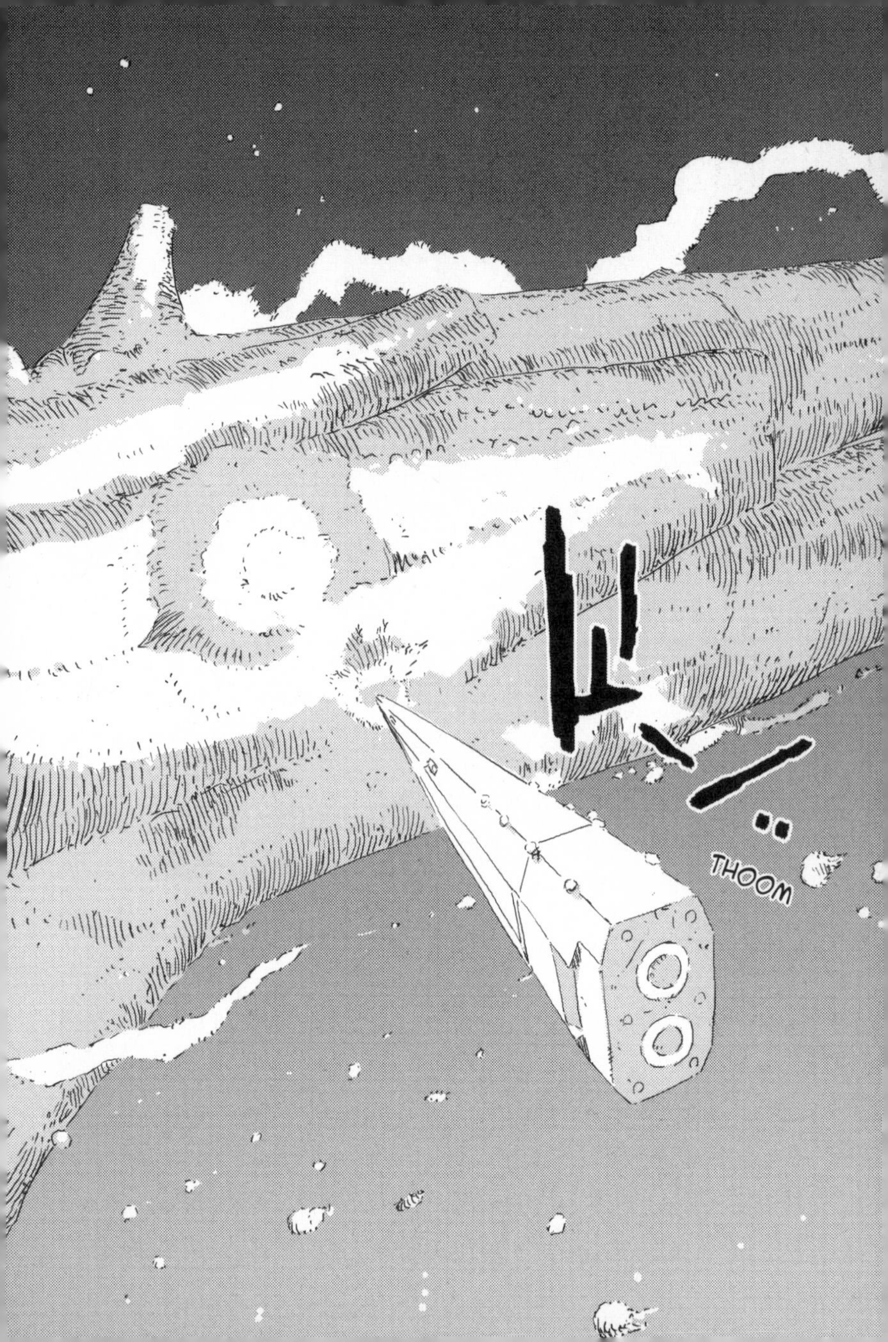
THOOM

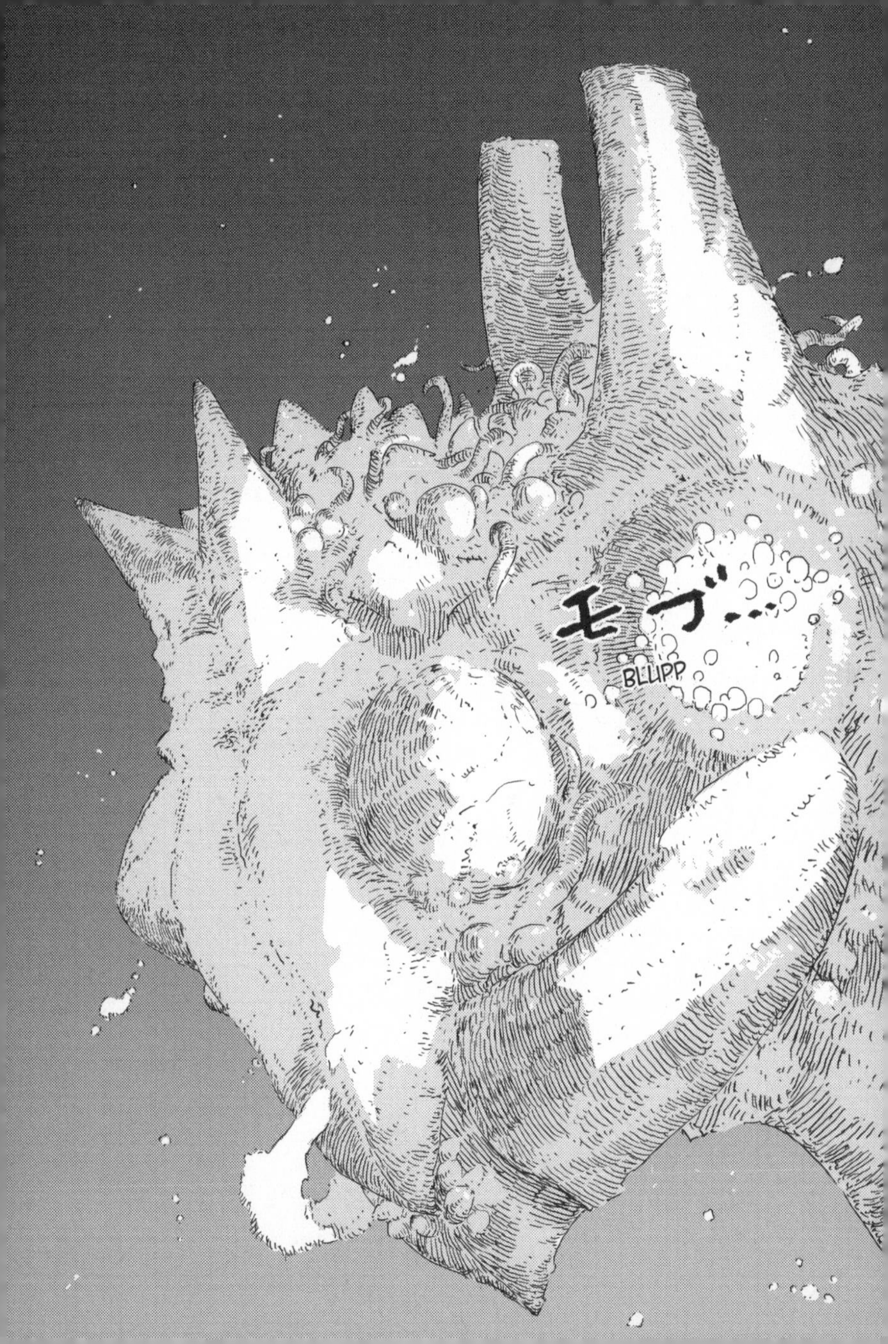
モヴ…
BLUPP

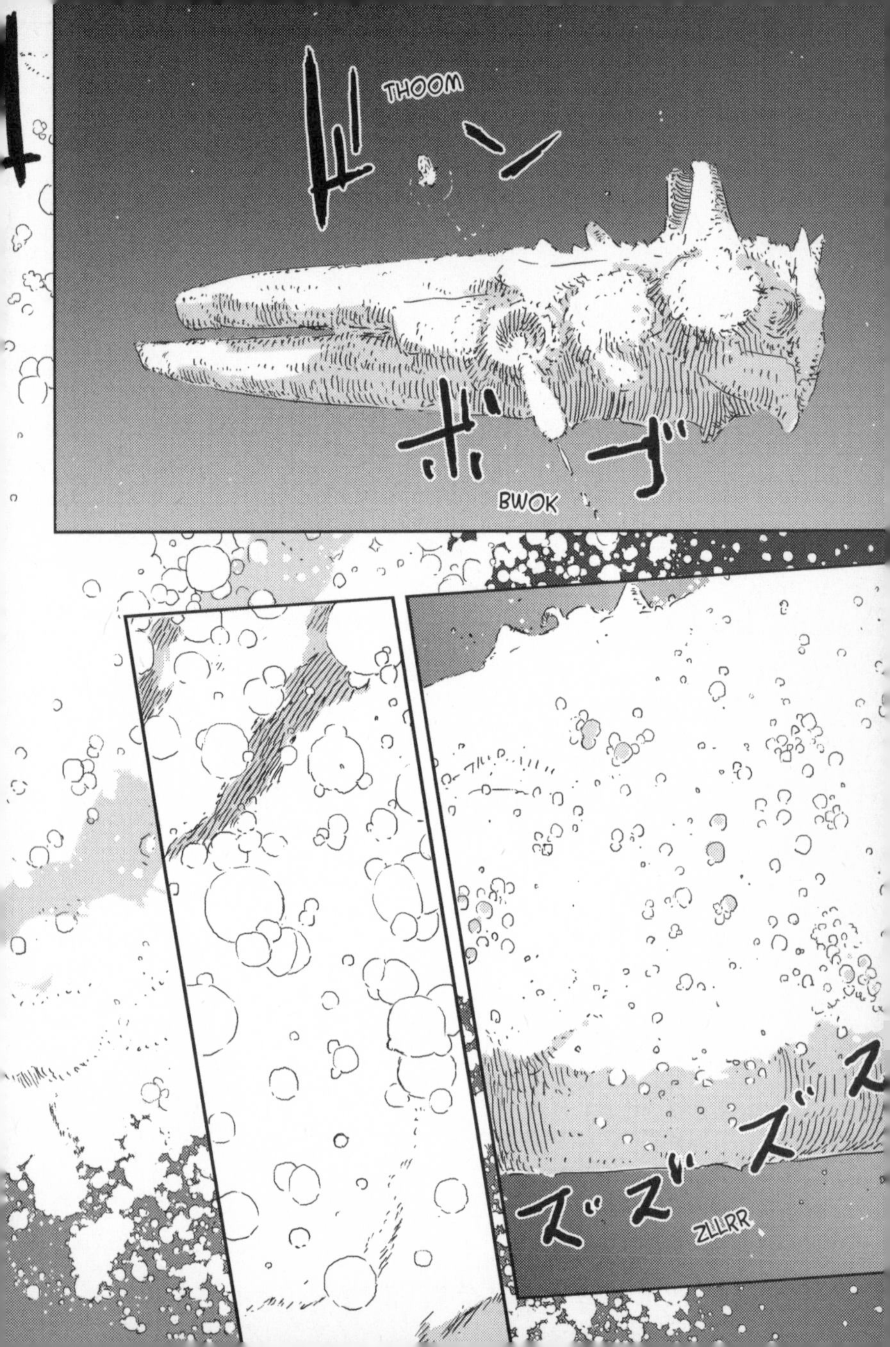
THOOM
BWOK
ZLLRR

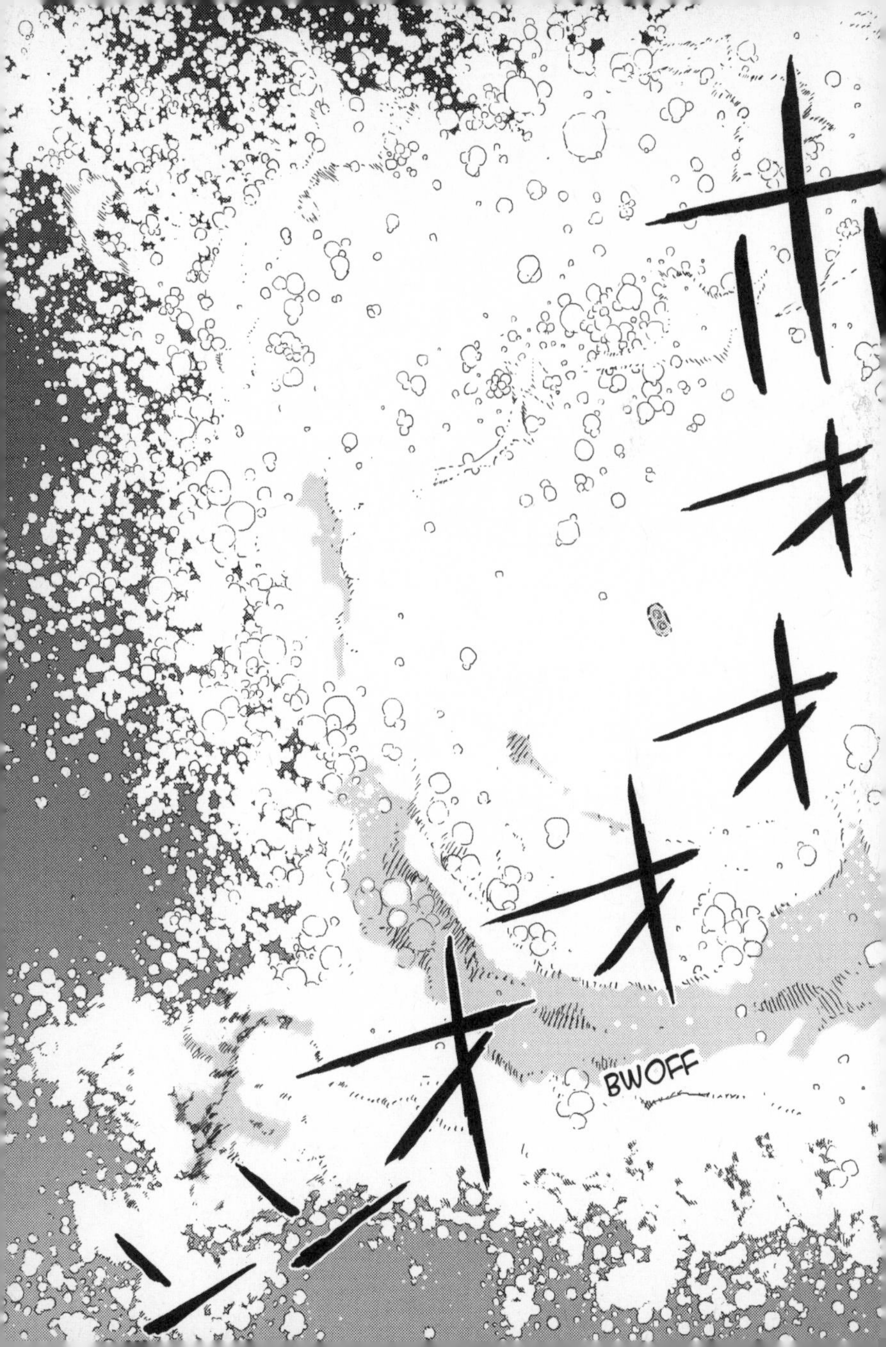
ホオオオオン
BWOFF

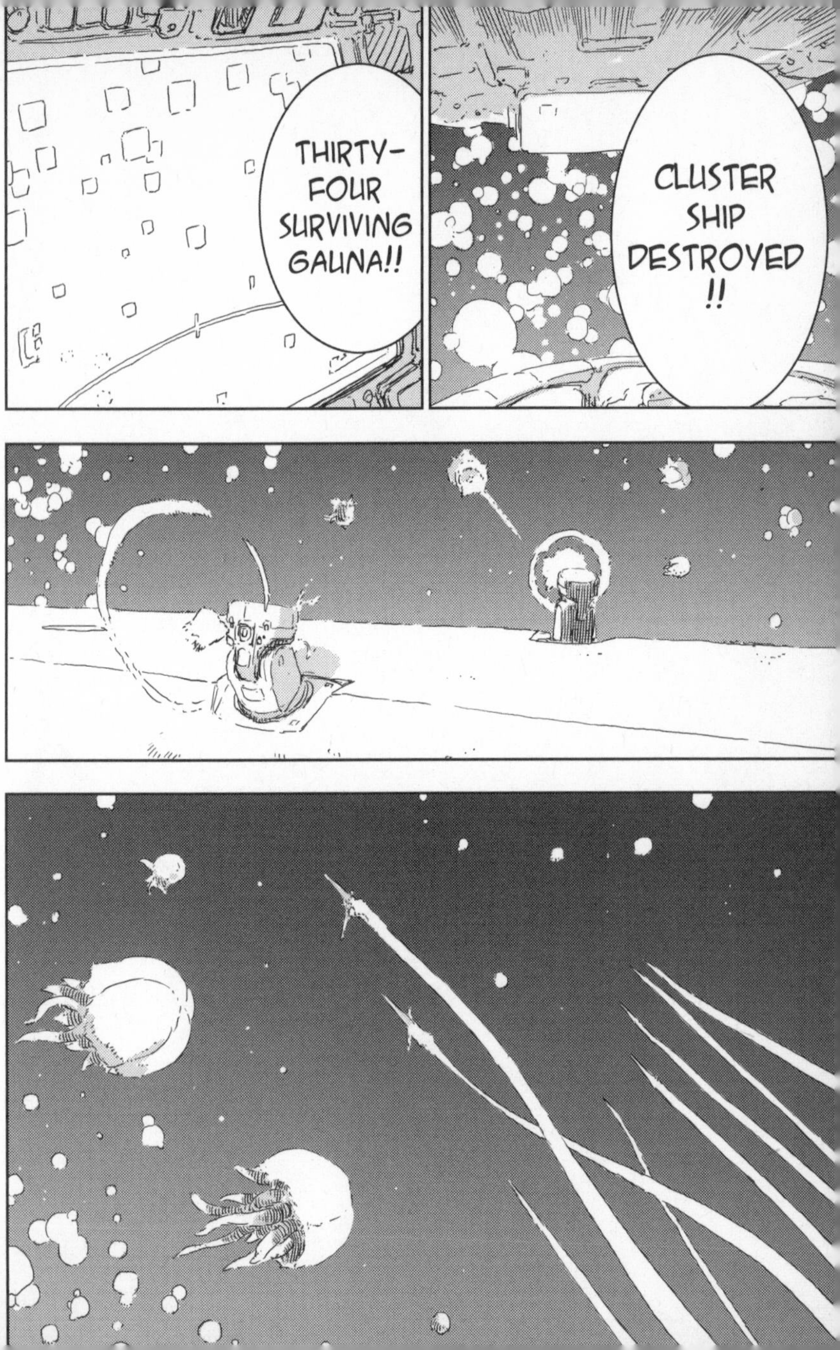
CLUSTER SHIP DESTROYED!!
THIRTY-FOUR SURVIVING GAUNA!!

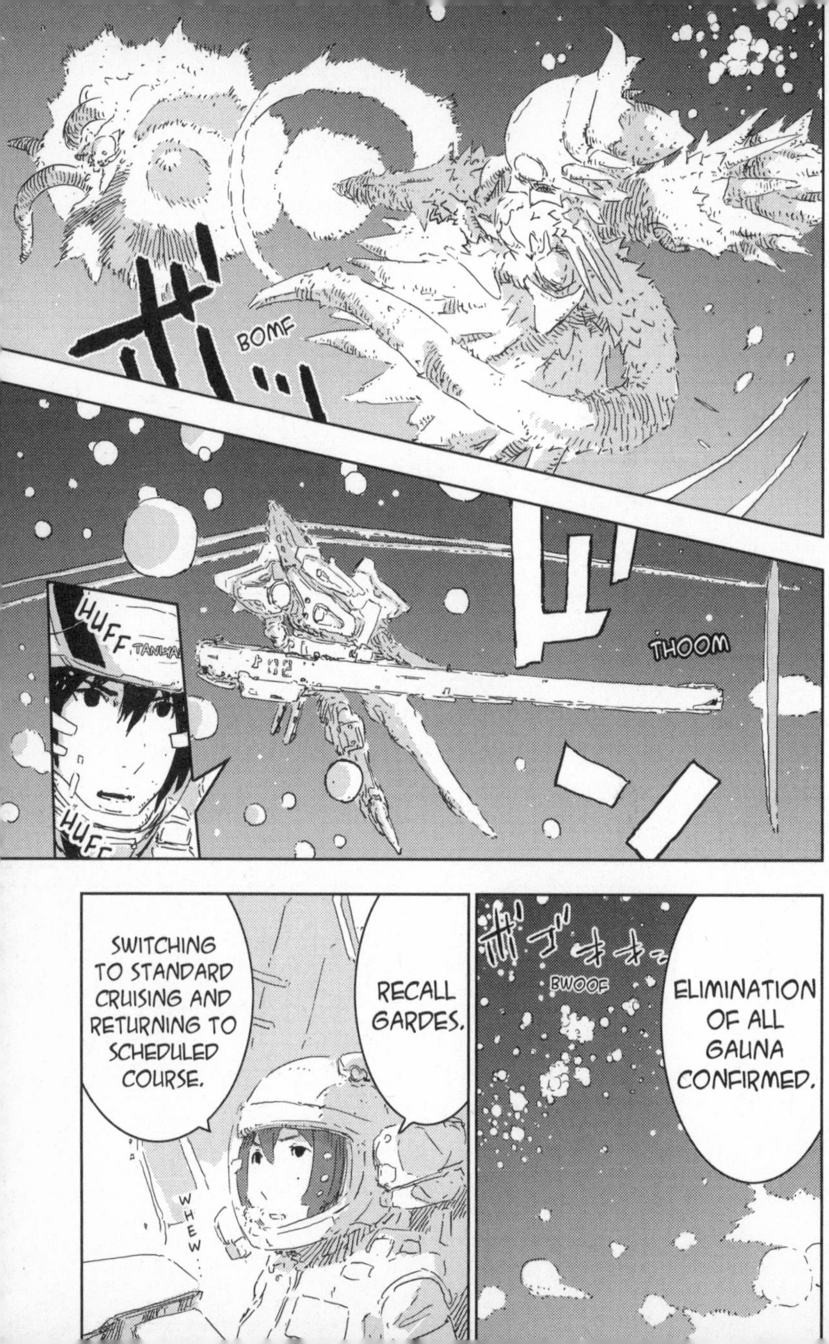
BOMF
THOOM
HUFF
HUFF
BWOOF
ELIMINATION OF ALL GAUNA CONFIRMED.
RECALL GARDES.
SWITCHING TO STANDARD CRUISING AND RETURNING TO SCHEDULED COURSE.
WHEW...

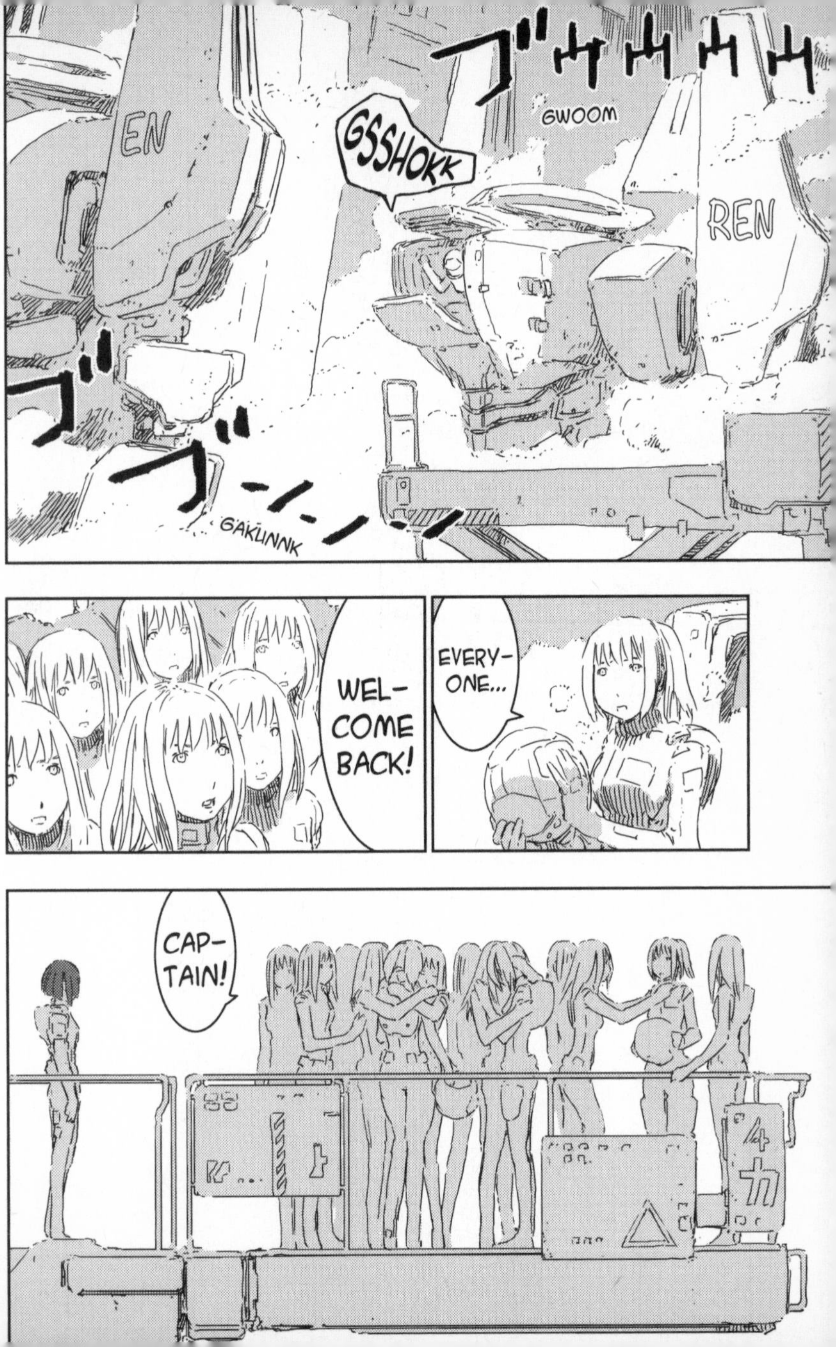
GWOOM
GSSHOKK
REN
EN
GAKUNNK
EVERY-ONE...
WEL-COME BACK!
CAP-TAIN!

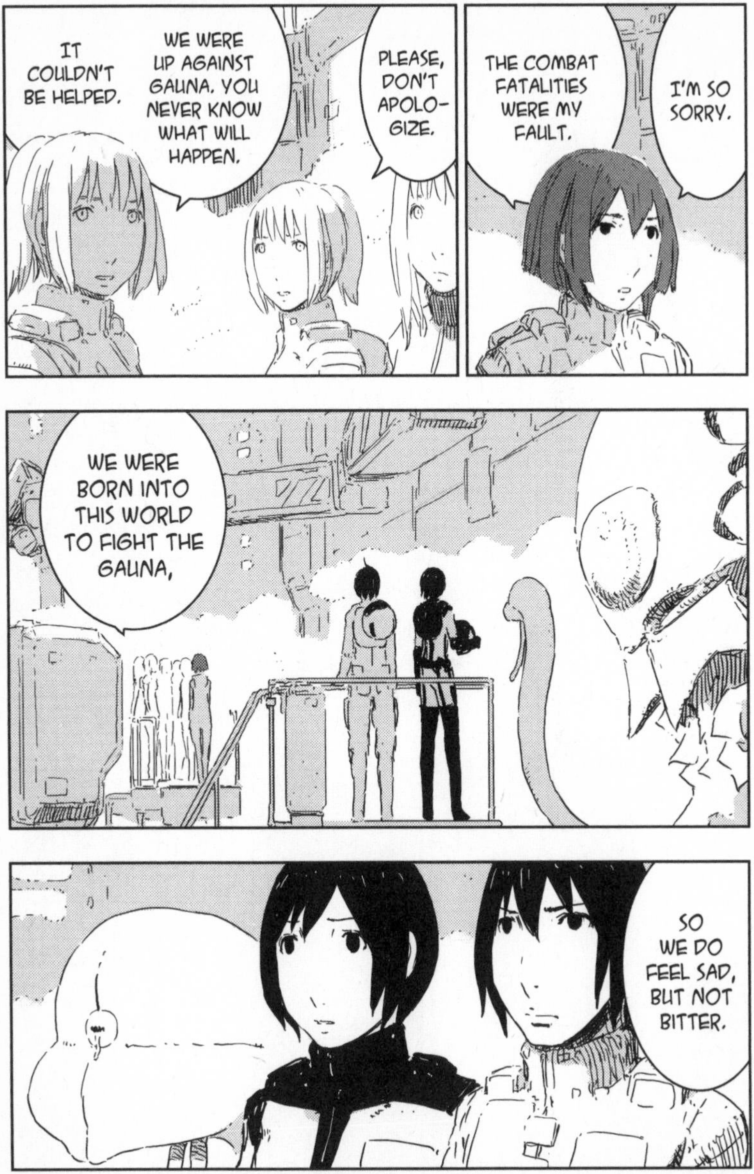
I'M SO SORRY.
THE COMBAT FATALITIES WERE MY FAULT.
PLEASE, DON'T APOLO-GIZE.
WE WERE UP AGAINST GAUNA. YOU NEVER KNOW WHAT WILL HAPPEN.
IT COULDN'T BE HELPED.
WE WERE BORN INTO THIS WORLD TO FIGHT THE GAUNA,
SO WE DO FEEL SAD, BUT NOT BITTER.

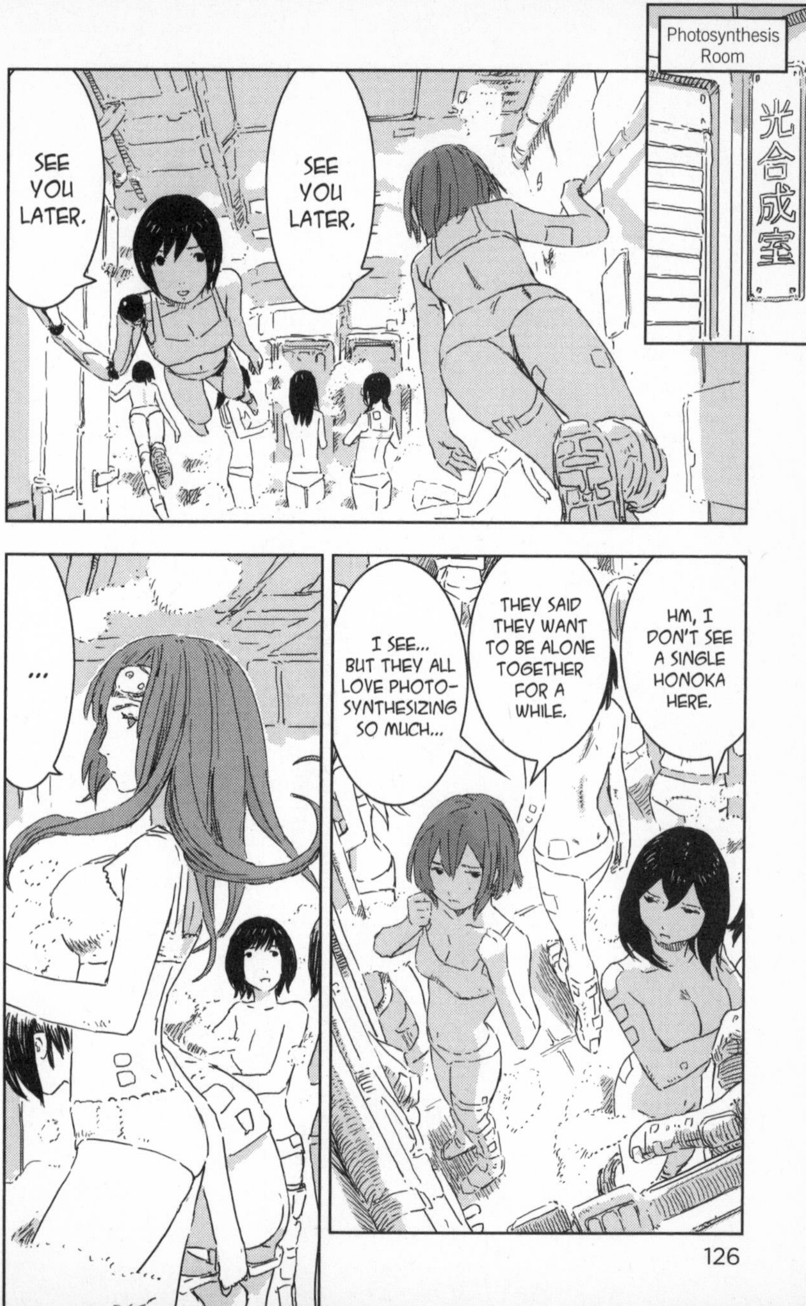
Photosynthesis Room
光合成室
SEE YOU LATER.
SEE YOU LATER.
HM, I DON'T SEE A SINGLE HONOKA HERE.
THEY SAID THEY WANT TO BE ALONE TOGETHER FOR A WHILE.
I SEE... BUT THEY ALL LOVE PHOTO-SYNTHESIZING SO MUCH...
...

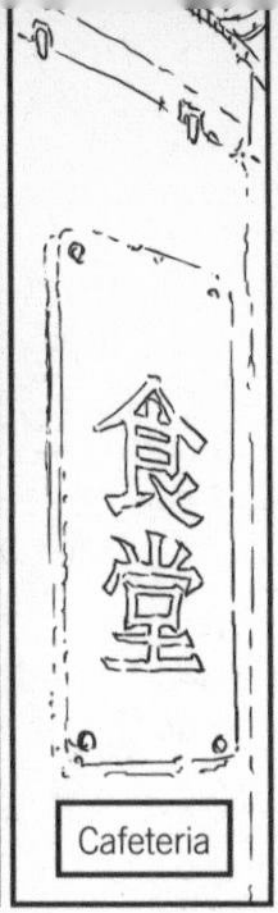
食堂
Cafeteria

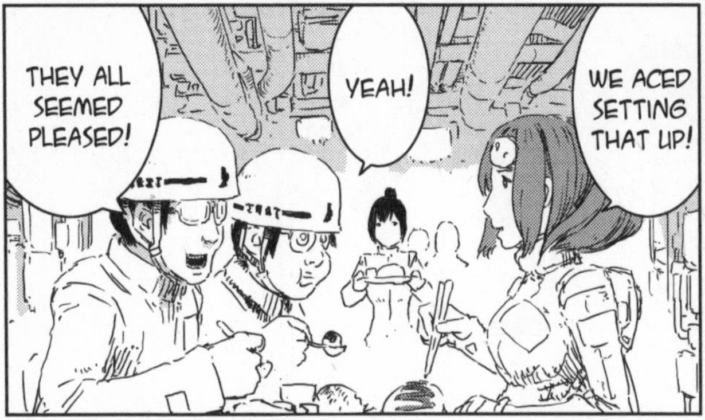
WE ACED SETTING THAT UP!
YEAH!
THEY ALL SEEMED PLEASED!

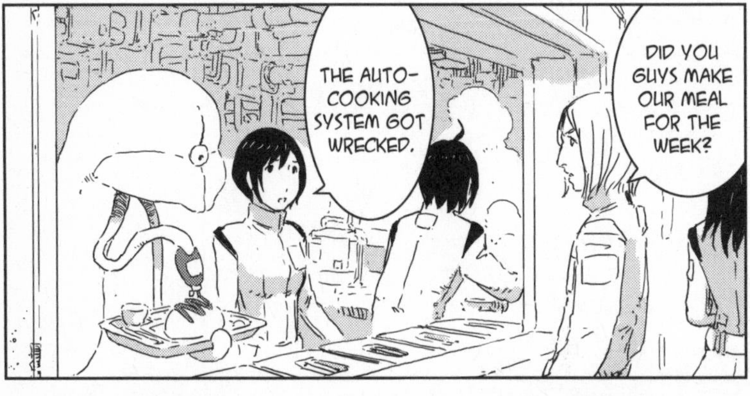
DID YOU GUYS MAKE OUR MEAL FOR THE WEEK?
THE AUTO-COOKING SYSTEM GOT WRECKED.

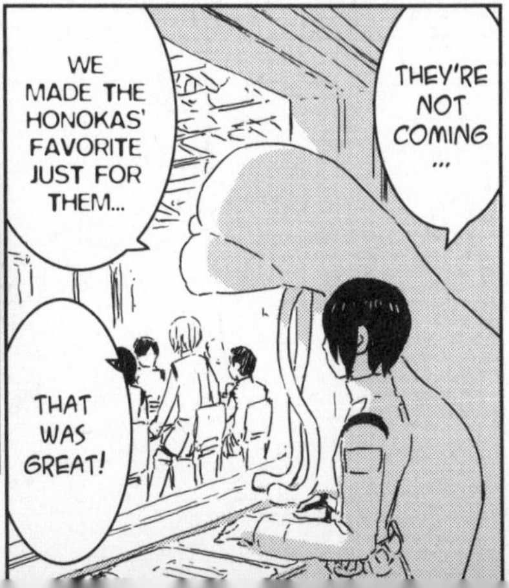
THEY'RE NOT COMING...
WE MADE THE HONOKAS' FAVORITE JUST FOR THEM...
THAT WAS GREAT!

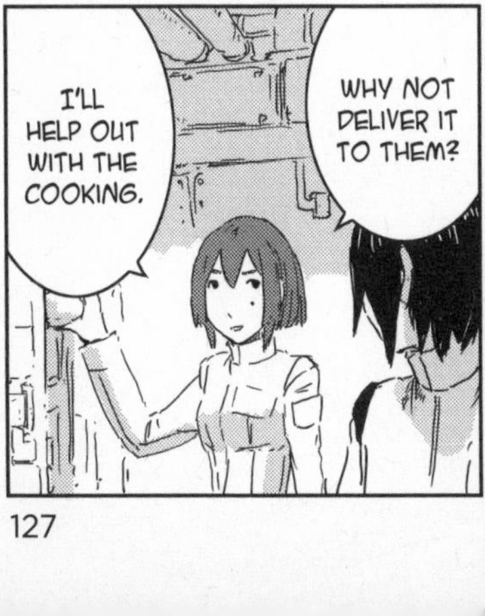
WHY NOT DELIVER IT TO THEM?
I'LL HELP OUT WITH THE COOKING.

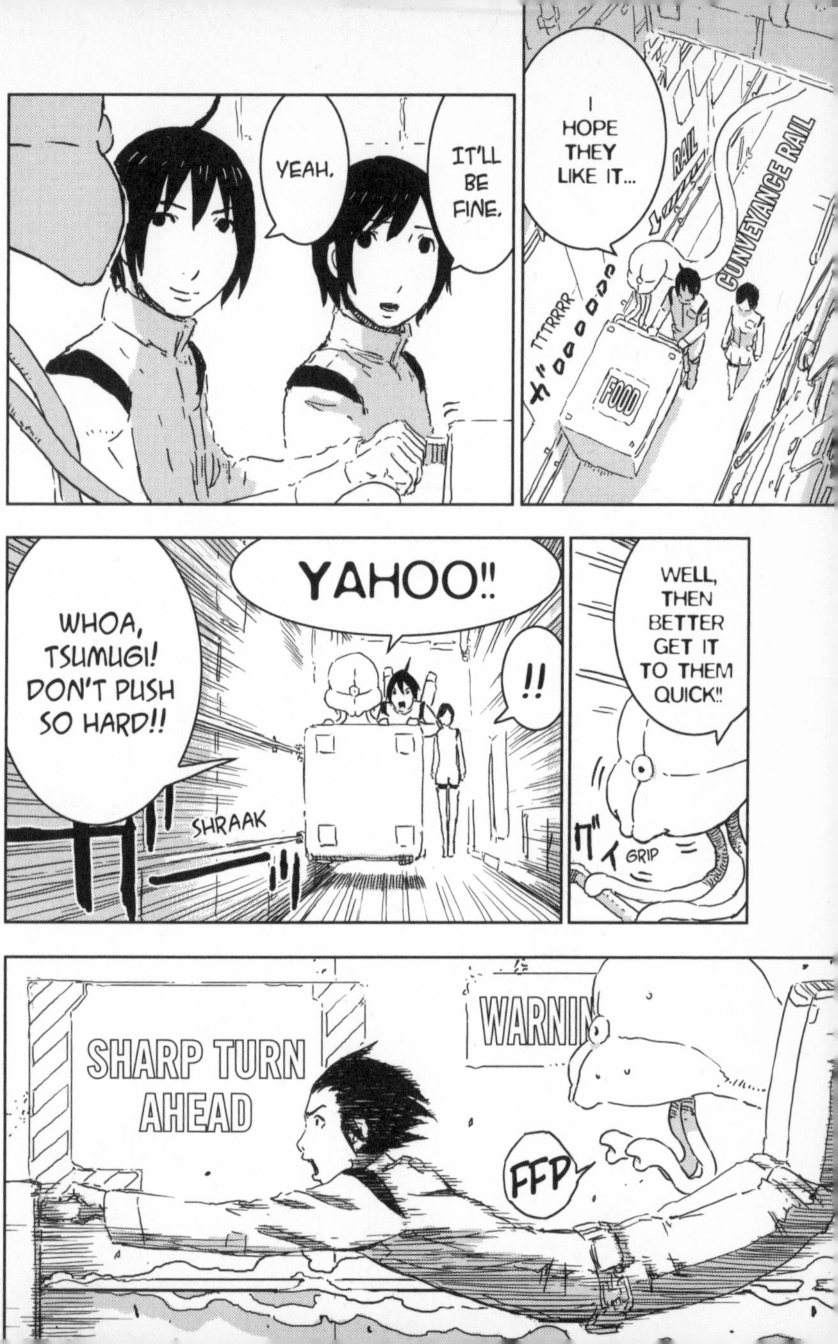
I HOPE THEY LIKE IT...
RAIL
CONVEYANCE RAIL
TTTRRRR
FOOD
IT'LL BE FINE.
YEAH,
WELL, THEN BETTER GET IT TO THEM QUICK!!
GRIP
!!
YAHOO!!
WHOA, TSUMUGI! DON'T PUSH SO HARD!!
SHRAAK
WARNIN
SHARP TURN AHEAD
FFP

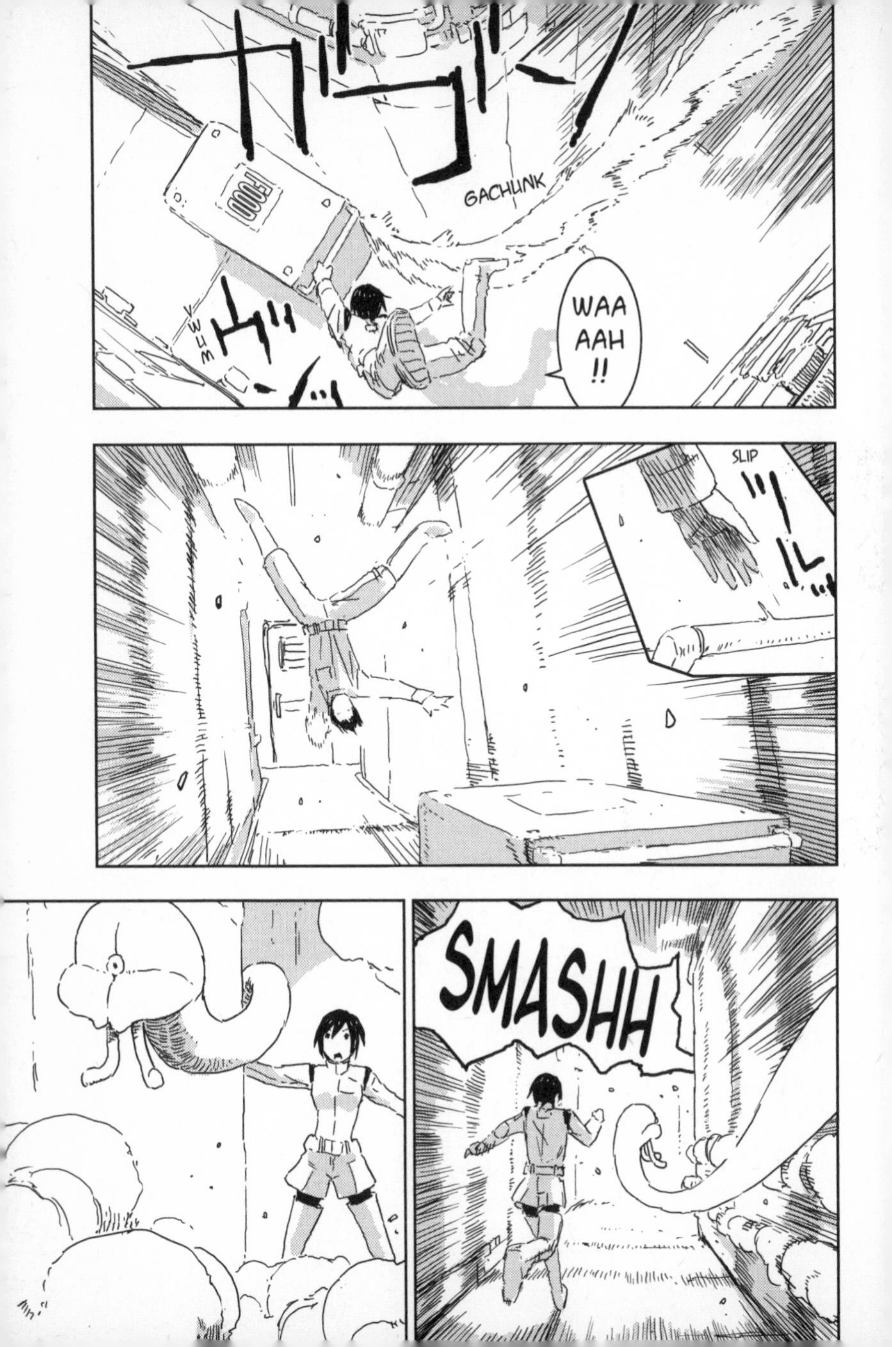
GACHUNK
WAA AAH !!
VWUM
SLIP
SMASHH

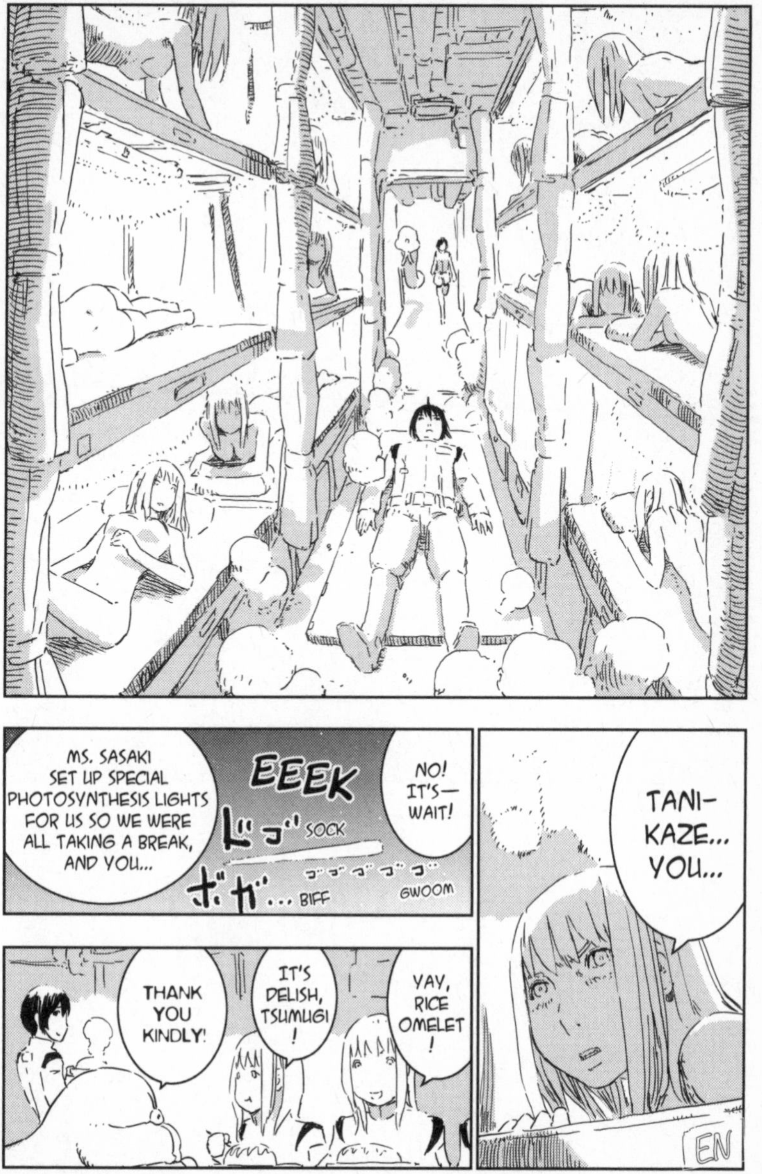
TANI-KAZE... YOU...
NO! IT'S— WAIT!
EEEK
ドゴ SOCK
ボガ... BIFF
ゴゴゴゴゴ GWOOM
MS. SASAKI SET UP SPECIAL PHOTOSYNTHESIS LIGHTS FOR US SO WE WERE ALL TAKING A BREAK, AND YOU...
YAY, RICE OMELET!
IT'S DELISH, TSUMUGI!
THANK YOU KINDLY!

Chapter 58: END

シドニアの騎士
KNIGHTS OF SIDONIA

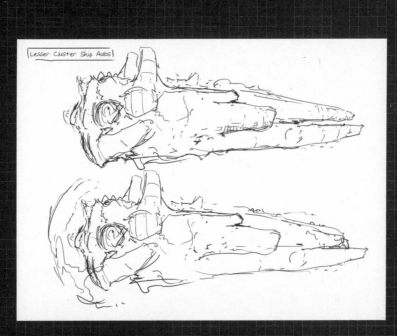

Lesser Cluster Ship Aulos

Chapter 59: The Sun Lem's Gravity

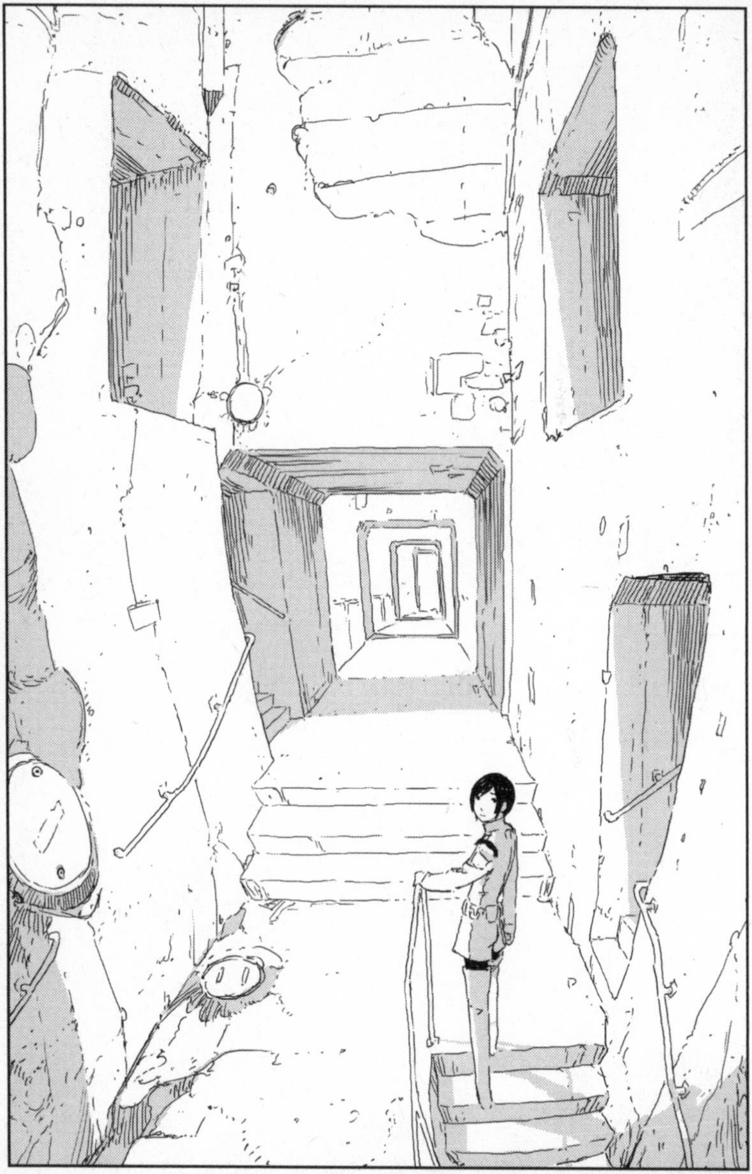

One Hundred Sights of Sidonia Part Forty-Five:
Circulation Corridor

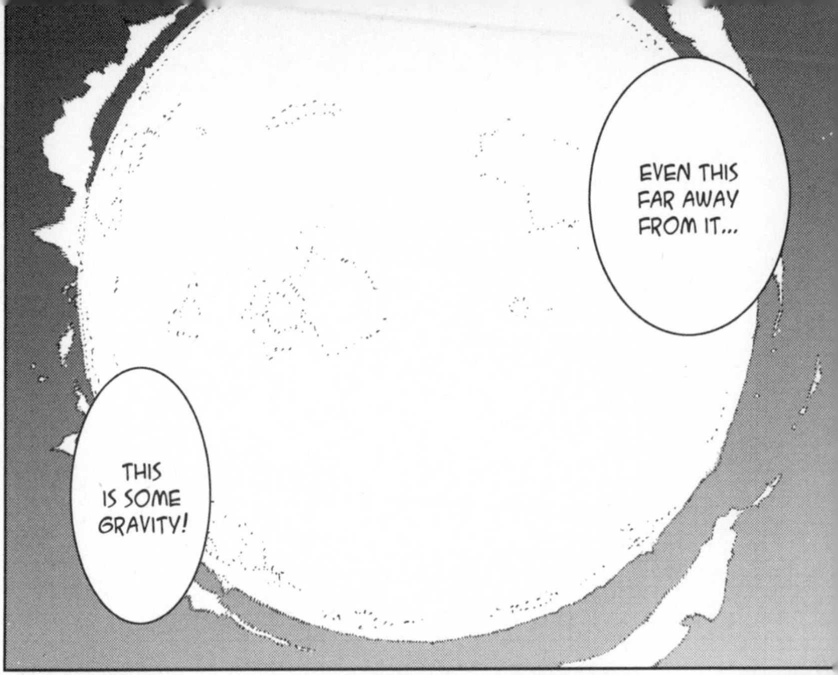
EVEN THIS FAR AWAY FROM IT...
THIS IS SOME GRAVITY!

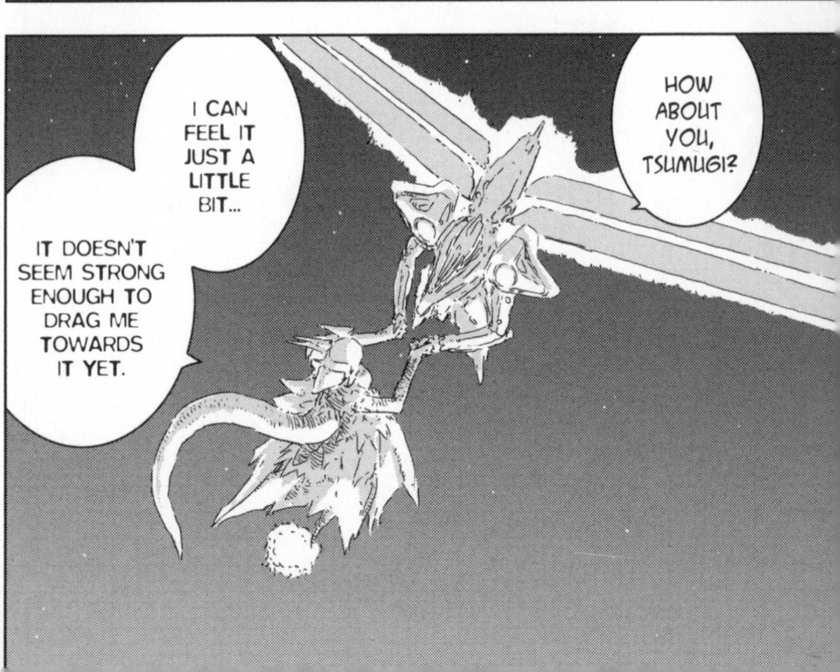
HOW ABOUT YOU, TSUMUGI?
I CAN FEEL IT JUST A LITTLE BIT...
IT DOESN'T SEEM STRONG ENOUGH TO DRAG ME TOWARDS IT YET.

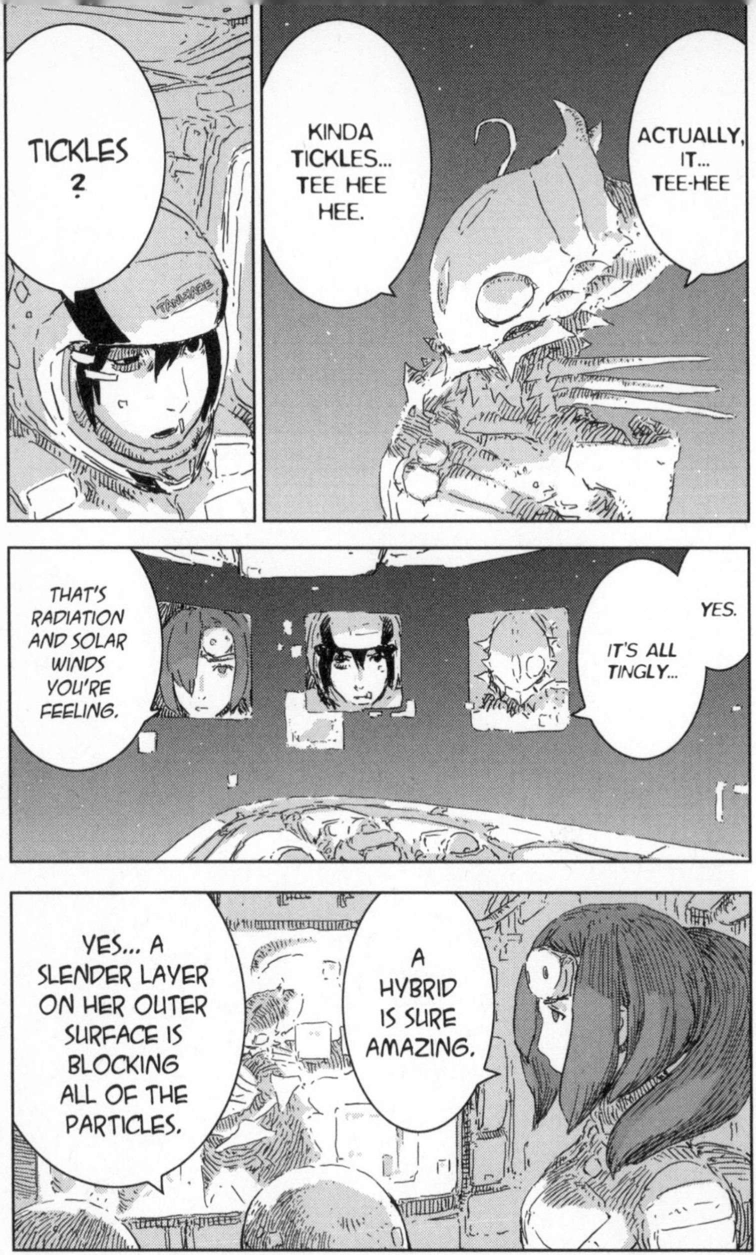
ACTUALLY, IT... TEE-HEE
KINDA TICKLES... TEE HEE HEE.
TICKLES?
YES.
IT'S ALL TINGLY...
THAT'S RADIATION AND SOLAR WINDS YOU'RE FEELING.
A HYBRID IS SURE AMAZING.
YES... A SLENDER LAYER ON HER OUTER SURFACE IS BLOCKING ALL OF THE PARTICLES.

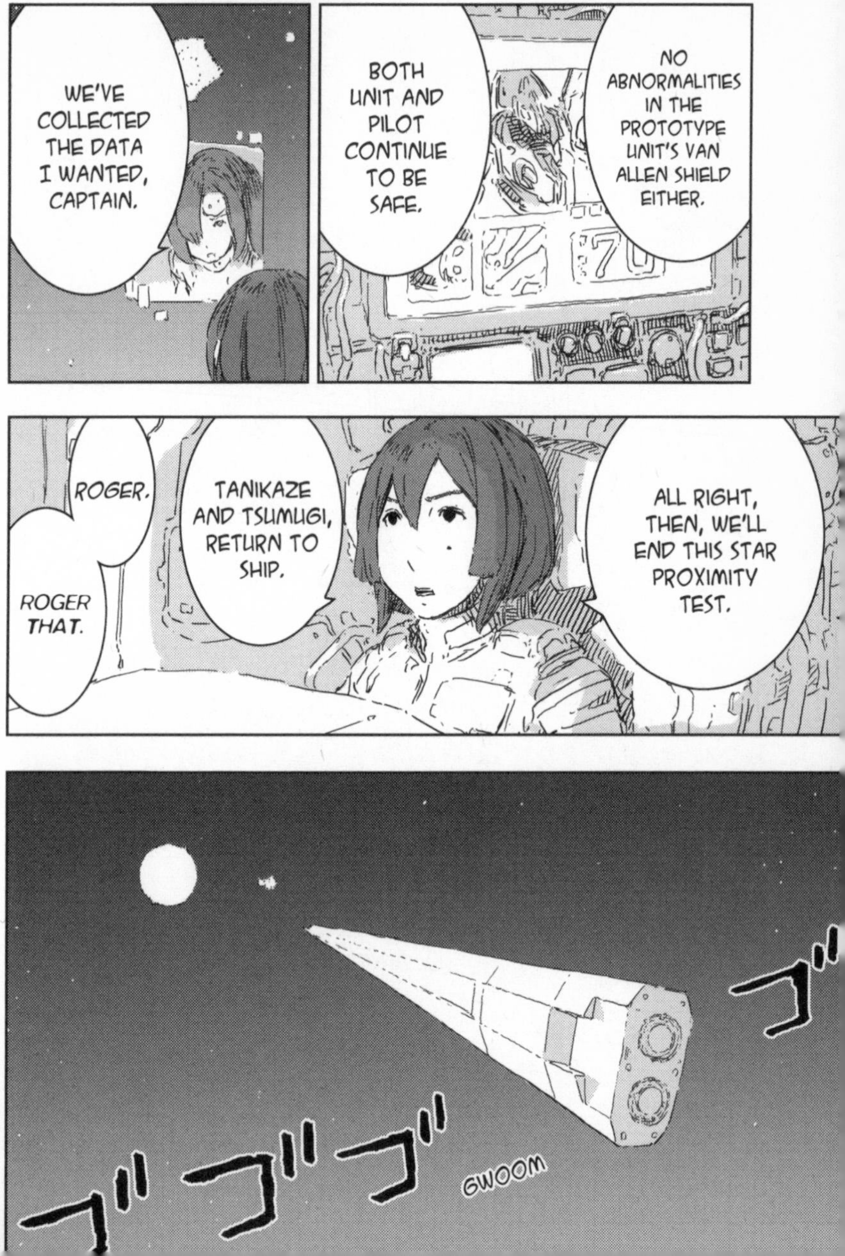
NO ABNORMALITIES IN THE PROTOTYPE UNIT'S VAN ALLEN SHIELD EITHER.
BOTH UNIT AND PILOT CONTINUE TO BE SAFE.
WE'VE COLLECTED THE DATA I WANTED, CAPTAIN.
ALL RIGHT, THEN, WE'LL END THIS STAR PROXIMITY TEST.
TANIKAZE AND TSUMUGI, RETURN TO SHIP.
ROGER.
ROGER THAT.
ゴゴゴゴ
GWOOM

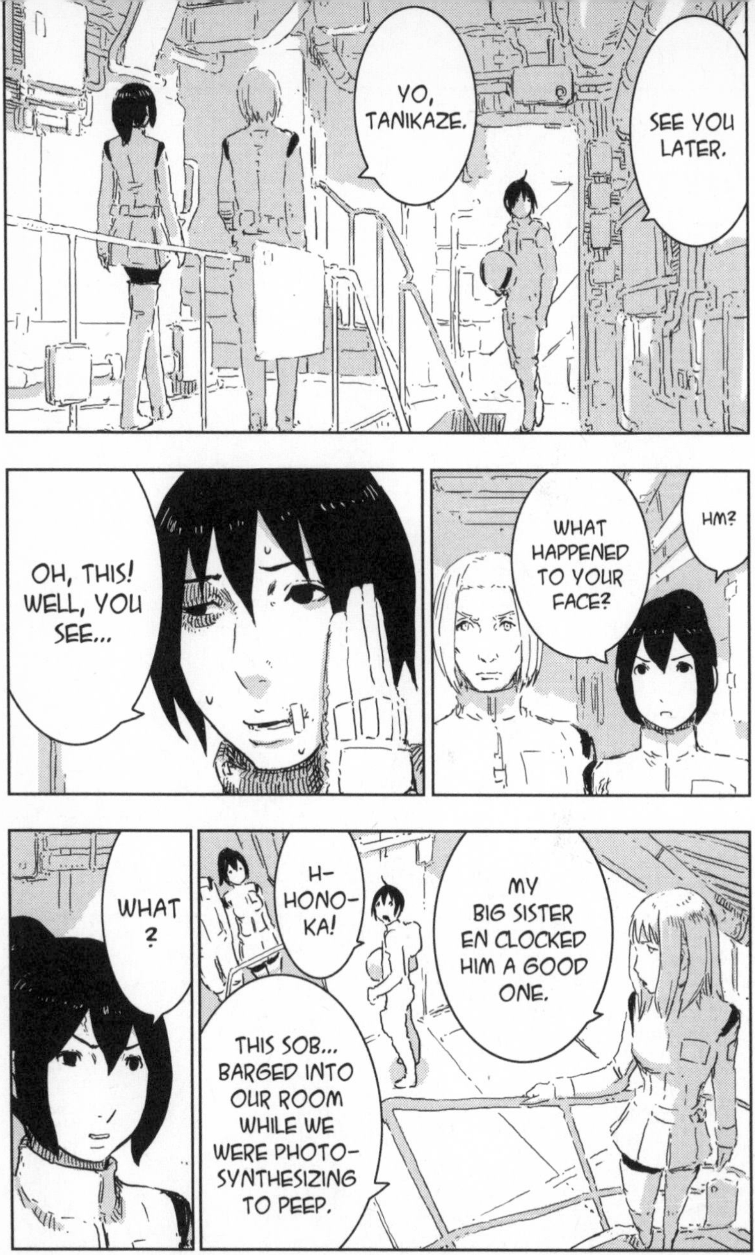
SEE YOU LATER.
YO, TANIKAZE.
HM?
WHAT HAPPENED TO YOUR FACE?
OH, THIS! WELL, YOU SEE...
MY BIG SISTER EN CLOCKED HIM A GOOD ONE.
H-HONOKA!
THIS SOB... BARGED INTO OUR ROOM WHILE WE WERE PHOTO-SYNTHESIZING TO PEEP.
WHAT?

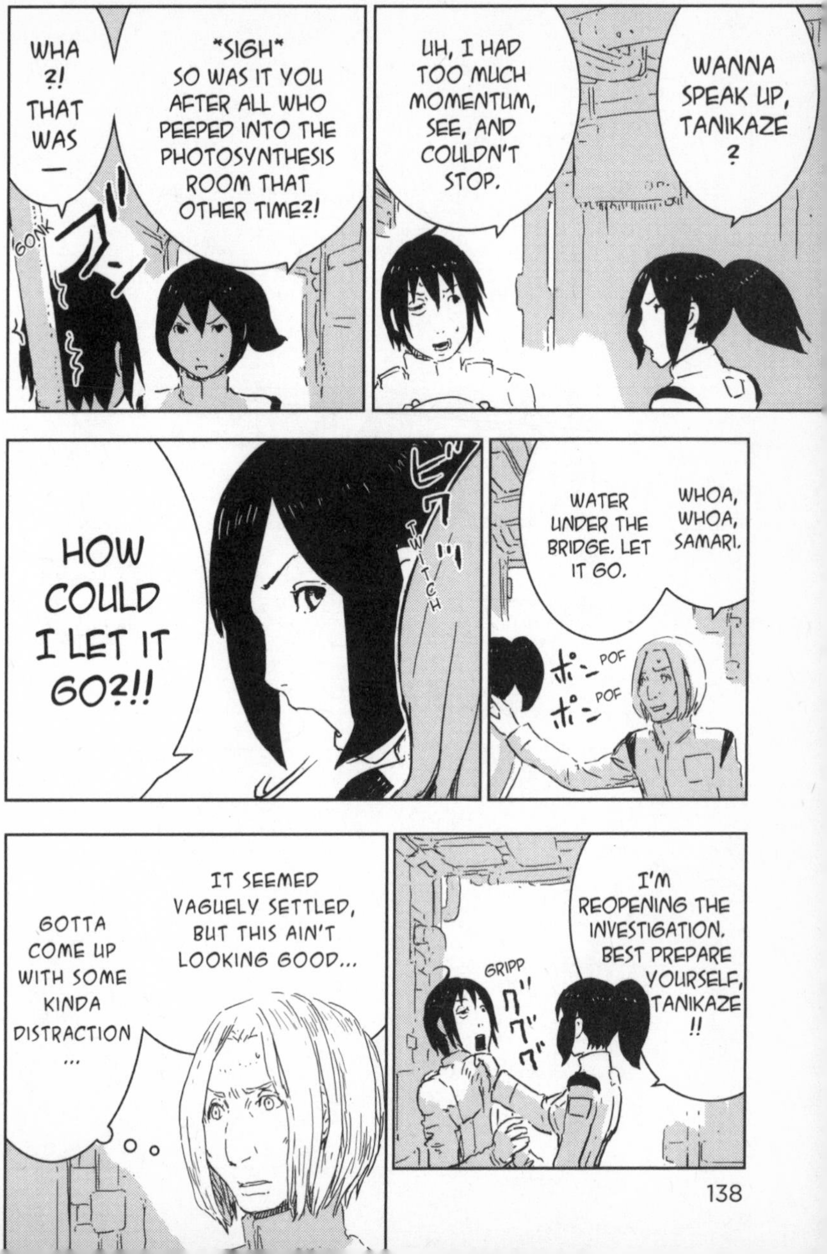
WANNA SPEAK UP, TANIKAZE?
UH, I HAD TOO MUCH MOMENTUM, SEE, AND COULDN'T STOP.
SIGH SO WAS IT YOU AFTER ALL WHO PEEPED INTO THE PHOTOSYNTHESIS ROOM THAT OTHER TIME?!
WHA?! THAT WAS—
GONK
WHOA, WHOA, SAMARI.
WATER UNDER THE BRIDGE. LET IT GO.
POF
POF
TWITCH
HOW COULD I LET IT GO?!!
I'M REOPENING THE INVESTIGATION. BEST PREPARE YOURSELF, TANIKAZE!!
GRIPP
IT SEEMED VAGUELY SETTLED, BUT THIS AIN'T LOOKING GOOD...
GOTTA COME UP WITH SOME KINDA DISTRACTION...

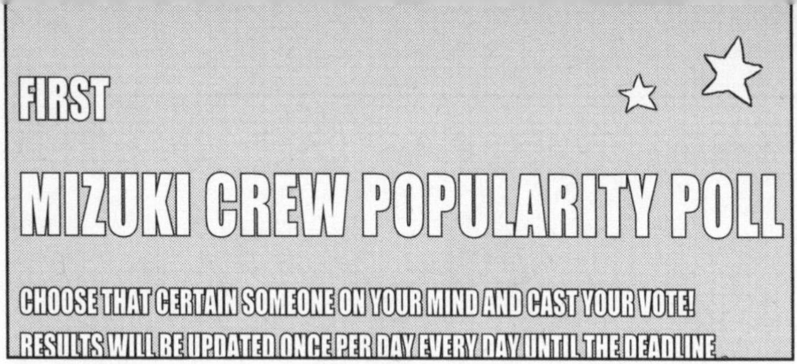
FIRST
MIZUKI CREW POPULARITY POLL
CHOOSE THAT CERTAIN SOMEONE ON YOUR MIND AND CAST YOUR VOTE!
RESULTS WILL BE UPDATED ONCE PER DAY EVERY DAY UNTIL THE DEADLINE

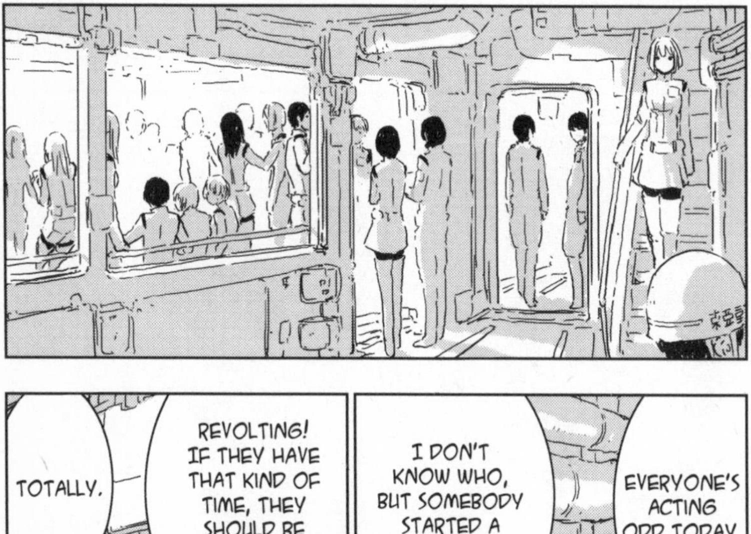

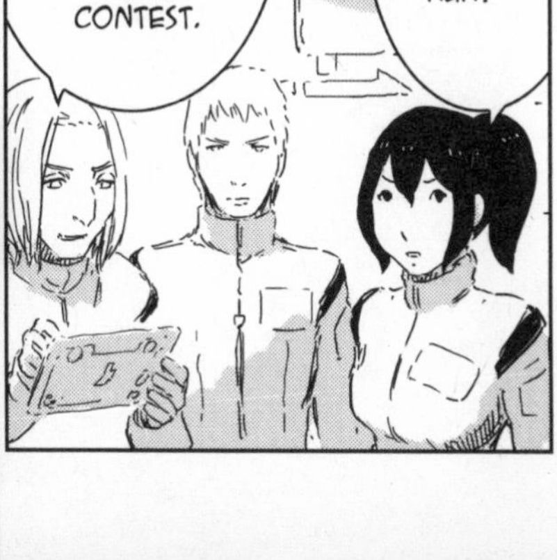
EVERYONE'S ACTING ODD TODAY, HUH?
I DON'T KNOW WHO, BUT SOMEBODY STARTED A POPULARITY CONTEST.

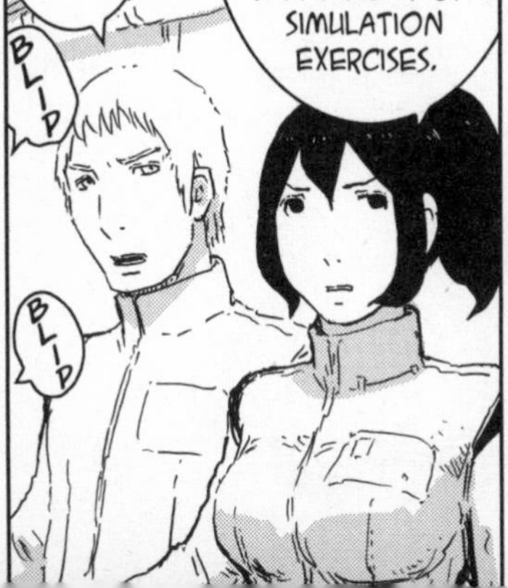
REVOLTING! IF THEY HAVE THAT KIND OF TIME, THEY SHOULD BE SPENDING IT ON SIMULATION EXERCISES.
TOTALLY.
BLIP
BLIP

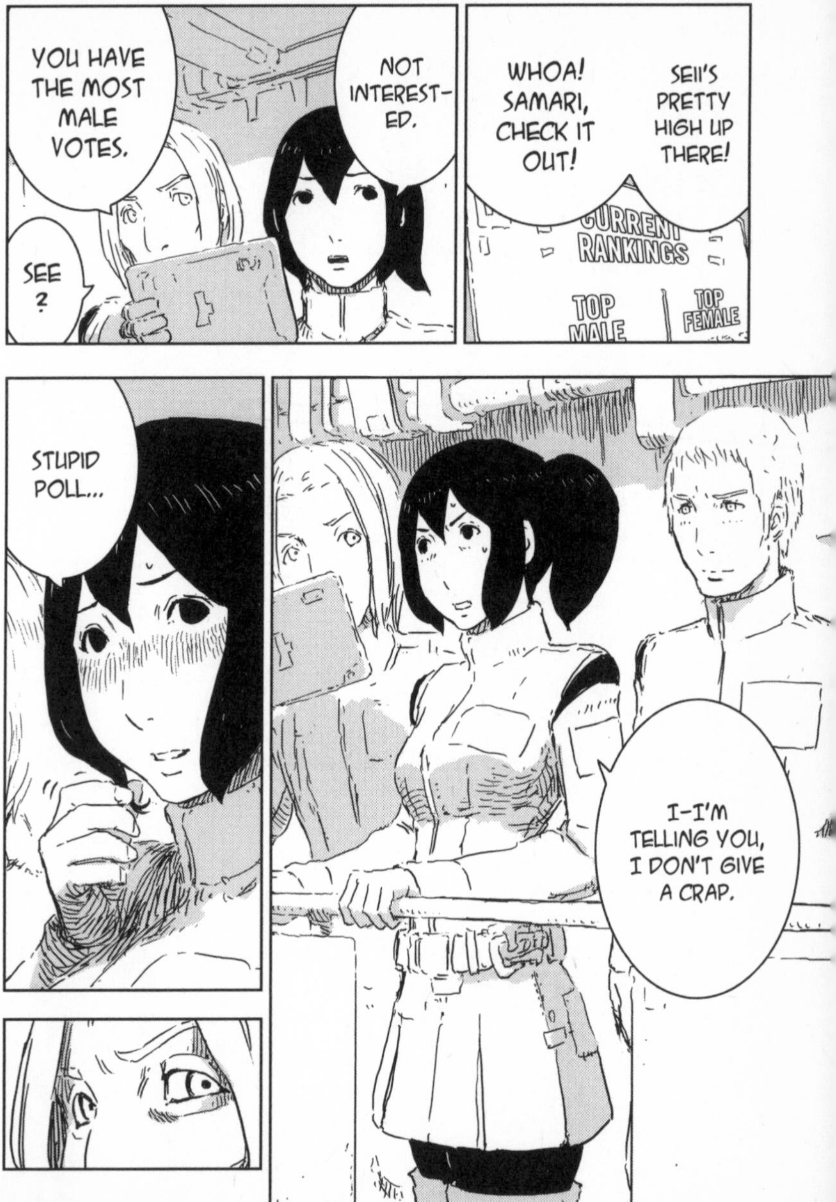
SEII'S PRETTY HIGH UP THERE!
WHOA! SAMARI, CHECK IT OUT!
CURRENT RANKINGS
TOP FEMALE
TOP MALE
NOT INTEREST-ED.
YOU HAVE THE MOST MALE VOTES.
SEE?
I-I'M TELLING YOU, I DON'T GIVE A CRAP.
STUPID POLL...

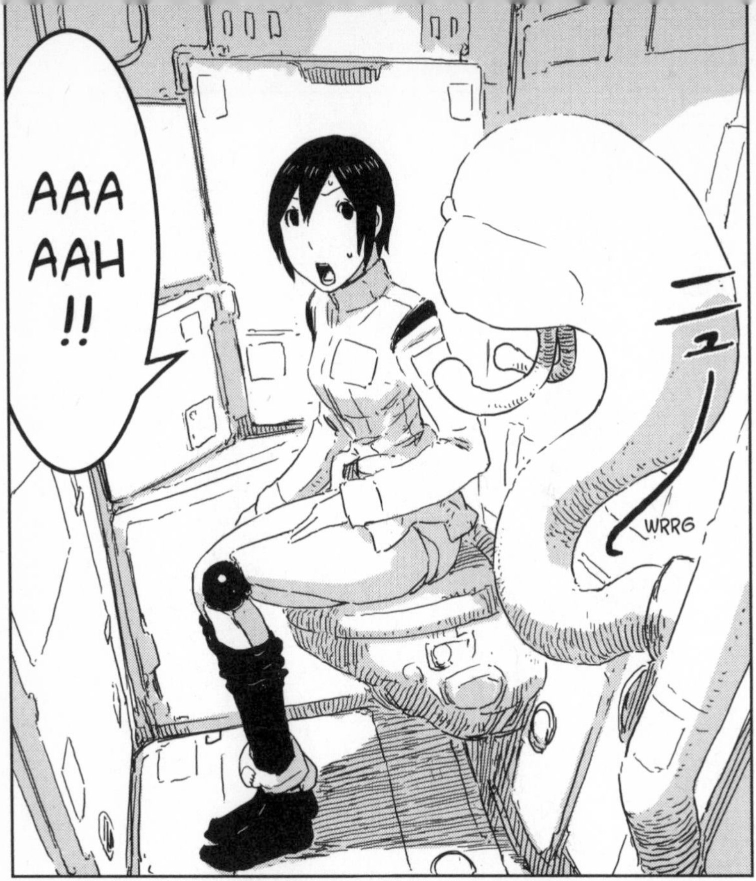
AAA AAH !!
ニュ
WRRG

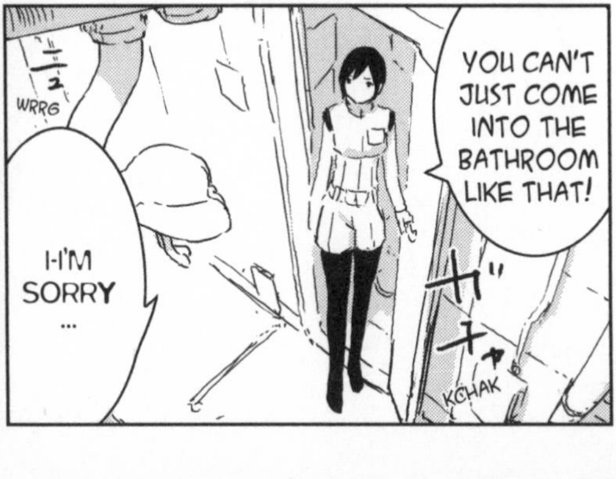
YOU CAN'T JUST COME INTO THE BATHROOM LIKE THAT!
ニュ
WRRG
I-I'M SORRY ...
ガチャ
KCHAK

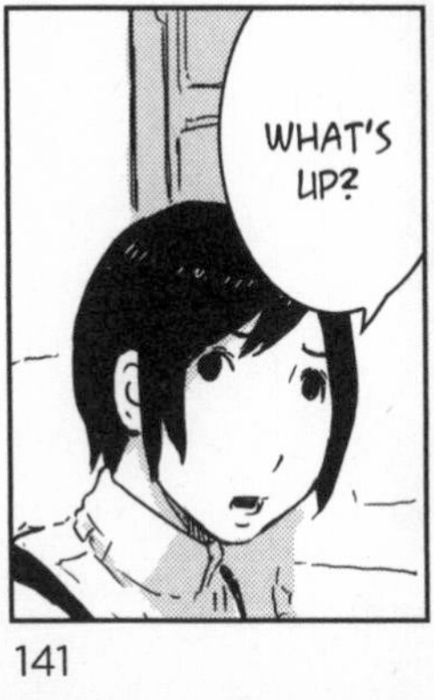
WHAT'S UP?

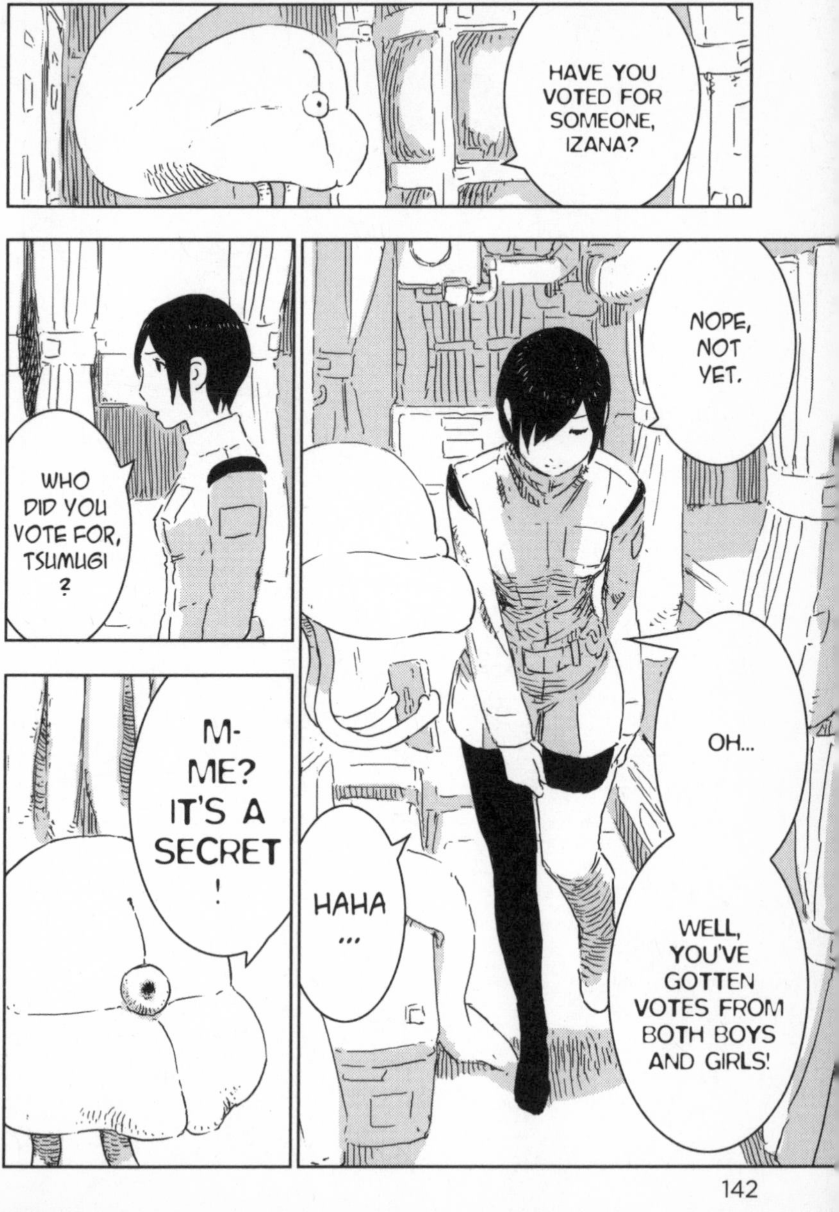
HAVE YOU VOTED FOR SOMEONE, IZANA?
NOPE, NOT YET.
OH...
WELL, YOU'VE GOTTEN VOTES FROM BOTH BOYS AND GIRLS!
HAHA...
WHO DID YOU VOTE FOR, TSUMUGI?
M-ME? IT'S A SECRET!

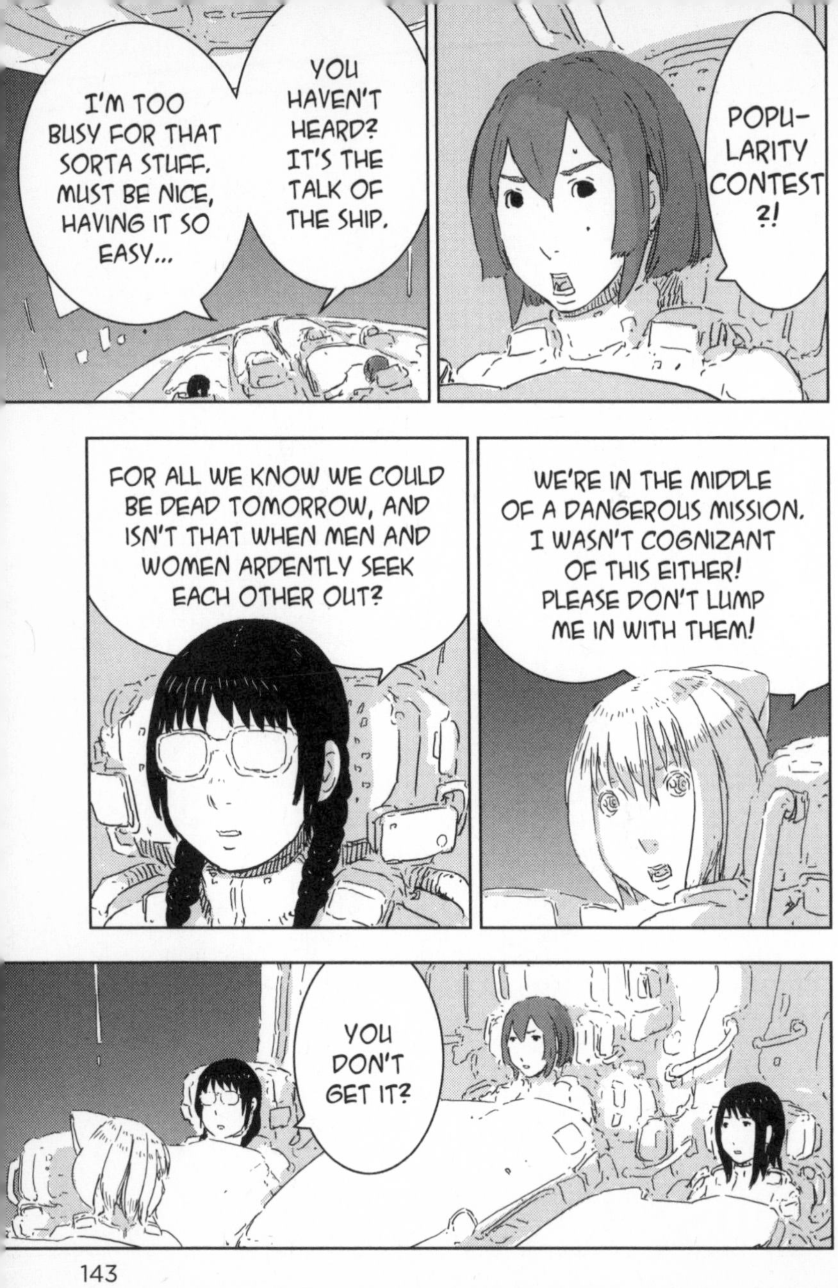
POPU-LARITY CONTEST?!
YOU HAVEN'T HEARD? IT'S THE TALK OF THE SHIP.
I'M TOO BUSY FOR THAT SORTA STUFF. MUST BE NICE, HAVING IT SO EASY...
WE'RE IN THE MIDDLE OF A DANGEROUS MISSION. I WASN'T COGNIZANT OF THIS EITHER! PLEASE DON'T LUMP ME IN WITH THEM!
FOR ALL WE KNOW WE COULD BE DEAD TOMORROW, AND ISN'T THAT WHEN MEN AND WOMEN ARDENTLY SEEK EACH OTHER OUT?
YOU DON'T GET IT?

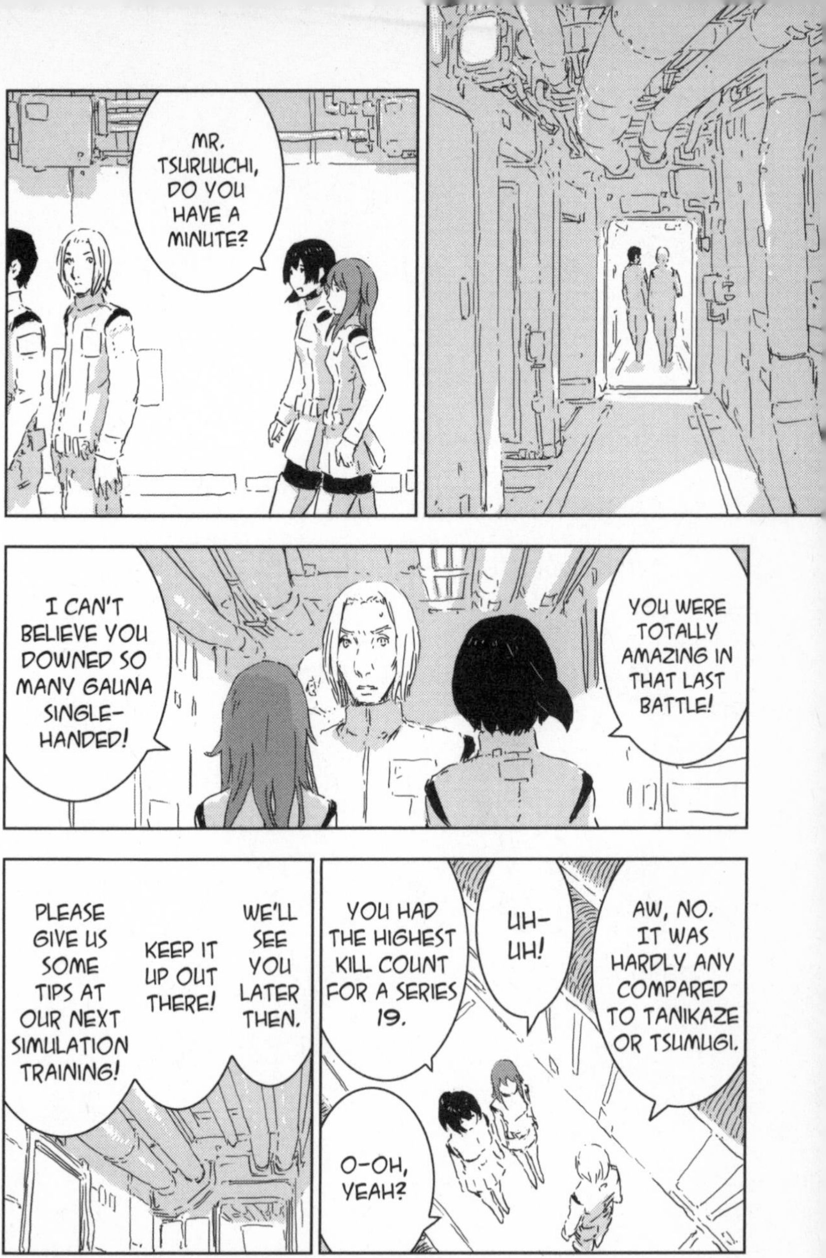
MR. TSURUUCHI, DO YOU HAVE A MINUTE?
YOU WERE TOTALLY AMAZING IN THAT LAST BATTLE!
I CAN'T BELIEVE YOU DOWNED SO MANY GAUNA SINGLE-HANDED!
AW, NO. IT WAS HARDLY ANY COMPARED TO TANIKAZE OR TSUMUGI.
UH-UH!
YOU HAD THE HIGHEST KILL COUNT FOR A SERIES 19.
O-OH, YEAH?
WE'LL SEE YOU LATER THEN.
KEEP IT UP OUT THERE!
PLEASE GIVE US SOME TIPS AT OUR NEXT SIMULATION TRAINING!

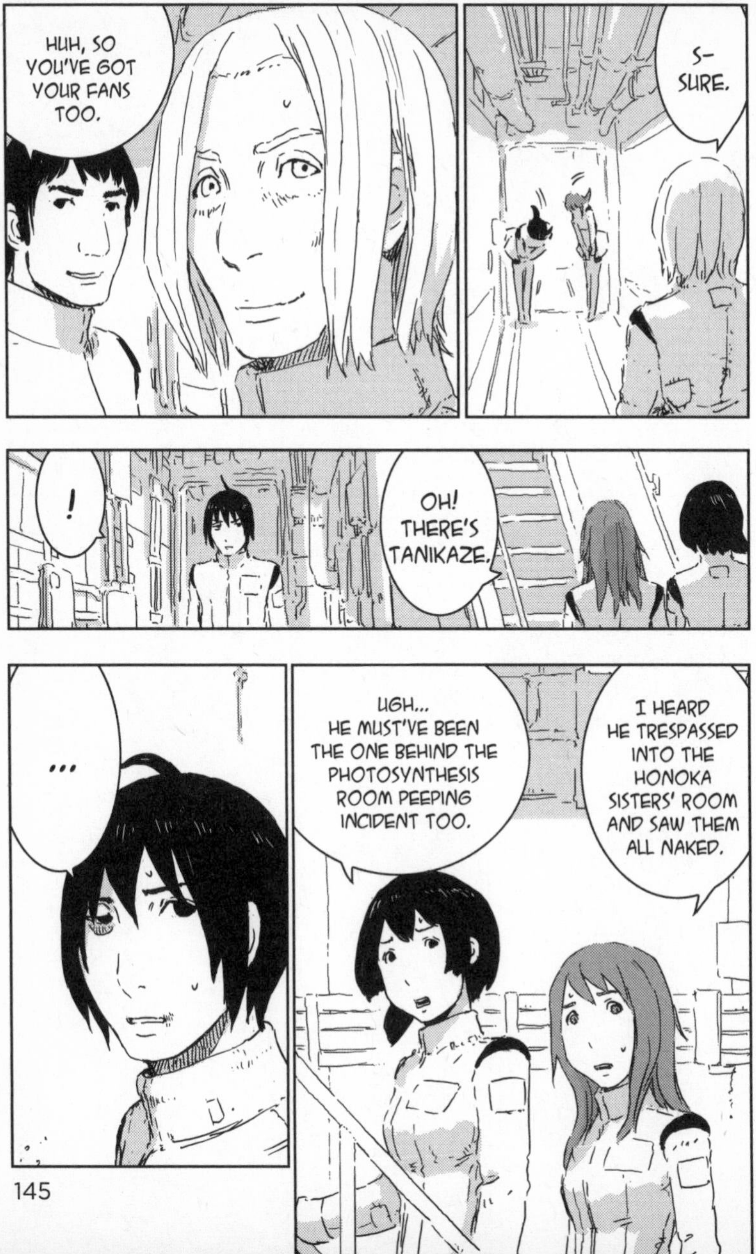
S- SURE.
HUH, SO YOU'VE GOT YOUR FANS TOO.
OH! THERE'S TANIKAZE.
!
I HEARD HE TRESPASSED INTO THE HONOKA SISTERS' ROOM AND SAW THEM ALL NAKED.
UGH... HE MUST'VE BEEN THE ONE BEHIND THE PHOTOSYNTHESIS ROOM PEEPING INCIDENT TOO.
...

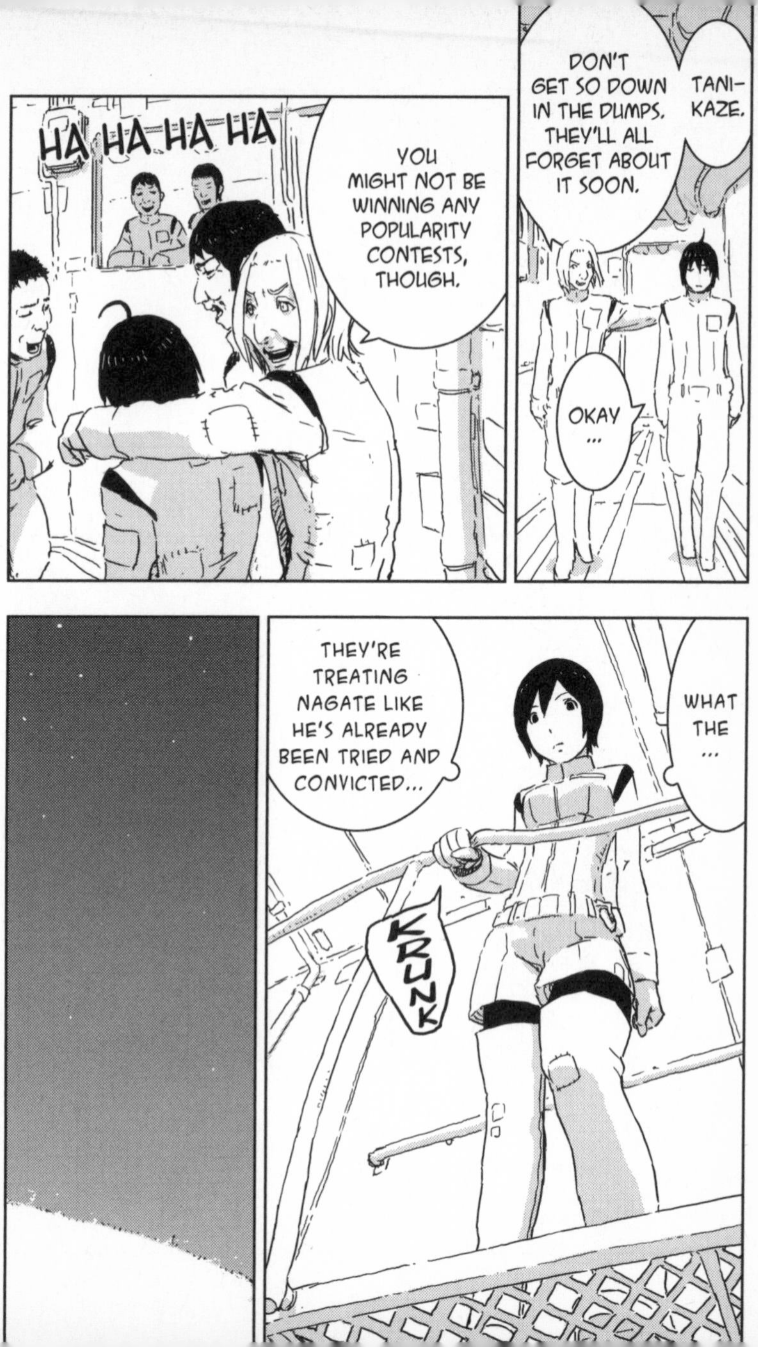
TANI-
KAZE.
DON'T GET SO DOWN IN THE DUMPS. THEY'LL ALL FORGET ABOUT IT SOON.
OKAY ...
YOU MIGHT NOT BE WINNING ANY POPULARITY CONTESTS, THOUGH.
HA HA HA HA
WHAT THE ...
THEY'RE TREATING NAGATE LIKE HE'S ALREADY BEEN TRIED AND CONVICTED...
KRUNK

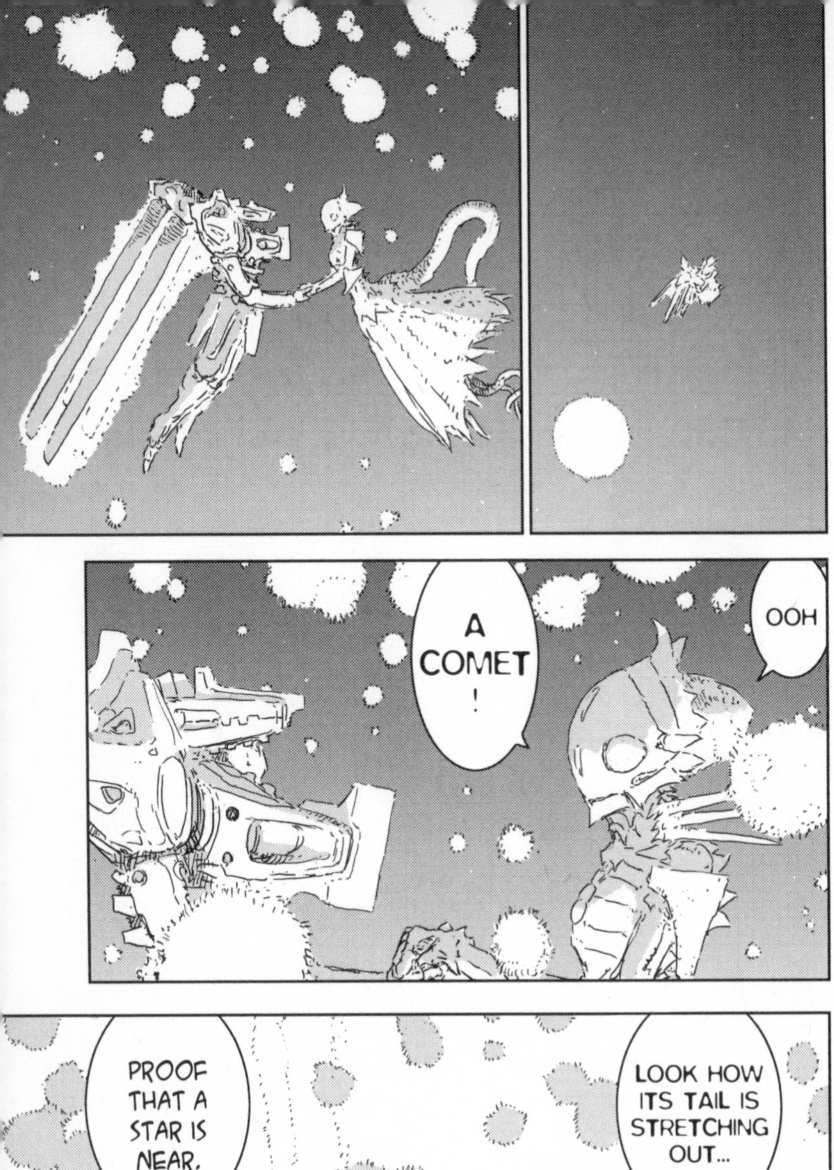
OOH
A COMET !
LOOK HOW ITS TAIL IS STRETCHING OUT...
PROOF THAT A STAR IS NEAR.

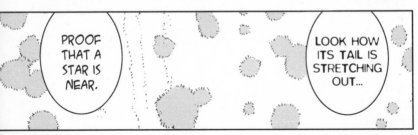

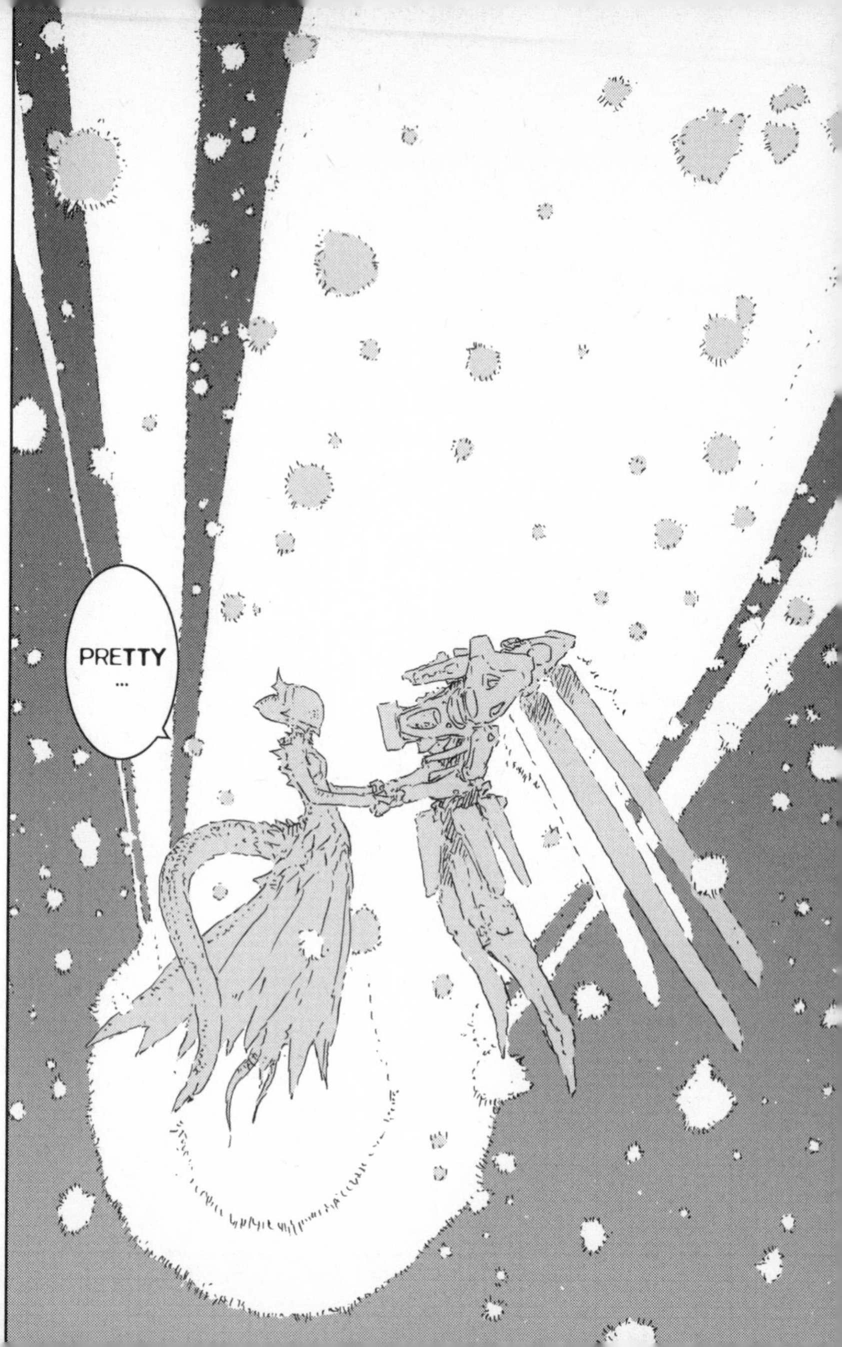
PRETTY
...

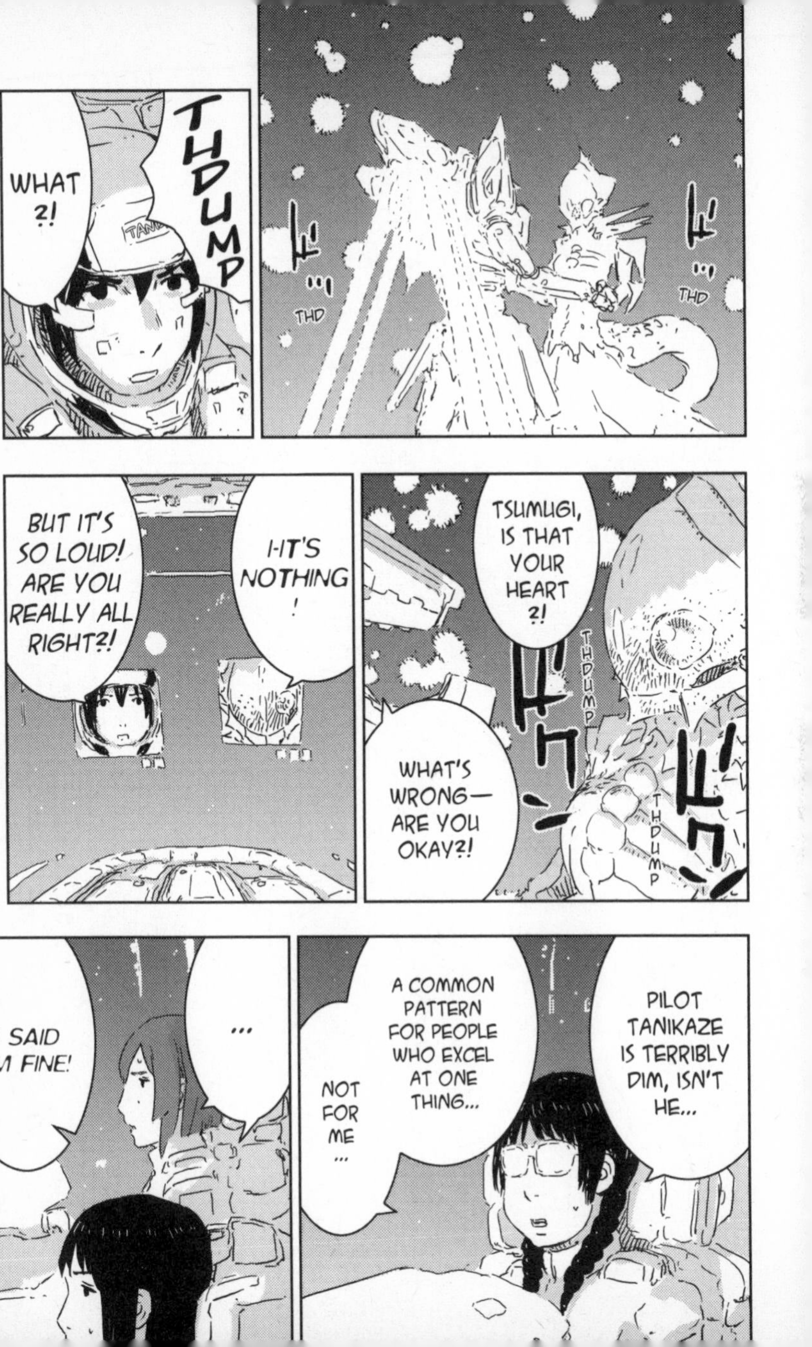
THD
THD
THDUMP
WHAT ?!
TSUMUGI, IS THAT YOUR HEART ?!
THDUMP
WHAT'S WRONG— ARE YOU OKAY?!
THDUMP
I-IT'S NOTHING !
BUT IT'S SO LOUD! ARE YOU REALLY ALL RIGHT?!
PILOT TANIKAZE IS TERRIBLY DIM, ISN'T HE...
A COMMON PATTERN FOR PEOPLE WHO EXCEL AT ONE THING...
NOT FOR ME ...
...
I SAID I'M FINE!

YOU RANKED **46**TH

PIPOP

WHAT ?!

DIDN'T EVEN KNOW HE WAS ON BOARD.

AWWW! YOU MEAN THAT MYSTERIOUS DUDE...

SO IT COMES DOWN TO WHO'S GOT A PRETTY FACE...

POPULARITY AMONG WOMEN	
1ST	OCHIAI
2ND	ICHIRO SEII
3RD	NAGATE TANIKAZE

THE SUPREME COMMANDER'S AIDE.

OCHIAI? WHO THE HELL IS THAT?

150

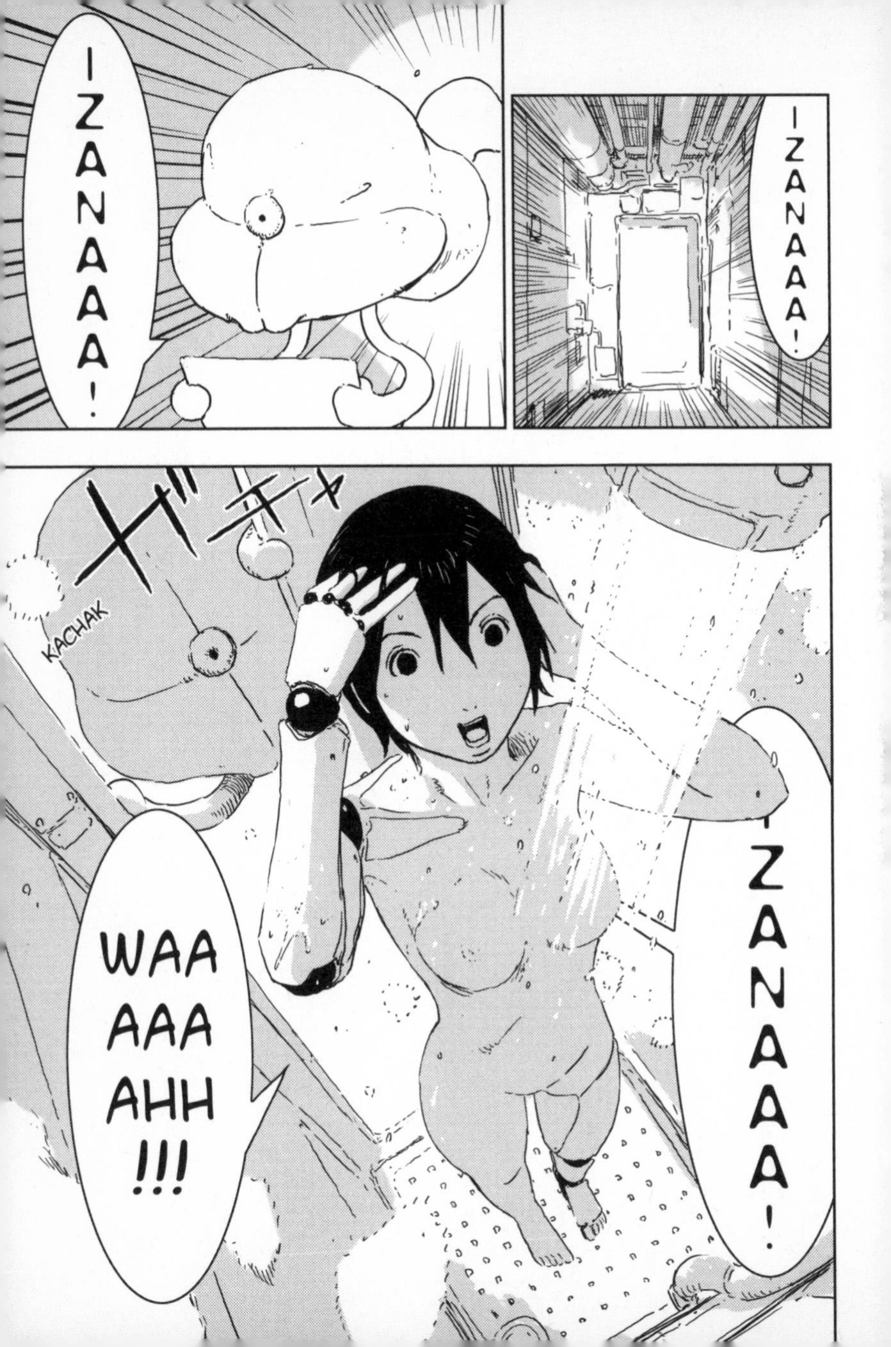
IZANAAA!
IZANAAA!
KACHAK
IZANAAA!
WAAAAAAHH!!!

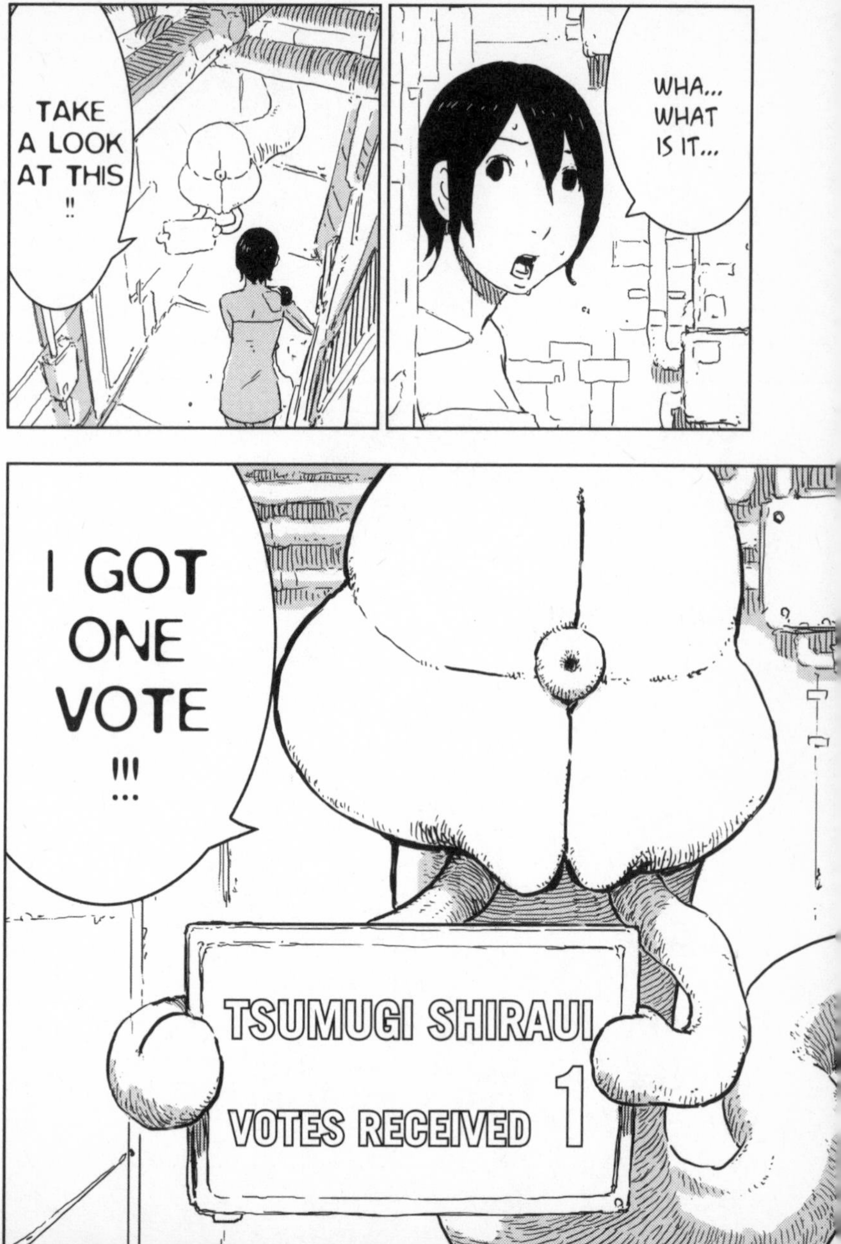
WHA... WHAT IS IT...
TAKE A LOOK AT THIS !!
I GOT ONE VOTE !!! ...
TSUMUGI SHIRAUI
VOTES RECEIVED 1

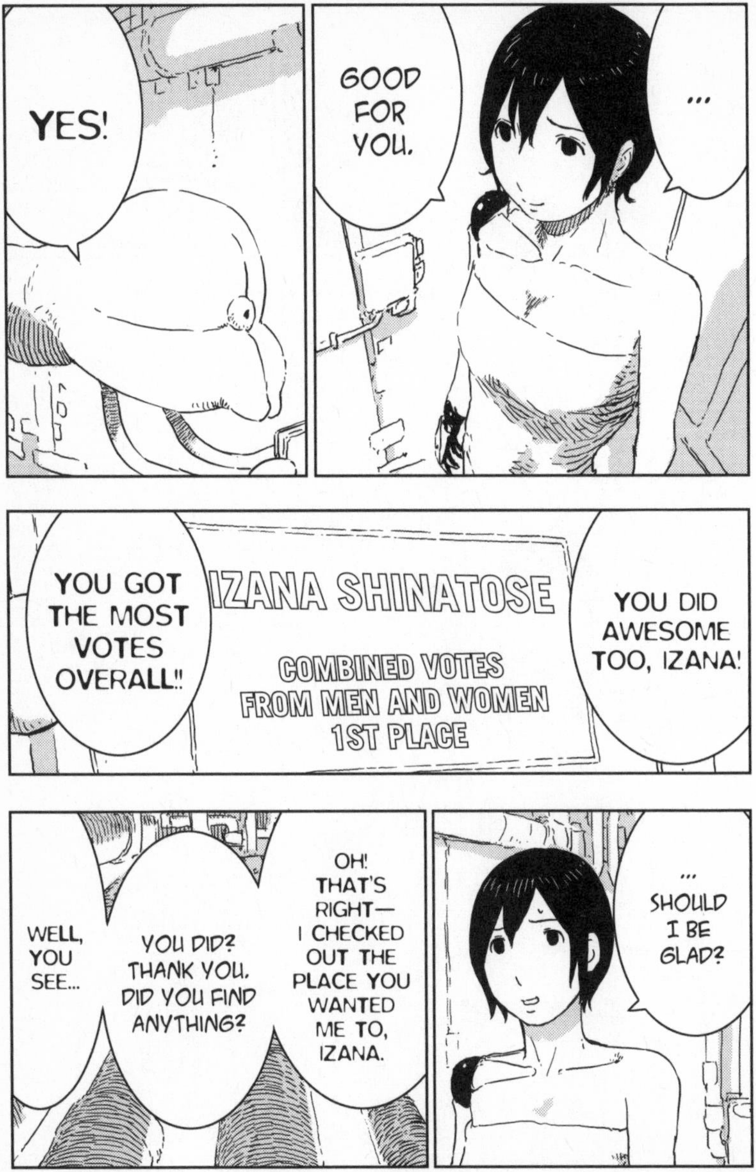
...
GOOD FOR YOU.
YES!
YOU DID AWESOME TOO, IZANA!
IZANA SHINATOSE
COMBINED VOTES FROM MEN AND WOMEN 1ST PLACE
YOU GOT THE MOST VOTES OVERALL!!
... SHOULD I BE GLAD?
OH! THAT'S RIGHT— I CHECKED OUT THE PLACE YOU WANTED ME TO, IZANA.
YOU DID? THANK YOU. DID YOU FIND ANYTHING?
WELL, YOU SEE...

POPULARITY AMONG MEN	
1ST	TERURU ICHIGAYA
2ND	ITTAN SAMARI
3RD	HONOKA SISTERS
4TH	YUHATA MIDORIKAWA
5TH	SASAKI

HOW DID THEY TALLY THESE?

"SISTERS" ...

... AN ARTIFICIAL LIFE FORM CAME IN FIRST PLACE ...

IT'S SICKENING! I WISH THEY'D STOP!

AREN'T THE MEN LOOKING AT ME A LITTLE TOO MUCH ?!

UH-UH, UH-UH. YOU KNOW EXACTLY WHAT YOU'RE DOING, DON'T YOU?

ICHI GAYA

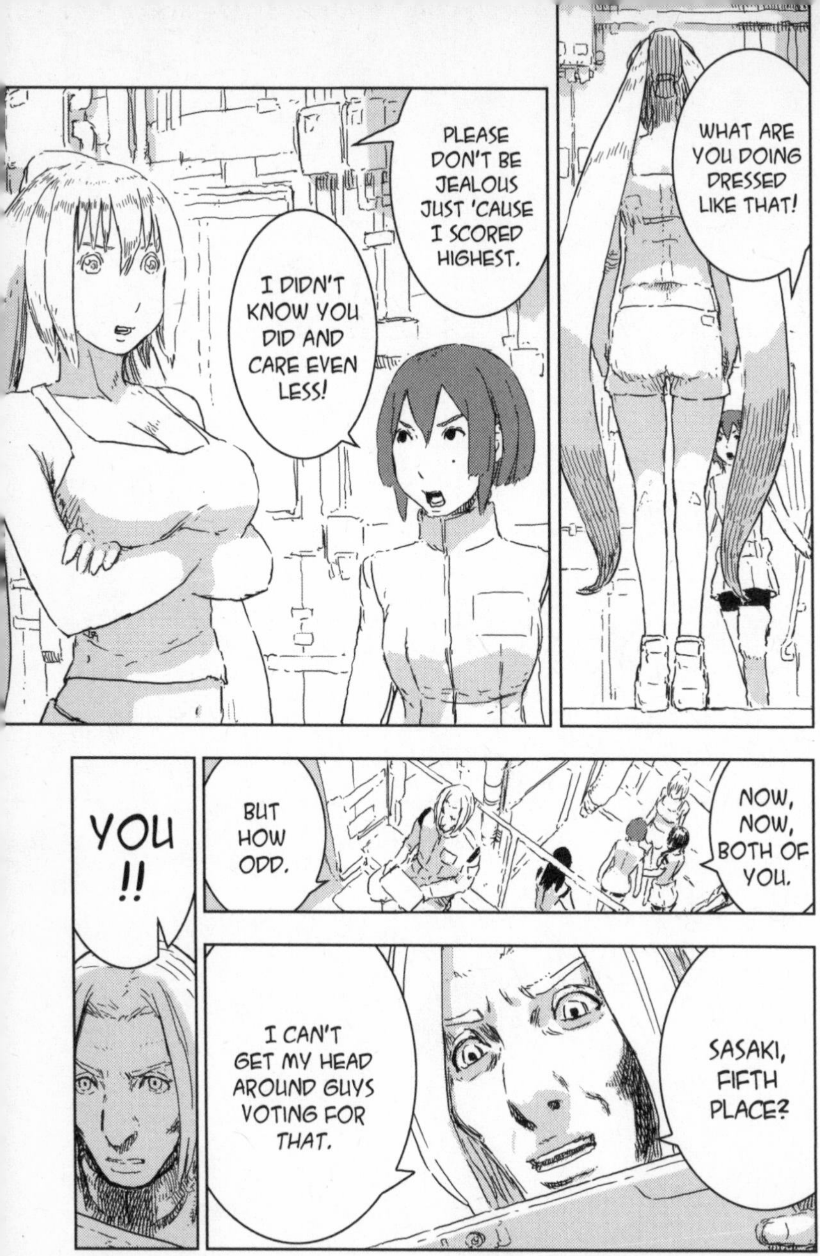
WHAT ARE YOU DOING DRESSED LIKE THAT!
PLEASE DON'T BE JEALOUS JUST 'CAUSE I SCORED HIGHEST.
I DIDN'T KNOW YOU DID AND CARE EVEN LESS!
NOW, NOW, BOTH OF YOU.
BUT HOW ODD.
SASAKI, FIFTH PLACE?
I CAN'T GET MY HEAD AROUND GUYS VOTING FOR THAT.
YOU !!

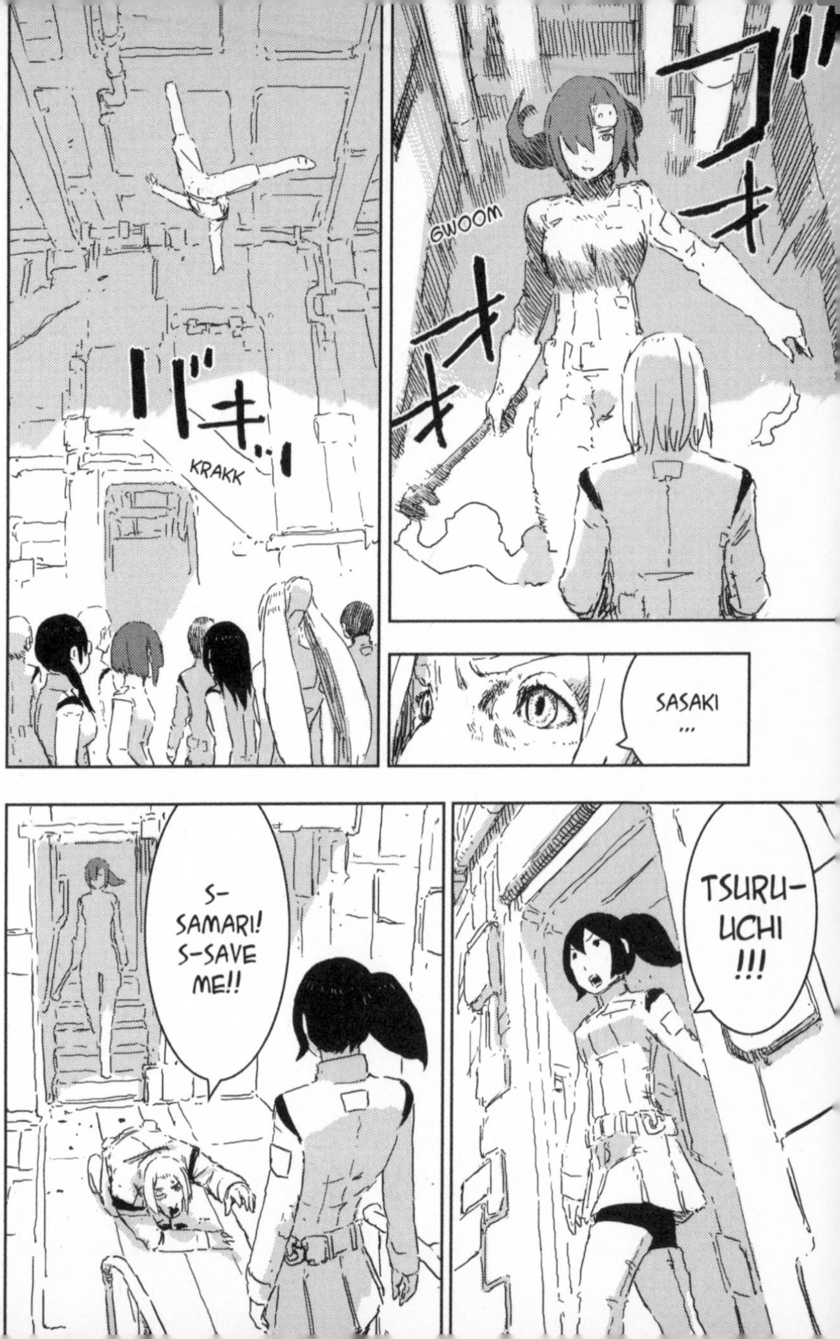
GWOOM
SASAKI ...
KRAKK
TSURU-UCHI !!!
S-SAMARI! S-SAVE ME!!

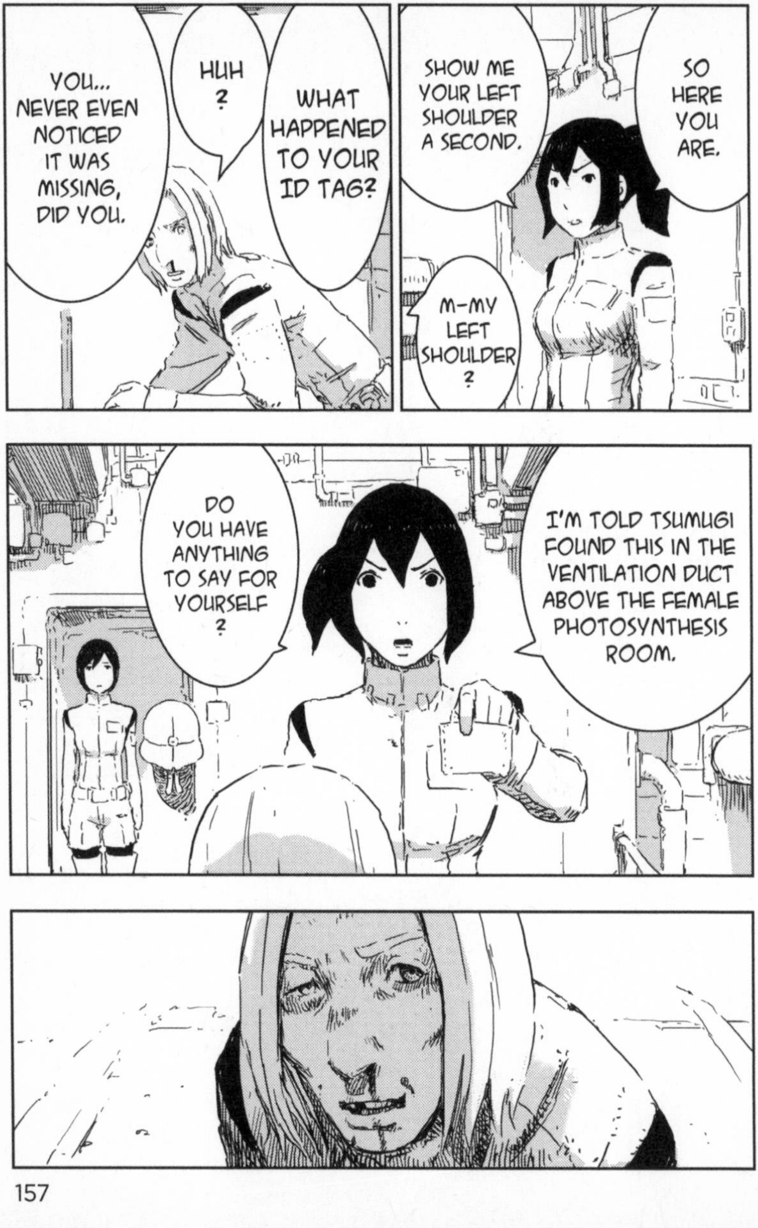
SO HERE YOU ARE.
SHOW ME YOUR LEFT SHOULDER A SECOND.
M-MY LEFT SHOULDER?
WHAT HAPPENED TO YOUR ID TAG?
HUH?
YOU... NEVER EVEN NOTICED IT WAS MISSING, DID YOU.
I'M TOLD TSUMUGI FOUND THIS IN THE VENTILATION DUCT ABOVE THE FEMALE PHOTOSYNTHESIS ROOM.
DO YOU HAVE ANYTHING TO SAY FOR YOURSELF?

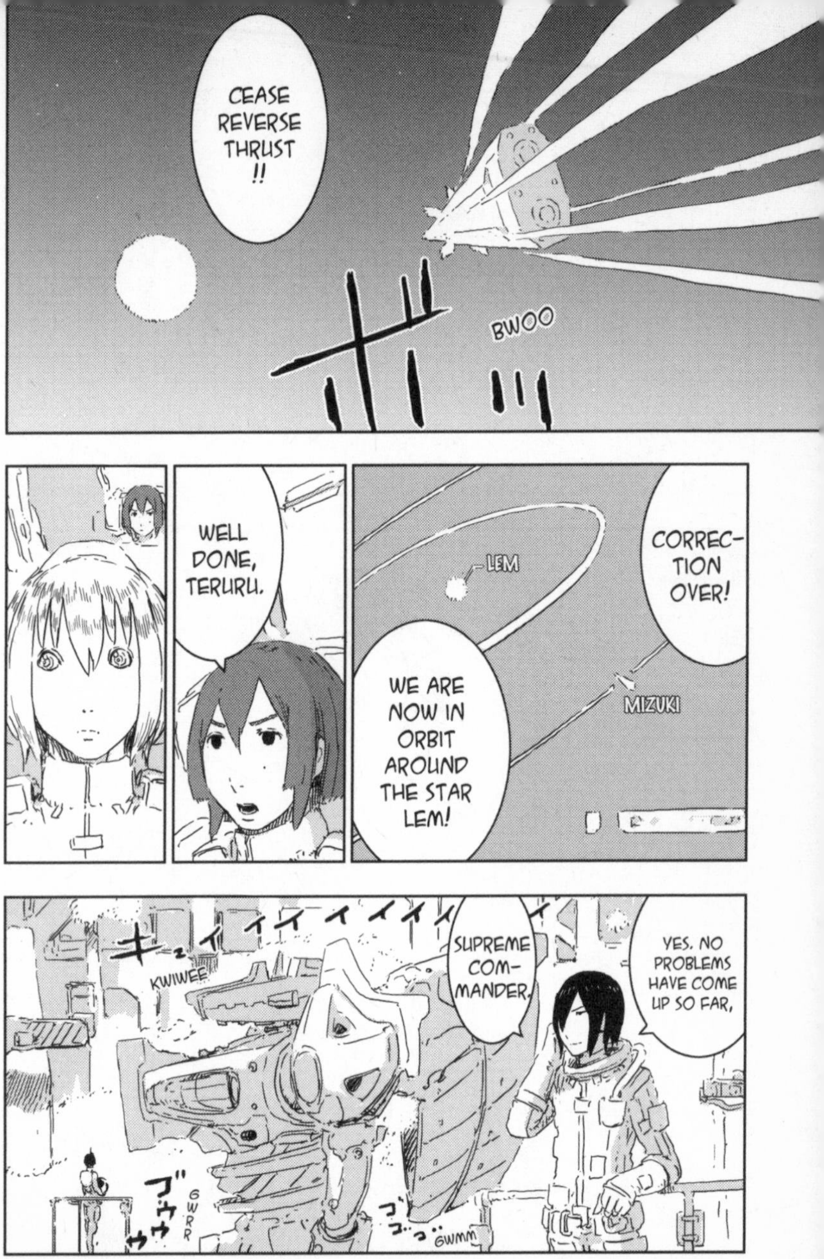
CEASE REVERSE THRUST !!
BWOO
CORREC-TION OVER!
LEM
MIZUKI
WE ARE NOW IN ORBIT AROUND THE STAR LEM!
WELL DONE, TERURU.
YES. NO PROBLEMS HAVE COME UP SO FAR,
SUPREME COM-MANDER.
KWIWEE
GWMM
GWRR

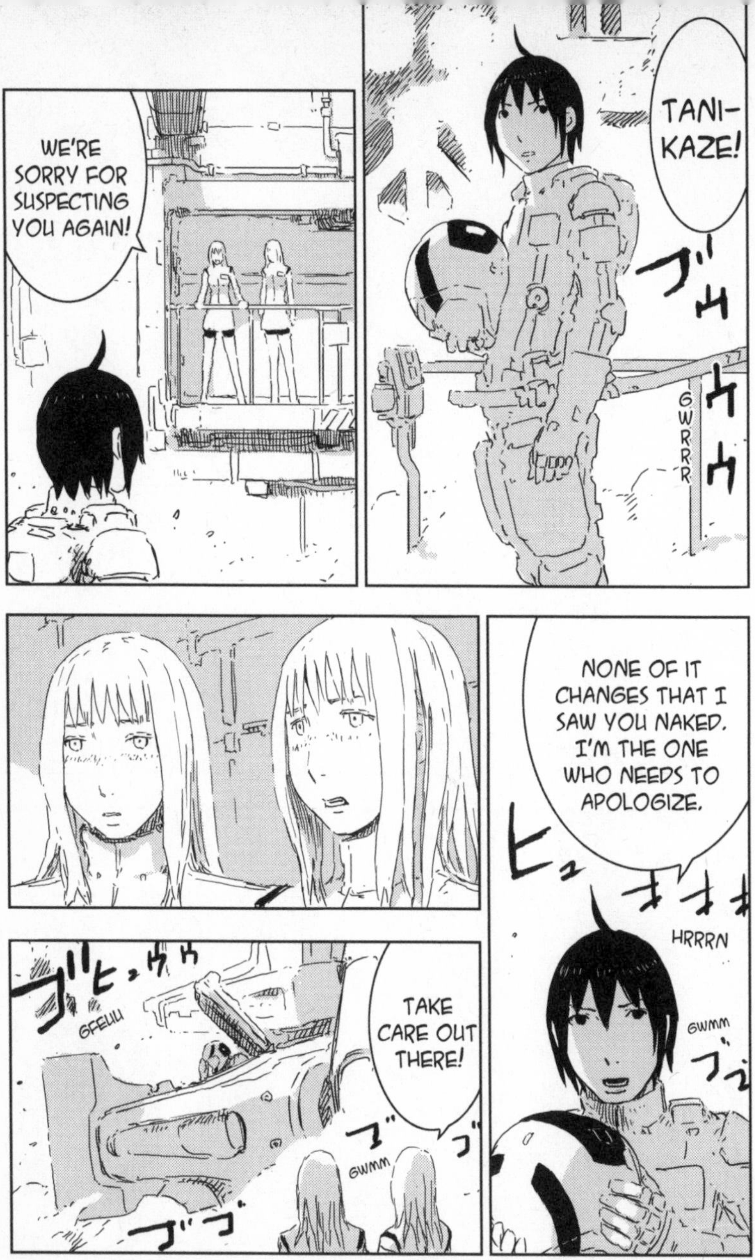
TANI-KAZE!
GWRRR
WE'RE SORRY FOR SUSPECTING YOU AGAIN!
NONE OF IT CHANGES THAT I SAW YOU NAKED. I'M THE ONE WHO NEEDS TO APOLOGIZE.
HRRRN
GWMM
GFEUU
TAKE CARE OUT THERE!
GWMM

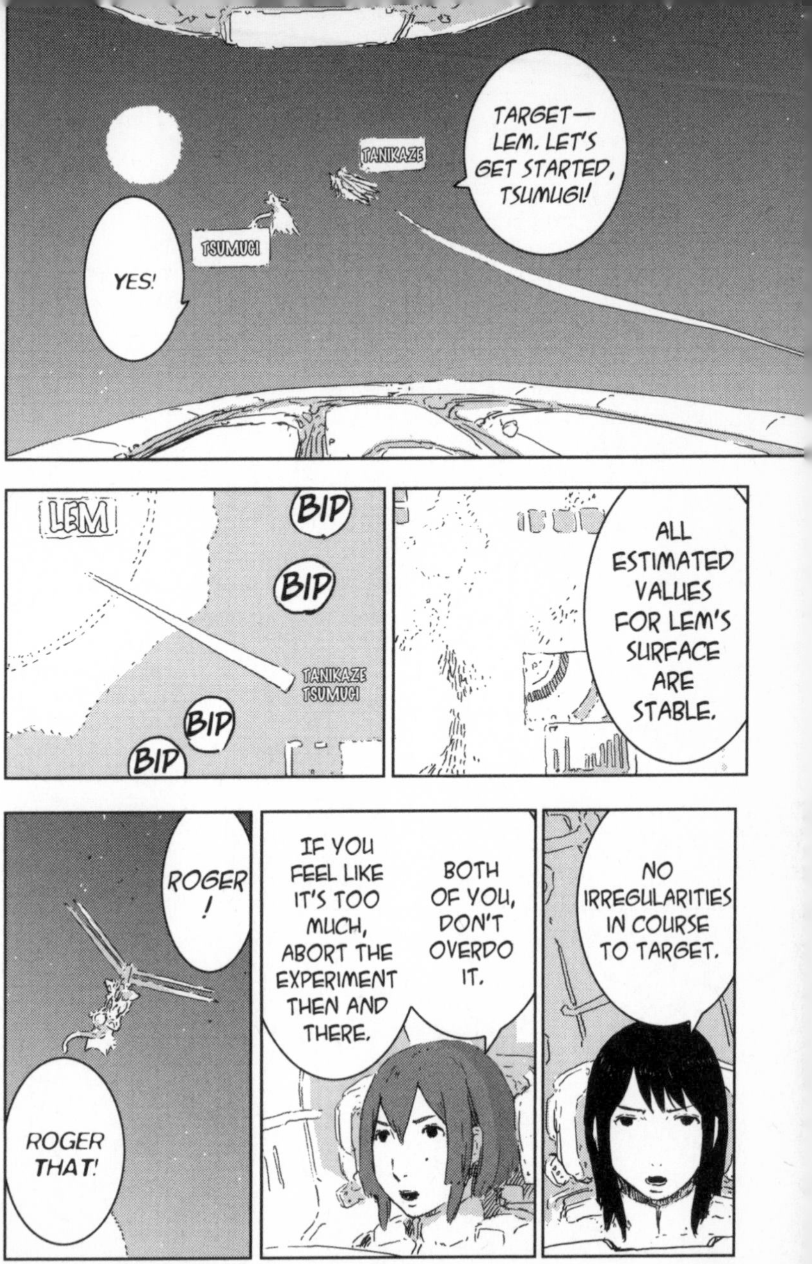

TARGET— LEM. LET'S GET STARTED, TSUMUGI!
TANIKAZE
TSUMUGI
YES!
ALL ESTIMATED VALUES FOR LEM'S SURFACE ARE STABLE.
LEM
BIP
BIP
TANIKAZE
TSUMUGI
BIP
BIP
NO IRREGULARITIES IN COURSE TO TARGET.
BOTH OF YOU, DON'T OVERDO IT.
IF YOU FEEL LIKE IT'S TOO MUCH, ABORT THE EXPERIMENT THEN AND THERE.
ROGER!
ROGER THAT!

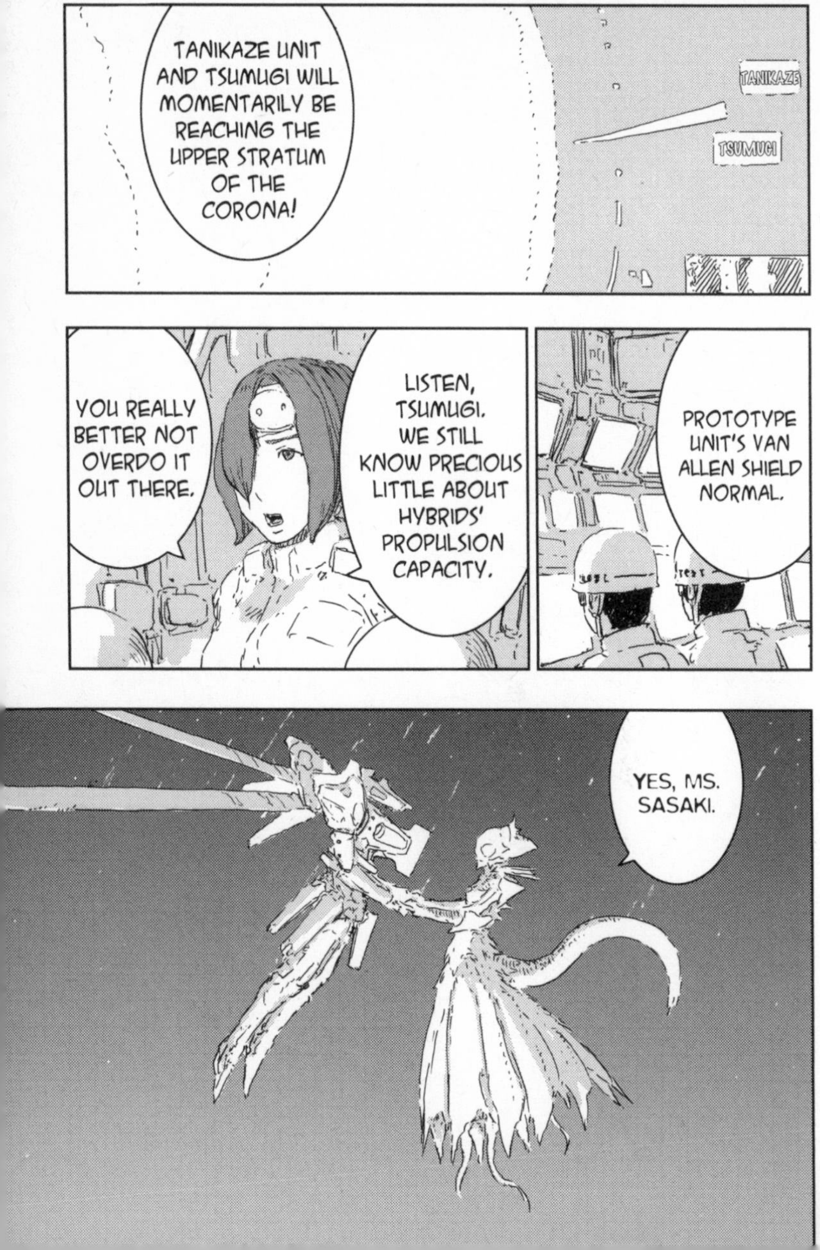

TANIKAZE UNIT AND TSUMUGI WILL MOMENTARILY BE REACHING THE UPPER STRATUM OF THE CORONA!
TANIKAZE
TSUMUGI
PROTOTYPE UNIT'S VAN ALLEN SHIELD NORMAL.
LISTEN, TSUMUGI. WE STILL KNOW PRECIOUS LITTLE ABOUT HYBRIDS' PROPULSION CAPACITY.
YOU REALLY BETTER NOT OVERDO IT OUT THERE.
YES, MS. SASAKI.

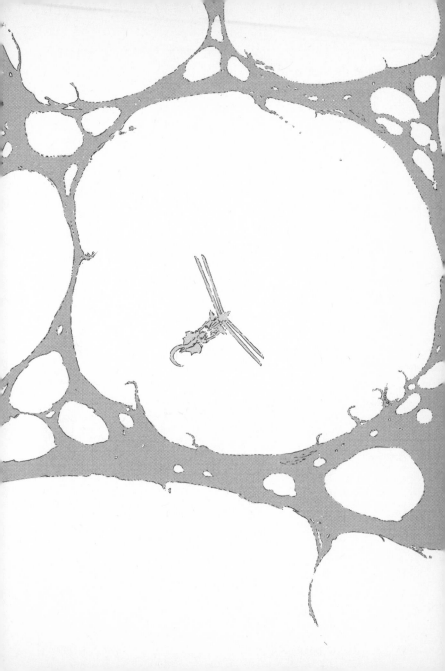

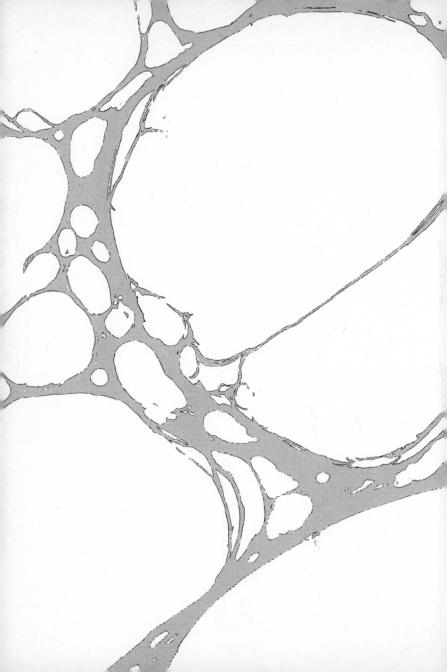

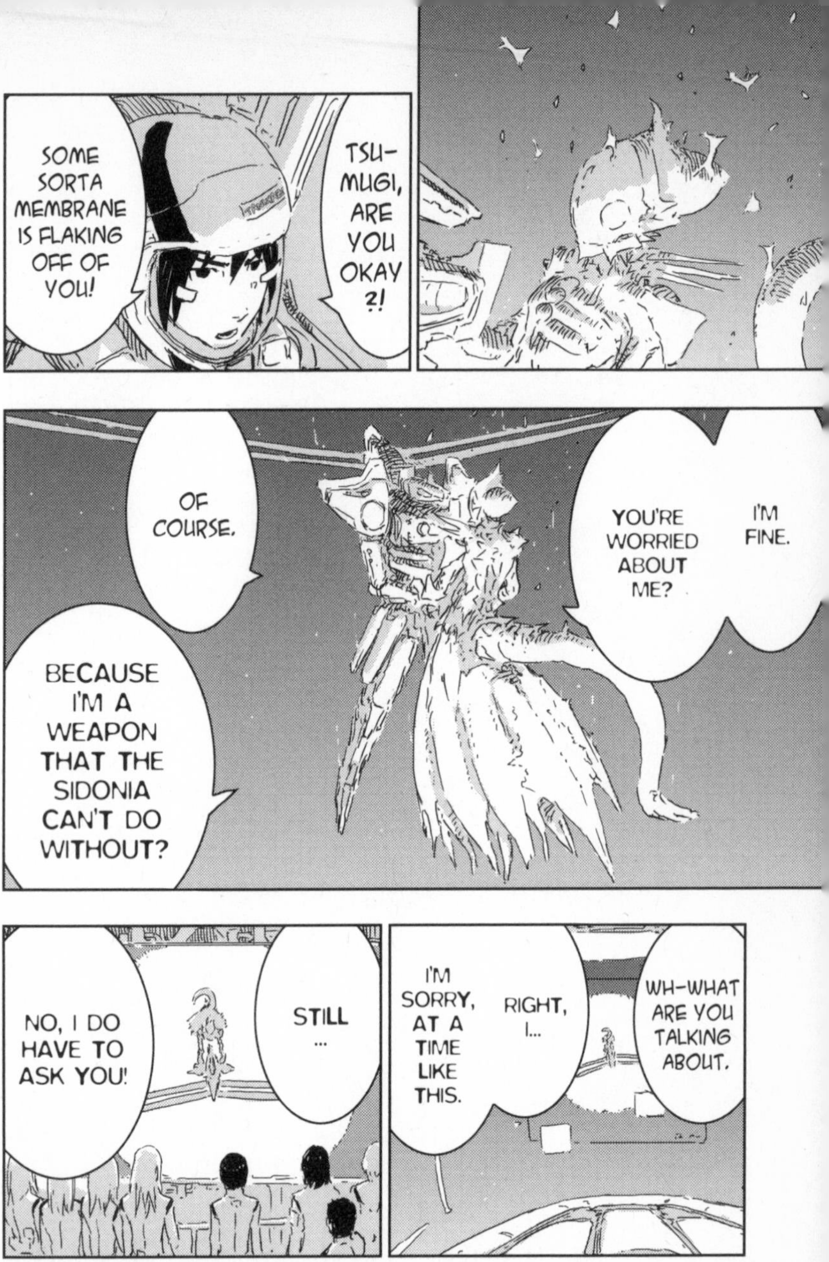
TSU-MUGI, ARE YOU OKAY ?!
SOME SORTA MEMBRANE IS FLAKING OFF OF YOU!
I'M FINE.
YOU'RE WORRIED ABOUT ME?
OF COURSE.
BECAUSE I'M A WEAPON THAT THE SIDONIA CAN'T DO WITHOUT?
WH-WHAT ARE YOU TALKING ABOUT.
RIGHT, I...
I'M SORRY, AT A TIME LIKE THIS.
STILL ...
NO, I DO HAVE TO ASK YOU!

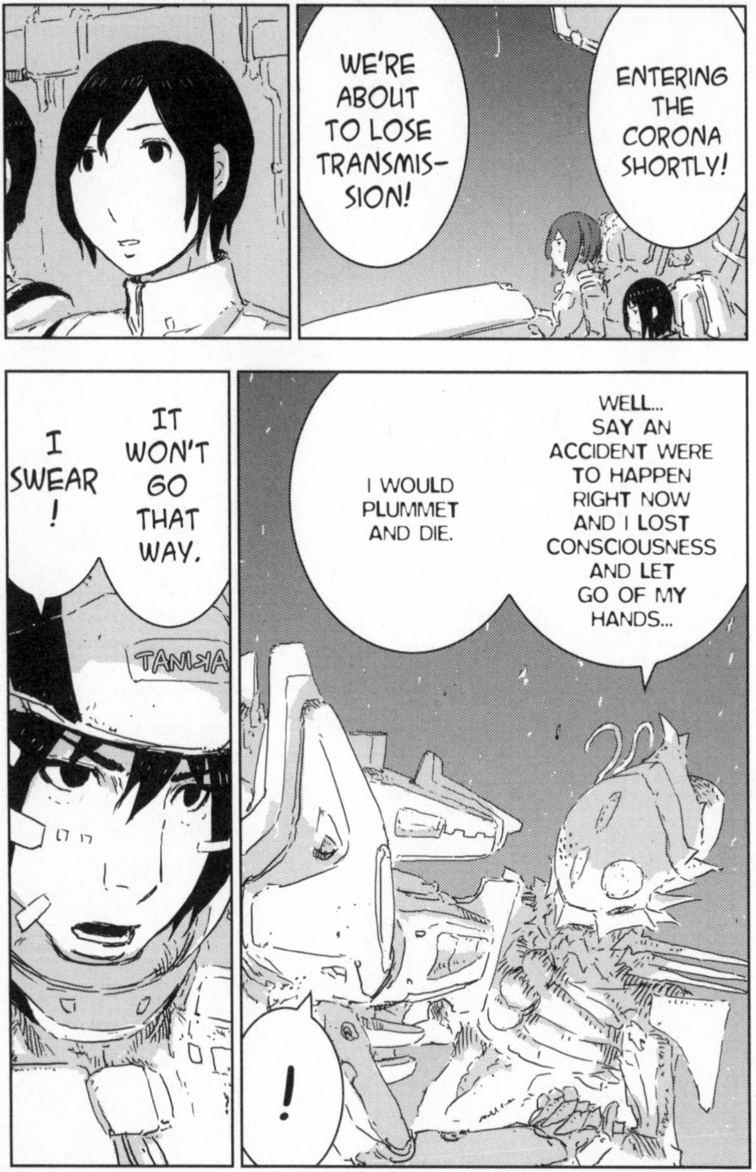
ENTERING THE CORONA SHORTLY!
WE'RE ABOUT TO LOSE TRANSMISSION!
WELL... SAY AN ACCIDENT WERE TO HAPPEN RIGHT NOW AND I LOST CONSCIOUSNESS AND LET GO OF MY HANDS...
I WOULD PLUMMET AND DIE.
!
IT WON'T GO THAT WAY.
I SWEAR!

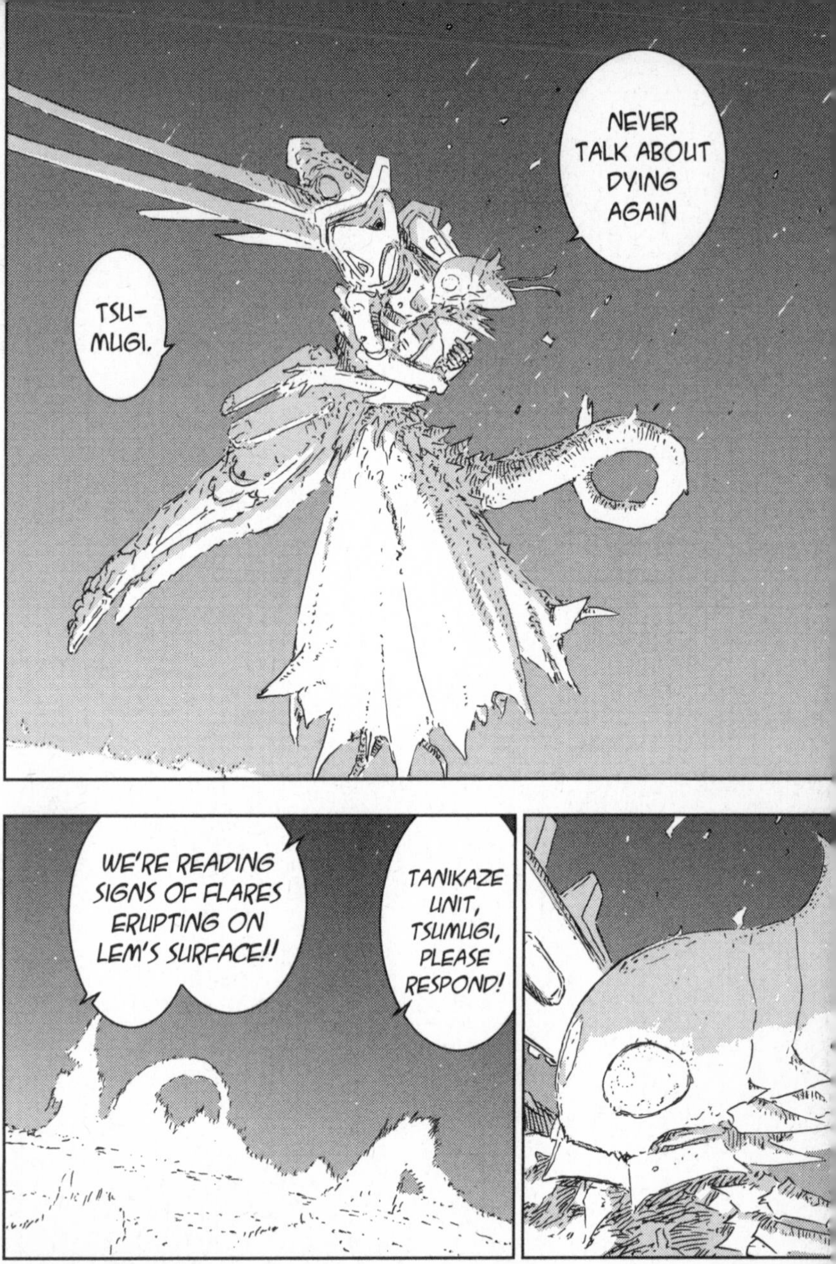
NEVER TALK ABOUT DYING AGAIN
TSU-MUGI.
TANIKAZE UNIT, TSUMUGI, PLEASE RESPOND!
WE'RE READING SIGNS OF FLARES ERUPTING ON LEM'S SURFACE!!

Chapter 59: END

KNIGHTS OF SIDONIA Volume ⑫ : END

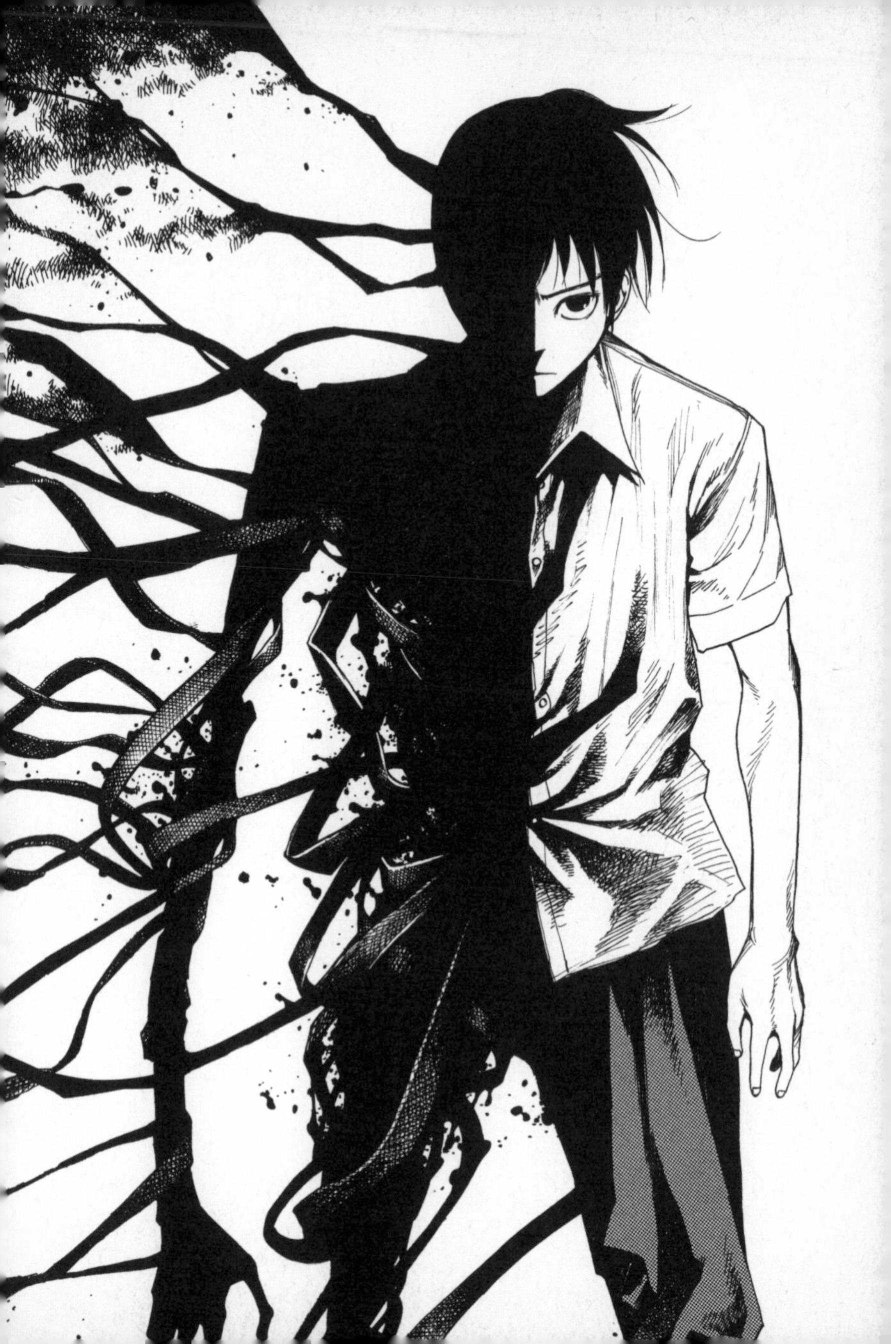

AJIN
DEMI-HUMAN

STORY: TSUINA MIURA
ART: GAMON SAKURAI

SAY YOU GET HIT BY A TRUCK AND DIE. YOU COME BACK TO LIFE. GOOD OR BAD?

FOR HIGH SCHOOLER KEI—AND FOR AT LEAST FORTY-SIX OTHERS— IMMORTALITY COMES AS THE NASTIEST SURPRISE EVER.

SADLY FOR KEI, BUT REFRESHINGLY FOR THE READER, SUCH A FEAT DOESN'T MAKE HIM A SUPERHERO. IN THE EYES OF BOTH THE GENERAL PUBLIC AND GOVERNMENTS, HE'S A RARE SPECIMEN WHO NEEDS TO BE HUNTED DOWN AND HANDED OVER TO SCIENTISTS TO BE EXPERIMENTED ON FOR LIFE—A DEMI-HUMAN WHO MUST DIE A THOUSAND DEATHS FOR THE BENEFIT OF HUMANITY.

VOLUME 1 AVAILABLE NOW!

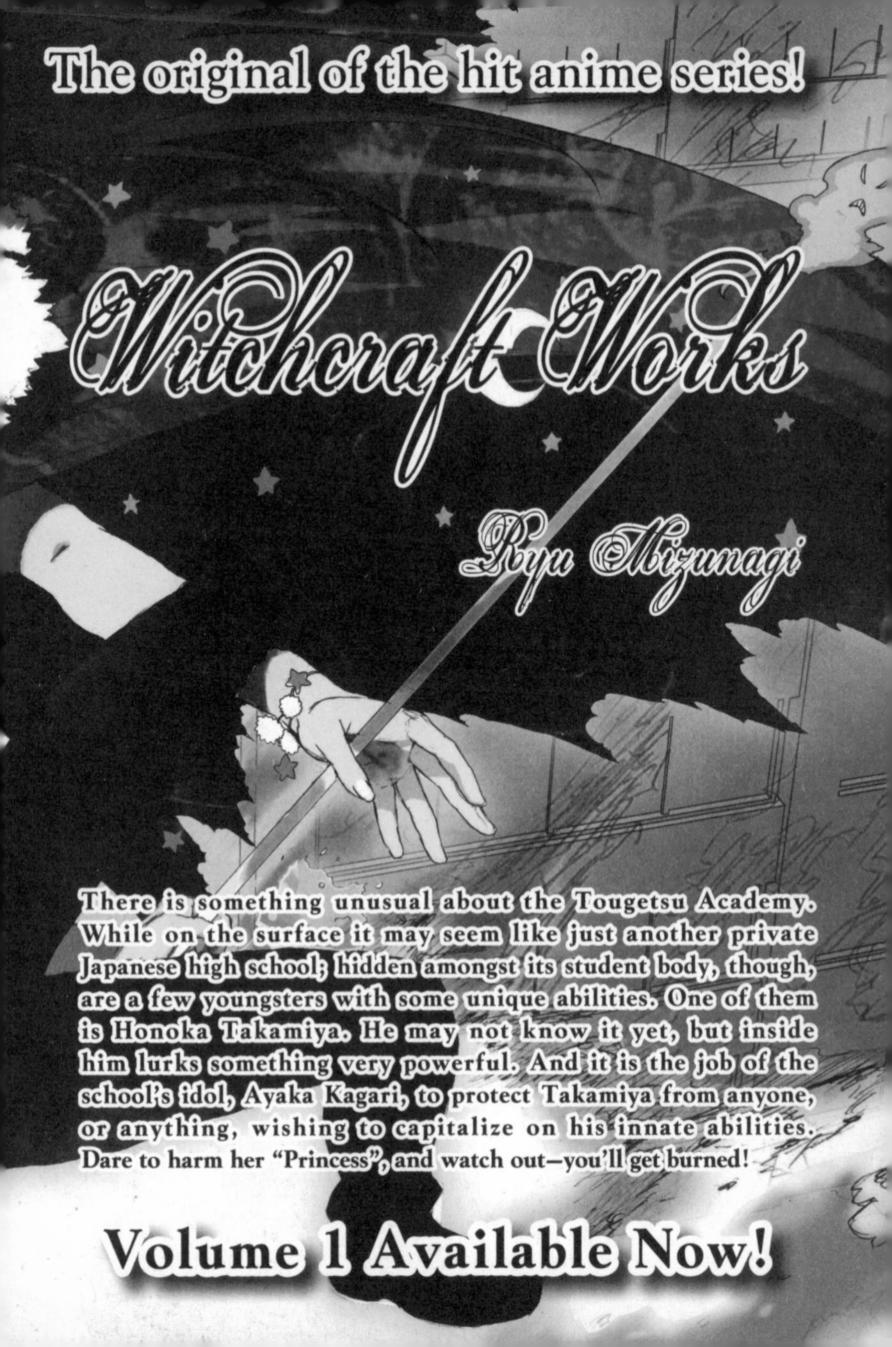
The original of the hit anime series!
Witchcraft Works
Ryu Mizunagi
There is something unusual about the Tougetsu Academy. While on the surface it may seem like just another private Japanese high school; hidden amongst its student body, though, are a few youngsters with some unique abilities. One of them is Honoka Takamiya. He may not know it yet, but inside him lurks something very powerful. And it is the job of the school's idol, Ayaka Kagari, to protect Takamiya from anyone, or anything, wishing to capitalize on his innate abilities. Dare to harm her "Princess", and watch out–you'll get burned!
Volume 1 Available Now!

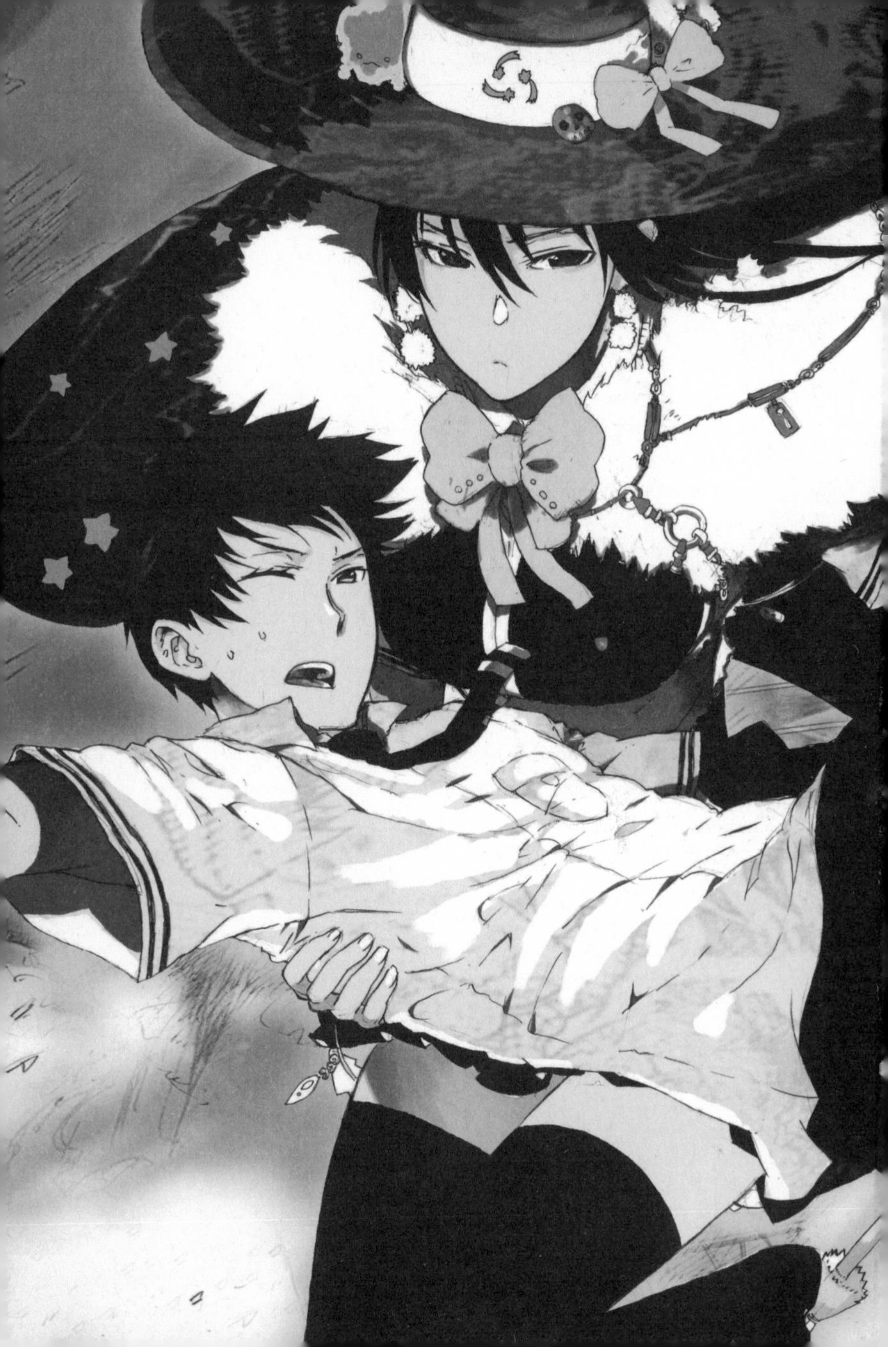

Knights of Sidonia, volume 12

Translation: Kumar Sivasubramanian
Production: Grace Lu
Daniela Yamada
Anthony Quintessenza

First published in Japan in 2014 by Kodansha, Ltd., Tokyo
Publication for this English edition arranged through Kodansha, Ltd., Tokyo
English language version produced by Vertical, Inc.

Translation provided by Vertical, Inc., 2014
Published by Vertical, Inc., New York

Originally published in Japanese as *Shidonia no Kishi 12* by Kodansha, Ltd.
Shidonia no Kishi first serialized in *Afternoon*, Kodansha, Ltd., 2009-

ISBN: 978-1-939130-99-0

Manufactured in Canada

First Edition

Vertical, Inc.
451 Park Avenue South
7th Floor
New York, NY 10016
www.vertical-inc.com